'9u,

WHEN
DOGMAS
DIE

WHEN
DOGMAS DIE

SUSANNA KRIZO

CREATION
HOUSE
A STRANG COMPANY

WHEN DOGMAS DIE by Susanna Krizo
Published by Creation House
A Strang Company
600 Rinehart Road
Lake Mary, Florida 32746
www.strangbookgroup.com

Unless otherwise noted, all Scripture quotations are from the New King James Version of the Bible. Copyright © 1979, 1980, 1982 by Thomas Nelson, Inc., publishers. Used by permission.

Scripture quotations marked KJV are from the King James Version of the Bible.

Scripture quotations marked NAB are from the *New American Bible with Revised New Testament and Revised Psalms* © 1991, 1986, 1970 Confraternity of Christian Doctrine, Washington, D.C. and are used by permission of the copyright owner. All Rights Reserved.

Scripture quotations marked NJB are from the *New Jerusalem Bible* © 1985 by Darton, Longman & Todd, Ltd. And Doubleday, a division of Bantam Doubleday Dell Publishing Group, Inc. All Rights Reserved.

Scripture quotations marked NAS are from the New American Standard Bible. Copyright © 1960, 1962, 1963, 1968, 1971, 1972, 1973, 1975, 1977 by the Lockman Foundation. Used by permission. (www.Lockman.org)

Scripture quotations marked NIV are from the Holy Bible, New International Version of the Bible. Copyright © 1973, 1978, 1984, International Bible Society. Used by permission.

Scripture quotations marked TLB are from The Living Bible. Copyright © 1971. Used by permission of Tyndale House Publishers, Inc., Wheaton, IL 60189. All rights reserved.

All italics within quotes are the author's emphasis.

Design Director: Bill Johnson

Cover design by Amanda Potter

Library of Congress Control Number: 2009931065
International Standard Book Number: 978-1-59979-865-3

First Edition

09 10 11 12 13 — 9 8 7 6 5 4 3 2 1
Printed in the United States of America

Contents

Acknowledgments

I WISH TO THANK Allen Quain, Ginny Maxwell, Atalie Anderson, and Amanda Lowell at Creation House for their excellent work, patience and faith.

I wish to also thank Katelyn Byrne, who despite her youth listened attentively as I contemplated the many great theological problems I had set out to solve; my dear friend Teri L. King who believed in this book before I did; and my husband, Ira, and our son, Jonathan, who endured patiently the many years of research and the final months of the writing process when the end seemed to elude all of us.

This book is written in remembrance of all the great unnamed men and women who braved the prejudices of their own time and paved the way for the return of biblical equality.

Finally, this book is dedicated with gratitude to my mother, Tuula, and my father, Esko, who taught me to love books by their own example.

Always ask why – not who, but why – for if you ask who gave the man authority over the woman, you may not find out why the man was given the authority, but if you ask why the man was given authority over the woman, you will find that it was the man's idea.

Introduction

Protestant Christians often believe that traditional theology has little or no effect on their interpretation of the Bible due to their commitment to *sola scriptura*. According to philosopher Erich Fromm, the erroneous assumption that one is not affected by the beliefs of others is common.

> Most people are not even aware of their need to conform. They live under the illusion that they follow their own ideas and inclinations, that they are individualists, that they have arrived at their opinions as the result of their own thinking – and that it just happens that their ideas are the same as those of the majority. The consensus of all serves as a proof for the correctness of "their" ideas.[1]

On the contrary, despite their commitment to *sola scriptura*, the Council of Biblical Manhood and Womanhood (CBMW) believes tradition is the supreme manifestation of the correctness of their complementarian theology which maintains that God gave the man authority over the woman.[2] In order

---

1. Erich Fromm, *The Art of Loving* (New York City: Bantam Books, 1956) 11.

2. "In 1987, a group of pastors and scholars assembled to address their concerns over the influence of feminism not only in our culture but also in evangelical churches. Because of the widespread compromise of biblical understanding of manhood and womanhood and its tragic effects on the home and the church, these men and women established *The Council on Biblical Manhood and Womanhood*. In opposition to the growing movement of feminist egalitarianism they articulated what is now known as the complementarian position which affirms that men and women are equal in the image of God, but maintain complementary differences in role and function. In the home, men lovingly are to lead their wives and family as women intelligently are to submit to the leadership of their husbands. In the church, while men and women share equally in the blessings of salvation, some governing and teaching roles are restricted to men." ("About Us," The Council of Biblical Manhood and Womanhood, http://www.cbmw .org/About-Us"[accessed June 29, 2009]).

to refute the theological position called egalitarianism,[3] which maintains men and women were created equal, CBMW created *Recovering Biblical Manhood and Womanhood* in 1991. The book, which is edited by John Piper and Wayne Grudem, contains twenty-five essays by twenty-four authors, and in his essay *Role Distinctions in the Church,* S. Lewis Johnson Jr. defines the influence the historical understanding of the Church should have on modern theology.

> To treat the church's historical understanding of Scripture lightly is to forget that it is the believing body that, through the centuries, carries on the theological enterprise with the Word in hand and accompanied by the enlightened Spirit. Thus, *the largest part* of any theologian's work comes from reverent consideration and response to the Christian theological tradition. The creeds of the church, the results of serious spiritual and theological strife, are more important than the views of individuals. We should *begin* our discussions *with the assumption that the church is probably right,* unless exegetical and theological study compels us otherwise.[4]

As has been noted before, assumptions make for sloppy scholars, for how can one know if exegetical and theological study will reveal the historical understanding to be incorrect if one *assumes* it to be correct and does not challenge it? Tradition is valuable, but it is not infallible, and we must guard ourselves against the conviction of the Roman satirist Juvenal that the present is *per se* evil and the past is good.[5] We should indeed reverently consider the traditional understanding of the church, but with the *knowledge* that the councils occasionally set the Bible aside.

---

3. "Disturbed by the shallow biblical premise used by organizations and mission groups to exclude the gifts of women, evangelical leaders assembled to publish their biblical perspective in a new journal, *Priscilla Papers,* in 1987. Included in the group were Gilbert Bilezikian, W. Ward Gasque, Stanley Gundry, Gretchen Gaebelein Hull, Catherine Clark Kreoger, Jo Anne Lyon, and Roger Nicole. The group determined that a national organization was needed to provide education, support, and leadership about biblical equality." ("Our Mission and History," Christians for Biblical Equality, http://www.cbeinternatioal.org./?q=content/our mission-and-history [accessed June 29, 2009]).

4. John Piper and Wayne Grudem, ed. *Recovering Biblical Manhood and Womanhood* (Wheaton: IL, Crossway, 1994), 164.

5. Edith Hamilton, *The Roman Way* (New York City: W.W. Norton & Company, 1964), 167.

They [bishops of Council of Nice] understood their position to be that of witnesses, not that of exegetes. They recognized but one duty resting upon them in this respect – to hand down to other faithful men that good thing the Church had received according to the command of God. The first requirement was not learning, but honesty. The question they were called upon to answer was not, What do I think probable, or even certain, from Holy Scripture? but, What have I been taught, what has been entrusted to me to hand down to others?[6]

William Weinrich recognizes in his essay *Women in the History of the Church* that not all councils followed the Bible, but he attempts to mitigate the fact by claiming that the misogynist (hatred of women) remarks were not determinative.

Sometimes it is asserted that the canonical prohibitions were motivated by misogyny and false evaluations of women's intellectual and moral capacities. Misogynous remarks and opinions of inferiority do exist. Yet, Manfred Hauke correctly notes that the language of Gennadius's *Statuta* – "however learned and holy" – and of Innocent III – whether Mary "stands higher than all the apostles " – indicates that ultimately and officially considerations of intellect and sanctity were not determinative. Determinative were the Biblical history, the example of Jesus, and the apostolic injunction.[7]

Weinrich is correct in affirming that the woman's restricted role was not based on sanctity or intellect, for it was her *whole nature* that was considered inferior. Clement of Alexandria (153-217) wrote it is "always proper for the one who is superior by nature to be over the inferior,"[8] a concept he borrowed from the Greek philosopher Aristotle (384-322 B.C.).

Aristotle outlined his political vision for the *polis* (state) in his work *Politica*. Slavery was being challenged during his time, wherefore Aristotle argued that some were by nature slaves and should be ruled by a master. He extended the same principle to women, arguing that "the male is by nature superior, and

---

6. Philip Schaff and Henry Wace, *Historical Introduction to the Council of Nice* (Ante Nice, 2nd Series, Volume XIV).

7. Piper and Grudem, 277.

8. Clement of Alexandria, *Stromata,* Book VII, Ch. II.

the female inferior; and the one rules, and the other is ruled; this principle, of necessity, extends to all mankind."[9] Aristotle did however not have the "why" for his argument, and Christine Allen describes his dilemma.

> If there is a common nature among human beings, and if a good person means living in accordance with this nature, it would follow that any person wishing to acquire practical wisdom would seek to exercise his rational faculty in the same way. In the *Politics* Aristotle realizes the consequence of his ethics when he is considering whether slaves can be good: "Since they are men and share in rational principle, it seems absurd to say that they have no virtue. A similar question may be raised about women and children" (1259b27-30). [10]

Allen explains how Aristotle resolved the problem by "introducing an observation about the nature of things, namely that some things naturally rule while other things naturally obey." The slaves, he maintained, had no deliberative faculty and women had one without authority, wherefore they could be virtuous "only in that measure of virtue which is proper to each of them."[11] Thus he concluded that the freeborn male ought to rule because he was superior in virtue. Allen explains further that, "the result of all this is that a woman is virtuous by obeying not commanding (1260a24), by being silent (1260a30), by preserving not acquiring (1277b21), by having true opinion not wisdom (1277b27) and by entering into friendships of inequality not equality (1158b11-13). In short, a good woman lives very differently from a good man." Ultimately, Aristotle's philosophy alone was not able to provide a definite reason why the woman was inferior, but his philosophy synthesized with theology was — *because God made her so.*

Clement of Alexandria was a former philosopher and one of the first theologians to synthesize Greek philosophy with theology: "The *Stromata* will contain the truth mixed up in the dogmas of philosophy, or rather covered over and hidden, as the edible part of the nut in the shell."[12] We should give

---

9. Aristotle, *Politica*, 1253b.20, 1254.20.

10. Christine Garside Allen, *Can a Woman be Good in the Same Way as a Man?* In Martha Lee Osborne, *Woman in Western thought*, (New York: Random House, 1979), 44-46.

11. *Politica*, 1255a20, 1260a12-14, 1260a20

12. *Stromata*, Book I, Ch. I.

due credit to Clement for his attempt to rescue Christianity from becoming largely a religion governed by superstition in the hands of the uneducated – which occurred in the Medieval Church – but we must also recognize the influence philosophy had on his theology. E.g., he explicitly approved of Euripides's poetic declaration of the woman's inferiority, which affected his interpretation of 1 Corinthians 11.

> "Women are therefore to philosophize equally with men, though the males are preferable at everything, unless they have become effeminate. To the whole human race, then, discipline and virtue are a necessity, if they would pursue after happiness. And how recklessly Euripides writes sometimes this and sometimes that! On one occasion, *"For every wife is inferior to her husband*, though the most excellent one marry her that is of fair fame." And on another, "for the chaste is her husband's slave, while she that is unchaste in her folly despises her consort … for nothing is better and more excellent, than when as husband and wife ye keep house, harmonious in your sentiments." *The ruling power is therefore the head"*.[13]

In his essay, Weinrich denies also that the general exclusion of women from leadership in the See of Constantinople was based on the natural inferiority of women,[14] but John Chrysostom (347-407), bishop of Constantinople, upheld the woman's inferiority: "Both the man falling into the woman's inferiority, and the woman rising up against the man by her outward habiliments."[15] Despite Chrysostom's brilliance and learning, or perhaps because of the latter, Aristotle's influence on his theology is unmistakable.

a) Aristotle considered every household a monarchy (*Politica*, 1255b20) in which the husband rules over his wife with a constitutional rule and over his children with a royal rule. A constitutional rule is between equals and the citizens rule and are ruled in turn, but although "the relation of the man to the woman is of this kind," the inequality between the two is permanent "because "the male is by nature fitter for command than the female" (*Politica*, 1259a37-1259b12). Chrysostom echoed Aristotle in his homily on Ephesians: "Every one's house is a city; and every man is a prince in his own house. … Does he

---

13. *Ibid.*, Book IV, Ch. VIII.
14. Piper and Grudem, 274.
15. John Chrysostom, *Homilies on First Corinthians*, Homily XXVI.

not seem to you to be, as it were, a sort of king, having so many authorities under his own authority. And thus the wife will be a second king in the house, lacking only the diadem" (Homily XXII).

b) Slavery was defended by Aristotle on the grounds that some were by nature slaves who should "practice obedience," while the masters should exercise "the authority and lordship which nature intended them to have" (*Politica*, 1255b5-10). He wanted the masters to avoid abuse, for the "interests of part and whole, of body and soul, are the same," seeing that the "slave is part of the master, a living but separated part of his bodily frame." Chrysostom interpreted Ephesians 5 with this concept in mind: "The wife is a second authority; let not her then demand equality, for she is under the head; nor let him despise her as being in subjection, for she is the body." He exhorted the man to "bring in love on his part as a counterpoise to obedience on her part," for "the hands and the feet, and all the rest of the members [are] given up for service to the head" (*Homily on Ephesians*, Homily XX).

c) According to Aristotle, the slave has to be ruled because he "has no deliberative faculty at all" (*Politica*, 1260a12-15), while the woman's reason is without authority. Both had to be ruled by the freeborn male because "the equality of the two or the rule of the inferior is always hurtful" (*Politica*, 1254b1-20). Chrysostom agreed with Aristotle for he wrote, "[I]n order that the one might be subject, and the other rule; (for equality is wont oftentimes to bring in strife) he [God] suffered it not to be a democracy, but a monarchy." Furthermore, Aristotle granted that the male child had authority, but that it was immature, and Chrysostom had an equivalent concept of a hierarchy among the children, in which "the female does not possess equal sway" (1 Corinthians, Homily XXXIV).

A millennium after Clement of Alexandria first synthesized philosophy with his theology, Thomas Aquinas (1225-1274) created *Summa Theologica*, a synthesis of medieval theology and Aristotle's philosophy. Through the *Summa*, the woman's inferiority would continue to be an inherent part of traditional theology, hidden as it was in the dogma of female subordination.

∽

According to Adrian Hastings, "the theological struggle from Nicaea in 325 to the Council of Chalcedon in 451 remains decisive for the evolution of both doctrine and the geographical shape of Christianity."[16] Jerome (347-420) provides an important insight into traditional theology and its development during this tumultuous era. Marriage followed guilt in Jerome's thinking because he believed nakedness and fig-leaves spoke of sexual passion, wherefore virginity – and chastity – was a return to the purity and equality which existed in the Garden before sin.[17] He concluded that, "in view of the purity of the body of Christ, all sexual intercourse is unclean,"[18] but he was careful to point out that he did not condemn marriage, or forbid it, but only subordinated it to virginity.[19] Hence, Jerome wanted virgins to remind themselves that Genesis 3.16 was only for the married woman, for the life they had accepted was independent from sexual differentiation.[20]

In Jerome's theology, the *married woman* was considered inferior and subjected to the man because of the sole guilt of Eve;[21] chaste women were equal to men in accordance with Galatians 3.28.

> And, indeed, when chastity is observed between man and woman, it begins to be true that there is neither male nor female; but, though living in the body, they are being changed into angels, among whom there is neither male nor female. The same is said by the same Apostle in another place: "As many of you as were baptized into Christ did put on Christ. There can be neither Jew nor Greek, there can be neither bond nor free, there can be no male and female: for ye are all one in Christ Jesus."[22]

Because Genesis 2.24 explicitly mentions marriage, Jerome explained that marriage is not found in the image of God, but is a metaphor of Christ and the Church. Since Christ had been a virgin in the flesh, husbands ought to

---

16. Adrian Hastings, ed. *A World History of Christianity*, (Grand Rapids: MI, Wm. B. Eerdmans Publishing Company, 1999), 47.

17. Jerome, "Letter XXII: To Eustochium," *The Letters of St. Jerome* 18-19.

18. Jerome, *Against Jovinianus*, Book I, 20.

19. "Letter XLVIII: To Pammachius" *The Letters of St. Jerome.*

20. "Letter XXII: to Eustochium" *The Letters of St. Jerome.* Irenaeus (180) believed Adam and Eve were virgins in the Garden but the exact reason for his belief is uncertain (Irenaeus, *Against Heresies*, Book III, XXII).

21. *Against Jovinianus*, Book I, 27.

22. *Apology of Jerome*, Book I, 28-29

love their wives as Christ – chastely,[23] wherefore even a married woman could become the man's equal through continence. Jerome explained further that "when difference of sex is done away, and we are putting off the old man, and putting on the new, then we are being born again into Christ a virgin."[24] I.e., we return to the time before the Fall.

> You have with you one who was once your partner in the flesh but is now your partner in the spirit; once your wife but now your sister; once a woman but now a man; once an inferior but now an equal. Under the same yoke as you she hastens toward the same heavenly kingdom.[25]

The equality of virgins is found already in the writings of Cyprian (200-258), the disciple of Tertullian.

> Hold fast, O virgins! hold fast what you have begun to be; hold fast what you shall be. A great reward awaits you, a great recompense of virtue, the immense advantage of chastity. Do you wish to know what ill the virtue of continence avoids, what good it possesses? "I will multiply," says God to the woman, "thy sorrows and thy groanings; and in sorrow shalt thou bring forth children; and thy desire shall be to thy husband, and he shall rule over thee." You are free from this sentence. You do not fear, the sorrows and the groans of women. You have no fear of child-bearing; nor is your husband lord over you; but your Lord and Head is Christ, after the likeness and in the place of the man; with that of men your lot and your condition is equal. It is the word of the Lord which says, "The children of this world beget and are begotten; but they who are counted worthy of that world, and of the resurrection from the dead, neither marry nor are given in marriage: neither shall they die any more: for they are equal to the angels of God, being the children of the resurrection."[26]

---

23. Ibid.
24. Jerome, *Against Jovinianus,* Book I, 16.
25. "Letter LXXI: To Lucinius," *The Letters of St. Jerome,* 3. Because his belief that sexual intercourse was caused by sin, Jerome felt compelled to transform the woman into a man for he no longer had a purpose for the sexual differentiation as a created order.
26. Cyprian, *Treatise II. On the Dress of Virgins,* 22.

Cyprian agreed with Jerome that Genesis 3.16 was a sentence for married women from which the virgin was exempted. Such distinction was possible only if the church taught the full equality of men and women as a created order and had to compromise in order to incorporate the inferiority and subjection of women into its teaching.

Although virginity was esteemed highly already during the apostolic era, the patristic rejection of marriage can be viewed as a reaction against the lax morality of Rome. As Christianity became an accepted religion of Rome in the fourth century and the church became somewhat worldly, celibacy became a requirement for the serious pursuit of holiness.[27] Celibacy took also the place of martyrdom as the persecution of Christians ceased with Emperor Constantine. Ambrose (340-397), bishop of Milan, who baptized Augustine, was one of the main advocates of celibacy in the fifth century and most of the great theological writers of the high patristic era followed his lead in endorsing celibacy as a means of recreating the simplicity and purity of the early church.[28]

∼

The belief that God subjected the woman to the man because of the sole guilt of Eve became an inseparable part of traditional theology through the Latin translation, the Vulgate, which Jerome finished in A.D. 404. In the Vulgate, Genesis 3.16 reads, "Sub viri potestate eris et ipse dominabitur tui." ("Under the man's authority will you be and he will rule over you") Jerome's translation did not follow the original Hebrew text – "Your turning shall be for the man and he shall rule over you" – for he interpreted the verse according to the

---

27. Also Jerome's contemporary Augustine (354-430) believed that temporary relationships, such as marriage, had become unimportant in the church, "For in that eternal kingdom to which He has vouchsafed to call His disciples, to whom He also gives the name of brothers, there are no temporal relationships of this sort. For 'there is neither Jew nor Greek, there is neither bond nor free, there is neither male nor female;' 'but Christ is all, and in all.' And the Lord Himself says: 'For in the resurrection they neither marry, nor are given in marriage, but are as the angels of God in heaven.' Hence it is necessary that whoever wishes here and now to aim after the life of that kingdom, should hate not the persons themselves, but those temporal relationships by which this life of ours, which is transitory and is comprised in being born and dying, is upheld" (Augustine, *Our Lord's Sermon on the Mount*, Book I, Ch. XV).

28. Hastings, 44-46.

fourth century belief that God punished the woman with subjection because she had displeased Him.

The Vulgate was *the* Bible for nearly a thousand years in Europe. No other translation existed although few spoke or understood Latin, which had become obsolete, and even fewer understood Greek or Hebrew, the original languages of the Bible. Benedicta Ward and G.R. Evans explain the development of theology during the millennium of the Vulgate.

> From the patristic period to the Reformation the Bible was the most important book in every monastic and cathedral library. That did not mean that ordinary people, or even most parish priests, had access to a copy, or any way of knowing exactly what it said. For most people, the Bible was literally a closed book. Those who did have a copy of it had it, of course, in the Vulgate, as only a handful scholars could read it in Greek.... Only those who had been educated as clerics or at the new universities could read it, and they had a pastoral responsibility to teach the uneducated masses what it said. The misinterpretation of the Bible could easily lead to heresy. Ordinary believers were therefore dependent on their parish priest to explain the Bible as well as he could, and many such priests were poorly educated and idle and did not do the job well. Until the later Middle Ages, when they could hear sermons preached by the friars, the faithful might have no other source of instruction. In worship week by week there was reading of the Bible, but a 'ministry of the Word' in Latin would tell people nothing unless there was some interpretation of the passage for them in their own language.... it is not surprising that for many people during the earlier Middle Ages their Christianity remained close to primitive superstition, and their ideas about God were often confused with beliefs of magic. Angels and devils and even saints could be hard to distinguish from the deities of paganism for those without education, as Augustine of Hippo and Gregory the Great both recognized.[29]

Because Thomas Aquinas by necessity used Jerome's interpretation of Genesis 3.16 in the thirteenth century, he believed that the subjection which began after the Fall was a proper punishment for the woman's sin. In the *Summa,* Thomas wrote, "As regards family life she was punished by being subjected

---

29. Ibid., 119-120.

to her husband's authority, and this is conveyed in the words, "Thou shalt be under thy husband's power." (Gen 3.16)"[30] In the same section, Thomas answered the question whether a wife was allowed to give alms without her husband's knowledge.

> I answer that, anyone who is under another's power must, as such, be ruled in accordance with the power of his superior: for the natural order demands that the inferior should be ruled according to its superior. Therefore in those matters in which the inferior is subject to his superior, his ministrations must be subject to the superior's permission.[31]

Thomas argued further that although the wife is "equal in the marriage act," she is under the husband's authority according to Genesis 3.16, and therefore not allowed to give alms without her husband's permission.

In the thirteenth century, equality as a created order was still recognized, wherefore Thomas had to answer the argument whether the woman should have been created before sin, because her subjection begun after the Fall.

> "Further, subjection and limitation were a result of sin, for to the woman was it said after sin (Genesis 3.16): "Thou shalt be under the man's power"; and Gregory says that, "Where there is no sin, there is no inequality." But woman is naturally of less strength and dignity than man; "for the agent is always more honorable than the patient," as Augustine says (Gen. ad lit. xii, 16). Therefore woman should not have been made in the first production of things before sin."[32]

Thomas answered, "as regards the individual nature, woman is defective and misbegotten [i.e. an impotent male]." But "as regards human nature in general, woman is not misbegotten, but is included in nature's intention as directed to the work of generation." He concluded that the woman's subjection is twofold: sin causes a subjection which is "servile, by virtue of which a superior makes use of a subject for his own benefit," but the subjection from

---

30. Thomas Aquinas, *Summa Theologica*, Second part of second part, Question 164, Article 2.
31. Ibid., Question 32, Article 8.
32. Ibid., First Part, Question 92, Objection 1.

creation is based on reason which predominates in the man, for good order can only be preserved if people are governed by those who are wiser.[33] In other words, because the woman is a defective human being, she cannot possess the man's reason, wherefore her subjection from Creation is due to her body, while the subjection which begun after the Fall was caused by her sin.

Notwithstanding the Aristotelian origin of Thomas's twofold subjection, it was accepted and incorporated into traditional theology. In the eighteenth and nineteenth century Protestant theology, the twofold subjection of the inferior woman was a central theme. Matthew Henry (1662-1714) believed the woman was equal due to her origin from the man (Gen 2.22) but also that the woman's creation for and from the man was the reason for her subjection (1 Tim 2.13; 1 Cor 11.8-0). Furthermore, Henry believed it was due to the Fall the woman was forbidden from usurping authority (Gen 3.16), for she who had been equal from creation, was made inferior due to sin. Yet, Henry maintained also that the subjection after the Fall "ought never to be complained of, though harsh; but sin must be complained of, that it made it so," for had the woman not taken the fruit she would never have complained of her subjection which begun at Creation. Because of Thomas Aquinas's twofold subjection, Henry used 1 Timothy 2 and 1 Corinthians 11 to create the subjection which he did not find in Genesis 2, which caused the contradiction in his theology.[34]

Adam Clarke (1760/2–1832) believed the woman was created neither inferior nor superior, for she was in all things like and equal to the man, (Gen 2.18) with equal powers, faculties and rights (Gen 2.21). And although the "woman had probably as much right to rule as the man" the subjection to the will of her husband is part of her curse (Gen 3.16). Yet, he believed also that because "Adam was first formed, then Eve," by "this very act God designed that he should have the pre-eminence." (1 Tim 2.13) But most importantly, Clarke adhered to the Aristotelian dogma according to which it is the structure of the woman's body which shows her inferiority to the man.[35]

Albert Barnes (1798–1870), who wrote as the women's rights movement was

---

33. Ibid., Question 92, Answer to Objection 2.

34. Matthew Henry, *Matthew Henry's Commentary on the Whole Bible: New Modern Edition,* Electronic Database, Hendrickson Publishers, Inc., 1991.

35. Adam Clarke, *Adam Clarke's Commentary on the whole Bible*, Electronic Database, Biblesoft, 1996.

being formed, made the woman a complete contradiction. Barnes believed that the woman's creation from the man made her the man's equal (Gen 2.20),[36] but because she took the lead in transgression, she was subjected to her husband's will (Gen 3.16). Although the woman was not to be regarded inferior in rank and nature because she was created from the man, Adam's prior creation signifies that "the woman should occupy a subordinate situation, and not usurp authority" (1 Tim 2.13), the veil being "the usual and appropriate symbol of their occupying a rank inferior to the man" (1 Cor 11.3, 9). It is not possible to reconcile the contradictions in Barnes's text, but if we remove 1 Timothy 2 and 1 Corinthians 11 from the equation, we find that Barnes affirms that the woman was created an equal and was subjected as a result of the Fall.

In conclusion, although the Council for Biblical Manhood and Womanhood portrays the man's authority as apostolic in origin and the current debate as an orthodox defense of the historical understanding of the church, the true subject of the debate is not whether egalitarianism is a pagan import, but whether egalitarians are correct in advocating for the rejection of the twofold subjection introduced by Thomas Aquinas.

---

36. Albert Barnes, *Barnes' Notes on the New Testament*, Electronic Database, Biblesoft, 1997.

CHAPTER 1

Gen 3.16

On such terms we might amuse ourselves without fear of offending each other in the field of Scripture, but I might well wonder if the amusement was not at my expense. For I confess to your Charity that I have learned to yield this respect and honour only to the canonical books of Scripture: of these alone do I most firmly believe that the authors were completely free from error. And if in these writings I am perplexed by anything which appears to me opposed to truth, I do not hesitate to suppose that either the Ms. is faulty, or the translator has not caught the meaning of what was said, or I myself have failed to understand it. As to all other writings, in reading them, however great the superiority of the authors to myself in sanctity and learning, I do not accept their teaching as true on the mere ground of the opinion being held by them; but only because they have succeeded in convincing my judgment of in truth either by means of these canonical writings themselves, or by arguments addressed to my reason. I believe, my brother, that this is your own opinion as well as mine. I do not need to say that I do not suppose you to wish your books to be read like those of prophets or of apostles, concerning which it would be wrong to doubt that they are free from error. Far be such arrogance from that humble piety and just estimate of yourself which I know you to have, and without which assuredly you would not have said, "Would that I could receive your embrace, and that by converse we might aid each other in learning!"

– AUGUSTINE[1]

∽

---

1. Augustine, "Letter LXXXII: To Jerome," *Letters of St. Augustine.*

THE EUROPEAN RENAISSANCE (ca. 1300-1600) revived the study of Greek and Hebrew, which indirectly led to the division of the Western Church in 1517. As the Reformation gained a following, and translations in the vernacular became readily available, the Council of Trent (1545-1563) declared that it would recognize only the Vulgate. The standardization of the Vulgate created the Clementine Vulgate (1592), which remained in use until the Second Vatican Council (1962-65) permitted liturgy to be performed in the vernacular.

In the Clementine Vulgate, Jerome's interpretation of Genesis 3.16 was preserved as it was also in Douay-Rheims (1610), the English translation of the Vulgate, still in use, albeit unofficially. The official Catholic Bible in the United States, the New American Bible with revised Psalms and New Testament (1988), replaced Jerome's translation with, "Yet your urge shall be for your husband, and he shall be your master." The most commonly used Catholic version outside of the United States, the New Jerusalem Bible (1985), translates Genesis 3.16, "Your yearning will be for your husband and he will dominate you."[2]

The sixteenth-century reformers rejected Jerome's Genesis 3.16 and translated *teshuwqah* with "desire." Although Wayne Grudem does not believe that the meaning of *teshuwqah* is sexual desire,[3] it appears that the origin of the English translation "desire" is "lust," which has a sexual connotation, as explained in the *Hard Sayings of the Bible*.

> It was Catherine C. Bushnell who did the pioneering research on this problem. She traced its genesis to an Italian Dominician monk named Pagnino who translated the Hebrew Bible. Pagnino, according to the infamous biblical critic Richard Simon, "too much neglected the ancient versions of Scripture to attach himself to the teachings of the rabbis." Pagnino's version was published in Lyons in 1528, seven years before Coverdale's English Bible. Now except for Wycliffe's 1380 English version and the Douay Bible of 1609, both of which were made from the Latin Vulgate, every English version from the time of Pagnino up to the present day has adopted Pagnino's rendering for Genesis 3.16. The older English Bibles, following Pagnino, rendered

---

2. See www.catholic.org.

3. Wayne Grudem, *Systematic Theology*, (Grand Rapids, MI: Zondervan, 1994), Footnote 20, 464.

this verse as "Thy lust [or lusts] shall pertayne [pertain] to thy husband." Clearly, then, the sense given to the word by Pagnino and his followers was that of libido or sensual desire. The only place that Bushnell could locate such a concept was in the "Ten Curses of Eve" in the Talmud.[4]

In the Ten Curses of Eve found in the Talmud, *teshuwqah* is given the meaning "sexual desire."[5] The same is found also in *The Jewish Study Bible*.[6]

Luther gave *teshuwqah* sexual overtones when he used the word *Verlangen* which means "longing, craving, yearning" in his German Bible (1545).[7] Similarly, Finland, a stronghold of Lutheranism, followed Luther's rendering; in the Finnish translation *teshuwqah* is translated with the word *haluta* which signifies "to desire or crave." In the neighboring Sweden, the translators chose the words *åtrå* (1917) and *lust* (1998); both have a sexual connotation.

The reformers accepted the word *desire* partly because of their rejection of the patristic legacy of equating sexuality with sin. In Augustine's theology, for example, the body, and by analogy the sexual woman, was sinful because of its tendency to draw the soul towards earthly pleasures. Despite the emphasis on celibacy and the strong monastic movement, the church was not able to eradicate sexual desire and as a result the sexual woman was seen as a threat for the celibate man, as described by Karen Jo Torjesen.

> But for the celibate males, the danger was not attacks of impotence, but, according to church authorities, the lure of female sexuality.

---

4. Kaiser, Davids, Bruce, Brauch, *Hard Sayings of the Bible* (Downers Grove, IL: Inter-Varsity Press, 1996), 98.

5. "*[6] And thy desire shall be to your husband' teaches that a women yearns for her husband when he is about to set out on a journey, [7] and he shall rule over thee' teaches that while a wife solicits [her husband to make love to her] with her heart [i.e. not explicitly], the husband does so with his mouth [i.e., he makes his desires known verbally]*" (Berel Dov Lerner, "*The Ten Curses of Eve*," http://jewishbible.blogspot.com/2005/10/ten-curses-of-eve-unpublishable.html [accessed June 29, 2009]).

6. "The woman will suffer pain in childbirth, experience sexual desire for her husband, yet be subordinate to him" (*The Jewish Study Bible* (New York: Oxford University Press, 2004), 17).

7. Reverso Dictionary, http://dictionary.reverso.net/german-english/Verlangen (accessed June 29, 2009), s.v. "Verlangen."

In 1484 the pope's fiery zeal to quench sexual desire ignited into a frightening conflagration. In this year a papal bull of Innocent VIII, "The Witches' Bull," enlisted the Inquisition as a judicial process for prosecuting witches who had allegedly given themselves to the devil sexually and had thereby become his instruments for inflaming, controlling, and obstructing sexual desire.... The inquisitors' view of women's dangerous sexuality should come as no surprise. Female sexuality appeared dangerous because men believed they had to control women, and in the end they were not able to. What was new was the fusion with Augustine's theology of sexuality. Sexual passion was in itself rebellion against the rational soul, and a rebellion against the rational soul was like rebellion against God.[8]

The belief that the woman was oversexed culminated in the witch craze (1560-1760), which swept through Europe and led to the destruction of over one hundred thousand women in the aftermath of the Reformation. Anne Llewellyn Barstow does not believe the witch craze was caused by the religious wars of Europe, but that they were connected to the wars as an outlet of religious anxiety.[9] The German-speaking lands, the birthplace of the Reformation, experienced the most severe persecutions, approximately three-fourths of the executions being carried out in the Holy Roman Empire. The Catholic territories in the German-speaking lands experienced the most attacks. But whereas the Catholics executed three times as many witches as Protestants,[10] they did not execute Protestant women - they killed their own.

Rejecting the Catholic association of witchcraft with female sexuality, Luther identified sorcery with the disobedient wife, thus freeing women to affirm their sexuality but putting them into the bind of an increasingly male-dominant family. What Protestantism gave women by encouraging them to become literate and to share religious life at home it took away with its ideal of the submissive wife. Catholicism, by maintaining its insistence on the dangerous nature of female

---

8. Karen Jo Torjesen, *When Women Were Priests, Women's Leadership in the Early Church and the Scandal of their Subordination in the Rise of Christianity* (San Fransisco, CA: Harper, 1993) 228-229, 233.

9. Anne Llewellyn Barstow, *Witchcraze* (San Francisco, CA: Harper San Francisco, 1994) 128-129.

10. Ibid., 58-59.

sexuality, kept the identification of all sexually active women with witches. All German women were endangered by the prevailing ideologies, but Catholic women had the most to fear.[11]

Martin Luther, a former Catholic monk, rejected celibacy in favor of marriage, and his translation of *teshuwqah* with *Verlangen* can be viewed as an affirmation of the goodness of marriage and the sexual nature of women, which Catholicism considered sinful.[12] But Luther's rejection of virginity created the all-encompassing vocation of marriage and motherhood for all women, which changed also Mary, the mother of Jesus, from an epitome of perpetual virginity into a submissive housewife.[13] As so often in theology, the truth is found in the middle. In 1 Corinthians 7, Paul wrote, "But I say to the unmarried and to the widows: It is good for them if they remain even as I am; but if they cannot exercise self-control, let them marry. For it is better to marry than to burn with passion" (1 Cor 7.8-9). Neither celibacy nor marriage is the perfect choice, for although it is good to marry, the unmarried can serve the Lord without distraction (1 Cor 7.35). To his disciples' objection that it is better not to marry if the man cannot divorce his wife at will, Jesus answered:

> "All cannot accept this saying, but only those to whom it has been given: For there are eunuchs who were born thus from their mother's womb, and there are eunuchs who were made eunuchs by men, and there are eunuchs who have made themselves eunuchs for the kingdom of heaven's sake. He who is able to accept it, let him accept it." (Matt 19.11-12)

---

11. Ibid., 59.

12. Most theological positions are a reaction against an excess of another, but due to the tendency of theologians to choose the polar opposite, another form of excess is created, only to be refuted later by others.

13. How Mary is viewed indicates how the church views women in general; in the early church, Mary was elevated into divinity in a direct correlation to the lowering of women's position in the church, for as women became inferior, it became inconceivable that God that could have been born of an sinful woman. In Protestantism, Mary is deprived from all distinctions to enforce the doctrine of the woman's subjection. But Mary was neither divine, nor the epitome of modern homemaking, for God was born of an ordinary woman whose faith was extraordinary, and who as a result has been called blessed by all generations (Luke 1:48).

~

Nearly four hundred years after Jerome's false translation was rejected by Protestant theologians, Genesis 3.16 was returned to its original position as a description of a consequence of sin. The Catholic response to the changing of the interpretation of Genesis 3.16 is seen in that although Rev. Regis Scanlon refers to Thomas's twofold subjection, he views the verse as a description of a "bad" subjection given to Eve as a punishment and "a constant threat" from which the married couple escapes, for the husband's authority is given to bring about mutual submission based upon their free commitment.[14] I.e., Scanlon no longer agrees with Thomas's view that Genesis 3.16 mandates the man to rule over the woman. Scanlon believes also that the virgin overcomes the negative effect of the Fall and "the threatened rule of the male over the female" by being under the authority of the Catholic Church, for in his view it is "the perfect fulfillment of that hierarchy of authority found in God's creation." But by this statement he contradicts himself, for the church has always been, and still is, considered feminine, and thus he makes a celibate man subject to a woman, so to speak. Perhaps Scanlon considers the celibate man to be subject to the authority of the bishop, who is always male, and not to the church *per se*. But even if we would allow for such a distinction, the celibate man's subjection does not fulfill the hierarchy in which a *man* has authority over a *woman*, unless we consider the celibate man to have become a woman.

If the church has always taught a creation based hierarchy, why does Scanlon refer only to the thirteenth-century theologian Thomas Aquinas? In fact, it is Scanlon's own argument which proves the impossibility of implementing such a hierarchy in the case of virgins, which accords well with the patristic belief that virgins and chaste women were equal with men. Thus we may conclude that the first-century church did not teach a creation based hierarchy in which the man had authority over the woman, for although virginity was highly esteemed, also marriage was approved of and not viewed as a consequence of sin.

The editors of *Recovering Biblical Manhood and Womanhood*, John Piper and Wayne Grudem, agree with Christians for Biblical Equality that Genesis

---

14. Rev. Regis Scanlon, *Women Deacons: At What Price? Catholic Culture*, http://www.catholicculture.org/culture/library/view.cfm?id=3439&repos=1&subrepos=0&searchid=482727 (accessed June 29, 2009).

3.16 is not a prescription of what should be.[15] However, Grudem does not believe that the verse is the beginning of the man's rule, but that it describes a distortion of the previously harmonious relationship due to man's harsh rule and the woman's desire to rebel against the man's authority.[16] Piper acknowledges that historically there has been "grave abuse" and that even in our days men are sometimes "too possessive, harsh, domineering, and belittling,"[17] but he cannot provide historical proof of a similar "grave abuse" of women controlling men, for women have never ruled over men;[18] instead, they have cooperated by "trying hard to live down to what is expected of them."[19] Most women have been, and still are, dominated by men and Raymond C. Ortlund Jr. believes there is a good reason for it.

> Because she usurped his headship in the temptation, God hands her over to the misery of competition with her rightful head. *This is justice,* a measure-for measure response to her sin.... First, God may be saying, "You will have a desire, Eve. You will want to control your husband, but he must not allow you to have your way with him, he must rule over you."... In this case, we would take "rule" as the exercise of godly headship.... Second, God may be saying, "You will have a desire, Eve. You will want to control your husband, But he will not allow you to have your way with him, He will rule over you." If this is the true sense, then, in giving the woman up to her insubordinate desire, God is penalizing her with domination by her husband. Accordingly, 3.16b should be rendered" "Your desire will be for your husband, and he will rule over you." The word "rule" would now be construed as the exercise of ungodly domination.[20]

Ortlund cannot choose either of the two options he gives, for the first option goes against Grudem's view that "he must rule over you" is not "a prescription of what should be."[21] The second option would make God, not sin,

---

15. Piper and Grudem, 409.

16. *Systematic Theology,* 463-464.

17. Piper and Grudem, 42.

18. Rosalind Rosenberg, *Beyond Separate Spheres: Intellectual Roots of Modern Feminism* (New Haven, CT: Yale University Press, 1982), 111.

19. Ibid., 172.

20. Piper and Grudem, 109.

21. Ibid., 409.

the source of the man's harsh rule, since God is seen as penalizing the woman with the man's ungodly dominion, which Ortlund himself calls "a monster and a virus," from which women need to be released.[22] That God punished Eve with subjection was the patristic interpretation based on the sole guilt of Eve which became the foundation for the twofold subjection of the woman in the thirteenth century. And as seen in Ortlund's theology, it is still a necessary component to support the subjection of woman as a created order.

Neither Grudem nor Ortlund are able to explain Genesis 3.16 for they give *teshuwqah* the meaning "desire to conquer or control" because of Genesis 4.7: "If you do well, will you not be accepted? And if you do not do well, sin lies at the door. And its desire is for you, but you should rule over it." Grudem finds a connection between the two verses because of the similarity of the language and he concludes that the woman has a desire to conquer the man just as sin has a desire to conquer humans.[23] But if the woman desires to control the man while the man becomes increasingly passive [24] how should one explain the conspicuous absence of matriarchs, especially since a society in which sin is ruled by humans does not exist? In addition, if the woman desires to conquer and control the man, she becomes an enemy who must be subjected and ruled as Ortlund perhaps unwittingly recognized.

Also Augustine made a connection between Genesis 3.16 and 4.7, but for a different reason.

> "Fret not thyself," or compose thyself, He says: withhold thy hand from crime; let not sin reign in your mortal body to fulfill it in the lusts thereof, nor yield your members instruments of unrighteousness unto sin. "For to thee shall be its turning," so long as you do not encourage it by giving it the rein, but bridle it by quenching its fire. "And thou shall rule over it;" for when it is not allowed any external actings, it yields itself to the rule of the governing mind and righteous will, and ceases from even internal motions. There is something similar said in the same divine book of the woman, when God questioned and judged them after their sin, and pronounced sentence on them all,—the devil in the form of the serpent, the woman and her

22. Ibid., 105.
23. *Systematic Theology,* Footnote 20, 464.
24. Piper and Grudem, 346.

husband in their own persons. For when He had said to her, "I will greatly multiply thy sorrow and thy conception; in sorrow shall thou bring forth children," then He added, "and thy turning shall be to thy husband, and he shall rule over thee." What is said to Cain about his sin, or about the vicious concupiscence of his flesh, is here said of the woman who had sinned; and we are to understand that the husband is to rule his wife as the soul rules the flesh. And therefore, says the apostle, "He that loveth his wife, loveth himself; for no man ever yet hated his own flesh." This flesh, then, is to be healed, because it belongs to ourselves: is not to be abandoned to destruction as if it were alien to our nature.[25]

Augustine was a Platonist before converting to Christianity [26] and he used Plato's body-soul dichotomy as the foundation for his doctrine on how men and women should relate to each.[27] In Augustine's theology, the soul will be restored to its proper nature only through its subjection to the spirit, and likewise, the body, which has become a nature that serves the law of sin, will be restored only through subjection to the soul. By analogy, the woman must be in subjection to the man to restore her to her proper nature, for Augustine believed that it was only after sin entered that "we are to understand that the husband is to rule his wife as the soul rules the flesh."[28]

Despite all efforts, it is not possible to create an analogy between the woman and sin, for as Rabbi Moshe Chaim Luzzatto explains, when the objects are found to be dissimilar, the analogy is invalid.[29] In chapter 3 God speaks to Eve about the man's rule, while in chapter 4 God speaks to Cain about his own rule over sin; one is acted upon while the other is the actor. In other words, Cain is warned that the he must resist sin to protect himself, but the woman is warned that the man is going to rule over her when she turns to him.

The pre-Christian Greek translation of the Old Testament, the Septuagint, (ca 250 B.C.) translated *teshuwqah* with *apostrophê*, which means "to turn," "to

---

25. Augustine, *City of God*, Book XV, Ch. 7.

26. Augustine, *Confessions,* Book VII, Ch. XX-XXI.

27. Augustine, *A Treatise on Faith and the Creed*, Ch. 10, 23.

28. *City of God*, Book XV, Ch 7.

29. Rabbi Moshe Chaim Luzzatto, *The Ways of Reason, New Revised Edition* (Jerusalem: Feldheim Publisher, 1997), 100.

resort, to recourse," and rhetorically, "when one turns away from all others to one, and addresses him specially."[30] The apostolic church used the Septuagint, but with the introduction of the sole guilt of Eve, the woman's turning to the man begun to be viewed as a sentence from God – a tradition begun, as far as can be ascertained, in the second century with Tertullian.

> If there dwelt upon earth a faith as great as is the reward of faith which is expected in the heavens, no one of you at all, best beloved sisters, from the time that she had first "known the Lord," and learned (the truth) concerning her own (that is, woman's) condition, would have desired too gladsome (not to say too ostentatious) a style of dress; so as not rather to go about in humble garb, and rather to affect meanness of appearance, walking about as Eve mourning and repentant, in order that by every garb of penitence she might the more fully expiate that which she derives from Eve, – the ignominy, I mean, of the first sin, and the odium (attaching to her as the cause) of human perdition. "In pains and in anxieties dost thou bear (children), woman; and toward thine husband (is) thy inclination [*conuersion*], and he lords it over thee." And do you not know that you are (each) an Eve? The sentence of God on this sex of yours lives in this age: the guilt must of necessity live too. *You* are the devil's gateway: *you* are the unsealer of that (forbidden) tree: *you* are the first deserter of the divine law: *you* are she who persuaded him whom the devil was not valiant enough to attack. *You* destroyed so easily God's image, man. On account of *your* desert – that is, death – even the Son of God had to die [31]

That all blame was placed on women was a decidedly Roman concept, which departed from the Grecian belief that the woman was helpless and therefore blameless, for the Roman woman was a force to be reckoned with. Even when the fault was clearly the man's, the woman had to accept the consequences, wherefore Lucretia committed suicide after being raped rather than be a living unchaste example. Although the woman's only option was to die if she fell for temptation, the man went ahead and married someone else, innocent as

---

30. Perseus Digital Library, www.perseus.tufts.edu (accessed June 29, 2009), s.v. "apostrophe."

31. Tertullian, *On the Apparel of Women*, Book I, Ch. I.

he was in the eyes of the world.[32] Ellen G. White, the founder of the Seventh Day Adventists, had a similar view of the superfluity of women, for she wrote, "Had Adam remained faithful God would have created another companion for him."[33]

Jerome knew *teshuwqah* meant "to turn,"[34] but he understood the woman's turning to signify her subjection to the man because of her sole guilt. Also Jerome's contemporary, Chrysostom, believed that the woman was subjected because "she made an ill use of her privilege and she who had been made a helper was found to be an ensnarer and ruined all then she is justly told for the future, 'thy turning shall be to thy husband.'"[35]

Sir Lancelot C.L. Brenton translated the Septuagint into English in 1851, but he followed the theology of his time (or the Vulgate) more than the Greek text for he wrote, "And thy submission shall be to thy husband, and he shall rule over thee."[36] Robert J.V. Hiebert (2007) followed the Greek literally and therefore translated the verse, "Your recourse will be to your husband and he will dominate you."[37] In *La Sagrada Biblia,* a Spanish translation of the Septuagint, *teshuwqah* is translated with the word "conversion," which is derived from the Latin *convertere* ("to turn around").[38]

Because modern theology rejects the sole guilt of Eve, and because the belief that the woman desires to conquer the man is clearly incorrect, how should we understand Genesis 3.16? The context is that of childbearing and the woman's relationship to the man. Caring for an infant in the hostile new world made Eve unable to provide for herself and her child, which caused her to turn to Adam for protection and provisions. According to Rabbi Samson

---

32. *The Roman Way,* 149-150.

33. Mercedes H. Dyer, ed. *Prove All Things, a response to Women in Ministry* (Berrien Springs, MI: Adventists Affirm, 2000), 118.

34. "And that after displeasing God she was immediately subjected to the man, and began to turn to her husband." (*Against Jovinianus,* Book I, 27).

35. *Homilies on 1 Corinthians 11,* Homily XXVI.

36. "Genesis," *English Translation of the Greek Septuagint Bible,* http://www.ecmarsh .com/lxx/Genesis/indExod.htm. (accessed June 29, 2009).

37. "Genesis," *A New English Translation of the Septuagint Bible* (Oxford University Press, 2007) http://ccat.sas.upenn.edu/nets/edition/01-gen-nets.pdf (accessed June 29, 2009).

38. "Y hacia tu marido, tu conversión, y él te dominará." (La Sagrada Biblia, Version de la Septuaginta al Espanol, Pbro. Guillermo Junemann Beckschaefer, http://www.synodia. org/libros/junemann/ [accessed June 29, 2009]).

Raphael Hirsch, "The new conditions of life that made sustenance the product of hard labor would naturally make women dependent on the physically stronger men."[39] But as the woman turned to the man, he had an opportunity to rule over her due to his greater physical strength. Childbearing and ruling have traditionally been considered the dividing difference between men and women due to the false interpretation of Genesis 3.16. But in reality it is only in the physical realm that men and women differ, for both men and woman are equally intelligent and capable of making decisions, although they may perform the tasks differently.

John Stuart Mill explained how man's strength became the source of his rule in *The Subjection of Women* (1869):

> And in the second place, the adoption of this system of inequality never was the result of deliberation, or forethought, or any social idea, or any notion whatever of what conducted to the benefit of humanity or the good order of society. It arouse simply from the fact that from the very earliest twilight of human society, every woman (owing to the value attached to her by men, combined with her inferiority in muscular strength) was found in a state of bondage to some man. Laws and system of polity always begin by recognising [sic] the relations they find already existing between individuals. They convert what was mere physical fact into a legal right, give it the sanction of society, and principally aim at the substitution of public and organized means of asserting and protecting these rights, instead of the irregular and lawless conflict of physical strength. Those who were already been compelled to obedience became in this manner legally bound to it.[40]

Mill explained that as "the law of the strongest" was abandoned and no one was allowed to practice it in the civilized nations, people forgot the true reason for the institution. He wrote, "People flatter themselves that the rule of mere force is ended; that the law of the strongest cannot be the reason of existence of anything which has remained in full operation down to the present time."

---

39. Rabbit Samson Raphael Hirsch, *The Chumash: The Stone edition* (Brooklyn, NY: Mesorah Publications, 1996), 8.

40. John Stuart Mill, *The Subjection of Women* (New York City: Source Book Press, 1970), 8-9.

Instead, they thought the institutions had "been preserved to this period of advanced civilization by a well-grounded feeling of its adaptation to human nature, and conductiveness to the general good."[41] But as Mill points out, the "unnatural generally means only uncustomary, and that everything which is usual appears natural." Thus Aristotle considered slavery natural; the divine right of the king was believed to have originated from God and the feudal nobility considered their power over the serfs to be "supremely natural" – as did the serfs themselves.[42]

The seductiveness of the man's rule over the woman is that it gives every man the opportunity to rule, even if they are subject to other men.

> Instead of being, to most of its supporters, a thing desirable chiefly in the abstract, or, like the political ends usually contended for by factions, of little private importance to any but the leaders; it comes home to the person and hearth of every male head of a family, and of every one who looks forwards to being so. The clodhopper exercises, or is to exercise, his share of the power equally with the highest nobleman. And the case is that in which the desire of power is the strongest: for every one who desires power, desires it most over those who are nearest to him, with whom his life is passed, with whom he has most concerns in common, and in whom any independence of his authority is oftenest likely to interfere with his individual preferences. It, in the other cases specified, powers manifestly grounded only on force, and having so much less to support them, are so slowly and with so much difficulty got rid of, much more it be so with this, even if it rests on no better foundation than those. We must consider, too, that the possessors of the power have facilities in this case, greater than in any other, to prevent any uprising against it. Every one of the subjects lives under the very eye, and almost, it may be said, in the hands, of one of the masters – in closer intimacy with him than with any of her fellow-subjects; with no means of combining against him, no power of even locally overmastering him, and, on the other hand, with the strongest motives for seeking his favor and avoiding to give him offence. In struggles for political emancipation, everybody knows how often its champions are bought off by bribes, or daunted

---

41. Ibid., 11.
42. Ibid., 21-23.

by terrors. In the case of women, each individual of the subject-class is in a chronic state of bribery and intimidation combined.[43]

The subject feels compelled to please the master, especially if she fears violence, and this has been true of women ever since their subjection to men began. Male violence against women is accepted in all societies in which women are excluded from lawmaking, but female violence against men is not equally tolerated.[44] As a result, few women have complained about the subjection openly. Most have accepted the rule, for "it is a political law of nature that those who are under any power of ancient origin, never begin by complaining of the power itself, but only of its oppressive exercise."[45] As women obtained the right to vote in the twentieth century, and the opportunity to change laws, they made male violence against themselves illegal and eventually felt safe enough to begin to challenge the rule itself, such as the false interpretation of Genesis 3.16 – the foundation of the twofold subjection.

---

43. Ibid., 18-20.
44. E.g. in England the old law used to condemn the wife who killed her husband (who was legally her Lord) to be burnt on the stake (Ibid., 54).
45. Ibid., 25.

CHAPTER 2

1 Cor 14.34-35

It is better for a man to be silent and be [a Christian],
Than to talk and not to be one. It is good to teach, if he who speaks also
acts.
There is then one Teacher, who spoke and it was done;
While even those things which He did in silence are worthy of the Father.
He who possesses the word of Jesus, is truly able to hear even His very
silence,
That he may be perfect, and may both act as he speaks,
And be recognized by his silence.

— IGNATIUS[1]

WEINRICH OBSERVES CORRECTLY that it was during the patristic and
medieval periods that "patterns of conduct and ecclesial behavior were
developed and solidified," and that the fathers of the Reformation adopted the
medieval practice of excluding women from the clergy "without question."[2]

> Martin Luther (d. 1547) consistently maintained a priesthood of all
> believers (especially on the basis of 1 Peter 2.9). This common priest-
> hood possesses the right and power to exercise all "priestly offices"
> (teach, preach, baptize, administer the Eucharist, bind and loose sin,
> pray for others, sacrifice, judge doctrine and spirits). Yet, Luther habit-
> ually combines 1 Corinthians 14.34 with Genesis 3.16 to assert that

---

1. Ignatius, Letter to the Ephesians, Ch. XV.
2. Piper and Grudem, 279.

women are excluded from the public exercise of the common priest-hood. In view of the "ordinance and creation of God" that women are subject to their husbands, Paul forbade women "to preach in the congregation where men are present who are skilled in speaking, so that respect and discipline may be maintained." However, if no man is present to preach, then "it would be necessary for the woman to preach." For Luther, the apostolic prohibition of 1 Corinthians 14.34 was determinative.[3]

But if Genesis 3.16 does not describe what should be, why did Luther connect the verse with 1 Corinthians 14.34 to affirm that women were excluded from the common priesthood? Because he followed tradition and not all traditions follow the Bible.

Luther's exclusion of women has it's origin in a tradition begun by Tertul-lian (145-220). Karen Jo Torjesen describes Tertullian's vision of the church as an essentially Roman institution.

> Tertullian's description of the Christian community dramatically marks the transition of the model of the church from the household or private association to the body politic. With him the church became a legal body (*corpus* or *societas*, the term the Romans used for the body politic) unified by a common law (*lex fidei*, "the law of faith") and a common discipline (*disciplina*, Christian morality). For Tertullian the church, like Roman society, united a diversity of ethic groups into one body under the rule of one law... Tertullian conceived the society of the church as analogous to Roman society, divided into distinct classes or ranks, which were distinguished from one another in terms of honor and authority.[4]

Only those who were full members of the political body could possess *ius docendi* (the legal right to teach) and *ius baptizandi* (legal right to baptize). Women could not be full members and therefore they were excluded from the clergy. But Tertullian excluded women also from the laity, for although the laity could perform the legal functions in the absence of the clergy, women could not.

---

3. Ibid., 278.
4. Torjesen, 162-3.

"It is not permitted to a *woman* to speak in the church; but neither (is it permitted her) to teach, nor to baptize, nor to offer, nor to claim to herself a lot in any manly function, not to say (in any) sacerdotal office."[5]

Weinrich considers Tertullian "a representative voice" of the universal church of the second century,[6] but he cannot do so without excluding women from the church altogether.

Thomas Aquinas continued to connect 1 Corinthians 14.34 to Genesis 3.16 in the Medieval Church.

The apostle says: "Let women keep silence in the churches," and "I suffer not a woman to teach." Now this pertains especially to the grace of the word. Therefore the grace of the word is not becoming to women.... First and chiefly, on account of the condition attaching to the female sex, whereby women should be subject to man, *as appears from Genesis 3.16.* Now teaching and persuading publicly in the church belong not to subjects but to prelates (although men who are subjects may do these things if they be so commissioned, because their subjection is not a result of their natural sex, as it is with women, but of some thing supervening by accident). Secondly, lest men's minds be enticed to lust, for it is written (Sirach 9.11): "Her conversation burneth as fire." Thirdly, because as a rule women are not perfected in wisdom, so as to be fit to be intrusted with public teaching."[7]

Luther inherited Thomas's theology, and the Protestant churches have continued Luther's habit of connecting Genesis 3.16 and 1 Corinthians 14.34-35, as seen in William MacDonald's *Believer's Bible Commentary.*[8]

---

5. Tertullian, *On the Veiling of Virgins,* Ch. IX.

6. Piper and Grudem, 273.

7. *Summa Theologica,* Second Part of Second Part, Question 177, Article 2.

8. MacDonald proposes *laleo* means "to speak authoritatively," which creates the absurd position of allowing children, but not women, to speak with authority: "When I was a child, I spake *[laleo]* as a child." (1 Cor 13.11, KJV; William MacDonald, *Believer's Bible Commentary,* [Nashville, TN: Thomas Nelson Publishers, Inc, 1980]).

We believe that the expression 'as the law also says' has reference to the woman's being submissive to the man. This is clearly taught in the law, which here probably means the Pentateuch primarily. Genesis 3.16, for instance says "your desire shall be for your husband, and he shall rule over you."[9]

But MacDonald cannot remain consistent in his theology, for Christian freedom from the law is one of the central themes of the New Testament.

The Christian has died to the law; he has nothing more to do with it. … Christians who desire to be under the law as a pattern of behavior do not realize that this places them under its curse. *Moreover, they cannot touch the law in one point without being responsible to keep it completely.* The only way we can live to God is by being dead to the law.[10]

∼

Although Tertullian believed women ought to be silenced in the church, he did not know what to make of the reference to the Law.

When enjoining on women silence in the church, that they speak not for the mere sake of learning (although that even they have the right of prophesying, he has already shown when he covers the woman that prophesies with a veil), he goes to the law for his sanction that woman should be under obedience. Now this law, let me say once for all, he ought to have made no other acquaintance with, than to destroy it.[11]

By the fourth century, the Law no longer posed a problem, for the inferiority of the woman and the sole guilt of Eve had changed the meaning of Genesis 3.16 from a consequence of sin to a commandment of God. Chrysostom combined 1 Corinthians 14.34 with Genesis 3.16 without discussion and maintained that women should be silent in the Church because "the woman is in some sort a weaker being and easily carried away and light minded."[12]

In the eighteenth- and nineteenth-century theology the inferiority of the

---

9. MacDonald, "1 Cor 14.34-35," 1802.
10. Ibid., "Gal 2.19," 1880.
11. Tertullian, *Five Books Against Marcion*, Book V, VIII.
12. *Homilies on First Corinthians,* Homily, XXXVII.

woman was the reason for her silence. Matthew Henry concluded that women ought to be silent and refrain from teaching in the church because, "it is the woman's duty to learn in subjection, it is the man's duty to keep up his superiority, by being able to instruct her."[13] Adam Clarke believed women prophesied in the Early Church because of 1 Cor 11.5, but because of the apparent contradiction with 1 Cor 14.34, he concluded that the latter forbade only asking questions, not all speech.[14] Clarke thought "the law" had reference to Genesis 3.16, as did Barnes and Tertullian, but although Tertullian allowed women to pray and prophesy, Barnes concluded that the silencing of women in the Church could not be disputed because the rule was "positive, explicit, and universal."[15] He equated foreign languages and prophesy with public speaking and therefore they were only for "the male portion of the congregation." And as to the contradiction between chapters 11 and 14, for Barnes there was none, for he thought Paul was forbidding women from speaking "on every ground."[16]

D.A. Carson disagrees with Weinrich's approval of Luther's habit of connecting Genesis 3.16 and 1 Corinthians 14.34 in his essay *Silent in the Churches*.

> By this clause [the law says], Paul is probably not referring to Genesis 3.16, as many suggest, but to the creation order in Genesis 2.20b-24, for it is to that Scripture that Paul explicitly turns to on two others occasions when he discusses female roles (1 Corinthians 11.8, 9; 1 Timothy 2.13).[17]

But the new connection is not without problems. The phrase "the law says" is found three times in the New Testament: Rom 3.19, 1 Cor 9.8, and 1 Cor 14.34. Carson concedes that Paul usually provides the actual verse from the Old Testament, which is true of the first two examples, but he believes Paul

---

13. "1 Cor 14.34-35," Matthew Henry's Commentary on the Whole Bible: New Modern Edition.

14. "1 Cor 14.34-35," *Adam Clarke's Commentary on the whole Bible.*

15. But if women are not allowed to speak in the church, why did Peter write if "anyone speaks, let him speak as the oracles of God" (1 Pet 4.11)? A similar prohibition against female speech is not found in his letters.

16. *Barnes' Notes on the New Testament.*

17. Piper and Grudem, 152.

has already provided the verse (Genesis 2.20-4) in 1 Corinthians 11. Carson believes also that the reference to the Law should be understood as *Scripture*, which includes the Creation account.[18] However, Genesis 1-3 is not called "the Law" or "Scripture" in the Bible; it is always called "the beginning."[19] Hence "the law" cannot refer to Genesis 2.20-24.

Carson recognizes the problem of reconciling 1 Cor 11.3-16 with 14.34-35 wherefore he suggests that the former allows women to prophesy but that the latter forbids them from evaluating prophecies. Because Carson acknowledges that the whole church should participate in the evaluation of teaching (Acts 17.11; Rev 2.2-3) he creates a distinction in which women are (1) allowed to prophesy, but not allowed to evaluate prophecy; and (2) disallowed to teach, but allowed to evaluate teaching. If "the careful weighing of prophecies falls under the magisterial function" of the teaching authority, why does not the evaluation of teaching considering Carson's belief that teaching is superior to prophesying?[20]

Also George W. Knight III recognizes that 1 Cor 11.3-16 allows women to pray and to prophesy in his essay *The Family and the Church*, but he views 1 Corinthians 14.34-35 as a prohibition for women to teach in a church setting.

> This is seen in Paul's treatment of the gifts in 1 Corinthians 11-14, where women are excluded only from speaking in church (1 Corinthians 14.34-5) where congregational "teaching" is involved (1 Corinthians 14.26; notice that the items listed in verse 26 correspond with the subjects dealt with in verses 27 and 35 [with only the first item, "a psalm," not dealt with in these verses] and in particular notice that "teaching" [NASB] in verse 26 is the one-word description for the "speaking" Paul will deal with when it comes to women in verses 34-35). These women are recognized as properly participating in praying and prophesying, for example, but are only asked not to throw off the cultural sign of their submission when they do so (1 Corinthians 11.1-6).[21]

---

18. Ibid., 148.

19. See Isaiah 40.2; 41.26; 46.10; Matthew 19.4-9; 24.19-21; Ecclesiastes 3.10-12; Mark 10.3-9; 13.18-19; Luke 11.49-51; 2 Thessalonians 2.13; 2 Timothy 1.9; Hebrews 1.10-12; 2 Peter 3.3-4; 1 John 3.8.

20. Piper and Grudem, 153.

21. Ibid., 351.

Knight does not explain how the "one-word description" of "speaking" (*laleo*) can be "teaching" in 1 Corinthians 14.26, considering *laleo* is connected to both tongues and prophecy three times in verses 27-29. Neither does he have a reason why women should learn *(manthano)* at home when the purpose of prophecy is that all may learn *(manthano)* at church (v. 31).

The context of 1 Corinthians 14 is speech. (*Laleo* is used twenty-four times in chapter 14.) In verses 1-25 Paul explains why the Corinthians should desire to prophesy rather than to speak in tongues; in verses 26-40 he explains the proper way of prophesying and speaking in tongues. Moreover, Paul considered prophesying, which both men and women participated in, equivalent to teaching, for he wrote, "But one who prophesies speaks [*laleo*] to men for edification [*oikodome*] and exhortation [*paraklesis*] and consolation... For you can all prophesy one by one, so that all may learn and all may be exhorted [*parakaleo*]" (Cor 14.3, 31, NAS). The purpose of their gathering together, the psalms, teachings, tongues, revelations and interpretations, was edification (*oikodome*, v. 26). Therefore prophesy was not distinguished from teaching as to its purpose. In addition, exhortation (*paraklesis*) is equivalent to declaring divine truths – such as the gospel, as seen in Acts 13.15-52, Hebrews 13.22, and 1 Thessalonians 2.2-3 – and people are expected to learn as a result. Since prophesying is a form of teaching, it is impossible that Paul excluded women from teaching, and consequently, the evaluation of prophesy.

~

Because of the difficulties associated with the former connection to Genesis 3.16, the meaning of "the law" and the impossibility to reconcile the two verses with chapter 11, it has been suggested that 1 Corinthians 14.34-35 is an interpolation (a later addition). Carson rejects the possibility on the grounds that "it is hard to believe that none of the earliest copies had any influence on the second-and third century textual traditions to which we have access."[22] But because all of the Western witnesses place 1 Corinthians 14.34-35 after verse 40, Carson concludes that it would take *only one* copyist to introduce a transposition of a verse "presumably early enough to capture the Western tradition."[23] If *one* copyist could create a uniform tradition by changing the

---

22. Ibid., 142.
23. Ibid., 142-143.

position of a verse without the earlier copies having an influence on the later textual tradition, why cannot the same be true of an interpolation?

It is likely that 1 Corinthians 14.34-35 was instrumental in changing the interpretation of Genesis 3.16, for it is connected to Genesis 3.16 only when the verse is viewed as a commandment. Because the interpretation of Genesis 3.16 was changed before the end of the second century, the interpolation must have been created in the early second century – early enough to change the textual traditions of the second and third centuries.

Carson is aware that the Western tradition knew of a variant position, but he is mistaken of the variant itself.

> The relevant textual evidence is quickly stated. Verses 34-35 appear in all known manuscripts, either in their present position, or in the case of all Western witnesses, after verse 40 (D F G 88* a b d f g Ambrosiaster Sedulius-Scotus). In addition, Codex Fuldensis (a Latin manuscript written between A.D. 541, and A.D. 546 by order of Bishop Victor of Capua) places the verses after verse 40, but also inserts them in the margin after verse 33. It appears that, despite the uniformity of the Western tradition, Victor, or those who worked at his bidding, became aware of the placement of the verses outside their own tradition and signaled their hesitation in this way. [24]

Carson believes the variant concerns the location of the two verses, but B.M. Metzger, whose error Carson perpetuates, admitted to Philip B. Payne that he had never seen the actual text. After viewing a photocopy of the manuscript, which shows that Bishop Victor ordered a rewriting of verses 36-40 in the bottom margin and not next to verse 33 and after verse 40, he admitted that "his statement in the *Textual Commentary on the NT* is in error."[25] As Payne explains, the scribe placed a symbol next to verse 33 to signal where to begin to read the text found in the bottom margin,

> I conclude that Bishop Victor ordered the rewriting of 1 Cor 14.34-40 in the margin of Codex Fuldensis with vv. 34-[3]5 omitted and that

---

24. Ibid.,141.

25. Philip B. Payne, *New Testament Study* (Edmonds, WA: Edmonds Publishing Group, 1995), 241-2.

there is a text-critical siglum that indicates the scribe's awareness of a textual variant at the beginning of 1 Cor 14.34 in codex Vaticanus. This text-critical evidence, plus the evidence from the non-Western ms 88* and Vulgate ms Reginensis with vv. 34-[3]5 transposed after v. 40, makes an already strong case for interpolation even stronger.[26]

Professor Metzger agreed that "the most natural explanation is that Victor ordered the rewriting of the text of 1 Cor 14.36-40 to replace all of vv. 34-40 in the text above and that this implies that Victor believed that 34-[3]5 was an interpolation."[27]

The Codex Fuldensis (A.D. 546) is the earliest dated manuscript of the New Testament and the only manuscript edited by "one of the eminent scholars of the early church," Bishop Victor, who combined Tatia's *Diatessaron* (the four Gospels) and Jerome's Vulgate, which he substituted for the Old Latin.[28] Payne concludes that "we must assume that Victor had sufficient evidence to convince him that the Vulgate text was wrong at 1 Cor 14.34-[3]5."[29] The Vulgate included also 1 John 5.7-8 with a preface claiming to be written by St. Jerome which "accuses the Latin translators of omitting this *testimonium*."[30] Bishop Victor omitted these verses, which supports the existence of interpolations in the Vulgate.

As noted before, Carson believes the second and third century textual traditions should have been affected by the first wherefore an early interpolation would have been impossible. But the incorrect rendering of Genesis 3.16 in the Vulgate was not challenged in the fifth century although Hebrew Bibles and the Septuagint were widely available. It is therefore not surprising that an interpolation of the same nature had been readily accepted and that the dissenting voices were few and far apart.

---

26. Ibid., 240.

27. Ibid., 245.

28. Tatian, a disciple of Justin Martyr, wrote the *Harmony of the Gospel* (*Diatessaron*) about A.D. 170. Tatian was an Assyrian and his work was used widely in Syria. "Scholars are inclined to make Tatian's to be the earliest Syriac translation of the Gospel" (www.newadvent.com).

29. Payne, 245.

30. Ibid., 241.

That a text bearing a striking similarity to 1 Corinthians 14.34-35 is found in the writings of Flavius Josephus, the Jewish historian, strengthens the likelihood of an early interpolation.[31]

> *The woman, says the law, is in all things inferior to the man. Let her accordingly be submissive,* not for her humiliation, but that she may be directed, for the authority has been given by God to the man.[32]

Josephus (born in A.D. 37) wrote *Against Apion* around A.D. 100, which makes Paul's letter to the Corinthians an earlier work. The context of the chapter in which the quote is found is marriage in Jewish Law. Because the husband's authority and the woman's inferiority are not found in the Old Testament, Josephus was most likely referring to the Jewish oral law, which he calls "our law." Josephus does not demand that the women be silent, for he affirms that all Jews knew the Law well and that anyone, women and servants included, could answer inquires.[33]

The silencing of women is found in a speech by Cato the Censor, the second century B.C. moral guardian of the Republican Rome.

> According to Livy, recorded in *The Early History of Rome*... Cato [the Censor] declared if every man had been concerned to ensure that his own wife looked up to him and respected his rightful position as her husband, we should not have [half of trouble with women en masse. Instead women have] become so powerful that our independence has been lost in our own homes and is now being trampled and stamped underfoot in public. We have failed to restrain them as individuals, and now they have combined to reduce us to our present panic... It made me blush to push through a positive regiment of women a few minutes ago in order to get here. My respect for the position

---

31. An alternative translation by William Whiston reads, "But then, what are our laws about marriage? ... For saith the Scripture, "A woman is inferior to her husband in all things." Let her, therefore, be obedient to him; not so, that he should abuse her, but that she may acknowledge her duty to her husband; for God hath given the authority to the husband." (Flavius Josephus Against Apion, in Josephus, The Complete Works, trans. by William Whiston [Nashville, TN: Thomas Nelson Publishers, 1998], 2.24).

32. Thomas Cahill, *Desire of the everlasting Hills* (New York: Random House, 2001), 233.

33. Josephus, 2.19.

and modesty of them as individuals – a respect which I do not feel for them as a mob – prevented me from doing anything as consul which would suggest the use of force. Otherwise I should have said to them, *"What do you mean by rushing out in public in this unprecedented fashion, blocking the streets and shouting out to men who are not husbands? Could you not have asked your questions at home, and have asked them of your husbands?"*[34]

The speech was given as a response to the upper-class women who had come to inquire of the Senate when the Oppian Laws, which had restricted the display of luxury during the war against Hannibal, were going to be abolished. Although Cato failed to retain the Oppian Laws, he became the icon of austere, moral living for all Romans. Tertullian, when defending the faith, asked the Romans, "Which of these gods of yours is more remarkable for gravity and wisdom than Cato."[35] And, Lactantius called Cato "the Chief of Roman wisdom."[36]

Cato's belief that women would not be content with equality makes him a likely source of an interpolation which mandates the subjection of women.

Woman is a violent and uncontrolled animal, and it is not good giving her the reins and expecting her not to kick over the traces. No, you have got to keep the reins firmly in your own hands... Suppose you allow them to acquire or to restore one right after another, and in the end to achieve complete equality with men, do you think that you will find them bearable? Nonsense. Once they have achieved equality, they will be your masters... [37]

A religion which made women equal with men would have not been welcomed by a patriarchal system which recognized only authority and subjection, for those who live in a hierarchical society seem woefully unable to trust that their subjects would not wish to rule them in turn if given a chance. Even today, equality between men and women is as abstract of a concept as eating grass is for the lion for those who fear the emerging of a matriarchy which has never existed in the past.

---

34. Jack Holland, *Misogyny* (New York City: Carroll and Graf Publishers, 2006), 43-44.
35. Tertullian, *The Apology*, Ch. XI.
36. Lactantius, *Of the False Wisdom of Philosophers*, Book III, Ch. XVIII.
37. Holland, 43-44.

CHAPTER 3

Gen 2.18-24

Reflection explains a lot of things.

— JAMES P. COMER[1]

~

AFTER GENESIS 3.16 was returned to its original position as a description of the consequence of sin at the end of the twentieth century, Genesis 2.18-24 became the only source for the woman's subjection. But because Genesis 1.26-27 clearly teaches equality, Ortlund suggests that a paradox exists in the creation account in his essay *Male-Female Equality and Male Headship*.

> There is a paradox in the creation account. While Genesis 1 teaches the equality of the sexes as God's image-bearers and vice-rulers on the earth, Genesis 2 adds another complex dimension to Biblical manhood and womanhood. The paradox is this: God created male and female in His image equally, but He also made the male the head and the female the helper.[2]

Since Ortlund's theology depends on this paradox, we must consider whether a paradox is a viable method of finding the truth. According to Philosopher George Berkeley, one resorts to a paradox to correct an error in one's thinking.

> But no sooner do we depart from sense and instinct to follow the light of a superior principle, to reason, mediate [sic], and reflect on

1. James P. Comer, *Beyond Black and White* (New York City: Quadrangle Book, 1972), 12.
2. Piper and Grudem, 99.

the nature of things, but a thousand scruples spring up in our minds concerning those things which before we seemed fully to comprehend. Prejudices and errors of sense do from all parts discover themselves to our view; and, *endeavoring to correct these by reason, we are insensibly drawn into uncouth paradoxes,* difficulties, and inconsistencies, which multiply and grow upon us as we advance in speculation. [3]

Ortlund recognizes that his theology has an error – the clear contradiction between Genesis 1 and 2 – and he tries to correct it by resorting to a paradox, but it is a perilous path, as philosopher Manuel Velasquez points out, "Once a single contradiction is allowed, it is easy to prove with rigorous logic that any statement whatsoever is true. That is anything can be proven once you accept a contradiction."[4] Accordingly, Ortlund and Grudem give two entirely different and contradictory meanings to *'ezer* ("help") which are both considered true.

Ortlund

It is the word "helper" that suggests the woman's supportive role. Spencer argues, however, that this description of Eve "does not at all imply inherent subordination." She adduces the fact that God Himself is portrayed in Scripture as our "Helper," which He is. She then interprets this fact: "If being 'one who helps' inherently implies subordination, then, in that case, God would be subordinate to human!" This reasoning is not really fallacious. The fallacy lies in the implication of what she says, namely, that God cannot be subordinate to human beings. He does so whenever He undertakes to help us. He does not "un-God" Himself in helping us; but stoops down to our needs, according to His gracious and sovereign will. Similarly, I subordinate myself to my children when I help them with their homework.... So it is with God. When He helps His people, He retains His glorious deity but (amazingly!) steps into the servant role, under us, to lift us up. He is the God who emptied Himself and came down to our level – below us, to the level of slavery – to help us supremely at the Cross. *Therefore, the fact that the Old Testament portrays God as our Helper proves only that the helper role is a glorious one, worthy even the*

---

3. Manuel Velasquez, *Philosophy, a Text with Readings*, (Belmont, CA: Thomson Wadsworth, 2008), 219.

4. Ibid., 405.

Almighty. This Biblical fact does not prove that the concept of helper excludes subordination. Subordination is entailed in the very nature of a helping role."[5]

Grudem

> It is true that God is often called our "helper," *but the word itself does not imply anything about rank or authority.* The context must decide whether Eve is to "help" as a strong person who aids a weaker one, or as one who assists a loving leader. The context makes *it very unlikely that helper should be read on the analogy of God's help,* because in Genesis 2.19-20 Adam is caused to seek his "helper" first among the animals.... Yet in passing through "helpful" animals to woman, God teaches us that the woman is a man's "helper" in the sense of a loyal and suitable assistant in the life of the garden. The question seems to assume that because the word (like helper) has certain connotations ("Godlikeness") in some places it must have them in every place.[6]

What becomes clear from the above quotes is that the analogy of God and woman can be used if it proves that the woman is subordinate, but not if it makes the woman superior to the man. Not surprisingly, Ortlund and Grudem never propose that the word *'ezer* means that the woman is an equal, for it would destroy their concept of male headship. Instead they focus on refuting a scenario in which the woman is the stronger and the man the weaker, which they perhaps expected to create an instant negative response as seen in Ortlund's response to Spencer's comment on Genesis 2. Ortlund expresses indignation that she would even suggest that the "helper" could be superior to Adam.[7] But however indignant Ortlund is, his own argument makes the woman superior, since he compares her to God *who stoops down* to help us and to a parent who comes down to the *child's level.* If God subordinates Himself, He must be under human authority, for subordination signifies occupying a lower position in a hierarchy. Tertullian refuted such a belief already in the third century when he wrote, "[Y]our divinity is put in subjection to Christians; and you can surely never ascribe deity to that which is under the

---

5. Piper and Grudem, 104.
6. Ibid., 87.
7. Ibid., 103.

authority of man."[8] Thus God does in fact "un-God" Himself if He subordinates Himself to human beings.[9]

Grudem is correct in his affirmation that the term *'ezer k^aneg^adow* itself doesn't imply anything about rank or authority but he makes the fallacy of concluding that the context does. If we agree with Grudem that the context makes it evident that the woman was "a loyal and suitable assistant for the life of the garden," we must explain how Adam concluded that he was looking for an "assistant" who was like the "helpful" animals, for the verb *matsa* ("to find") in Genesis 2.20 is active wherefore it is Adam who does not find the *'ezer k^aneg^adow* among the animals. If we understand his search for an *'ezer k^aneg^adow* in terms of his loneliness, which is the only context given, it becomes clear that Adam was not looking for an assistant, but another human. W. Gunther Plaut observes, "The process of naming the animals, Adam realizes that he needs a helpmate (Gen 2.20). How are the two related? Man discovers his solitude when he begins to give names, i.e. to use words, and cannot say 'man' to any other creature."[10] Humans were not created to live in solitude and the naming of the animals highlighted the man's loneliness and his need for human companionship.

Later Biblical poetry describes the reward of companionship and kinship, and the feeling of futility of the lonely human.

> There is one alone, without companion: He has neither son nor brother.
> Yet there is no end to all his labors, Nor is his eye satisfied with riches.
> But he never asks, "For whom do I toil and deprive myself of good?"
> This also is vanity and a grave misfortune.

---

8. *The Apology*, Ch. XXIII.

9. John M. Frame, on the other hand cannot decide whether the word *help* implies subordination or not in his essay *Men and Women in the Image of God*. He writes, "Humans beings are to help God (1.28); woman is to help man (2.20)," (Piper and Grudem, 227) and he believes "the very submission of the woman also images God. God the Lord is not too proud to be our "helper." (230) But suddenly and somewhat inexplicably he agrees with those "who say that 'helper' does not in itself connote any subordination," for although God is the helper of Israel He was not created for Israel as the woman was for the man (Footnote 19, 507). Frame does not explain how the woman's submission can image God's if God does not submit.

10. W. Gunther Plaut, *The Torah, Genesis, A Modern Commentary* (New York: Union of American Hebrew Congregations, 1974), 24.

Two are better than one, because they have a good reward for their
labor.
For if they fall, one will lift up his companion. But woe to him who
is alone when he falls,
For he has no one to help him up. (Eccl 4.8-10)

The second fallacy Grudem commits is that he assumes that we should be
looking for a *similarity* between the woman and the animals, when in fact
we should be looking for the *difference*. The woman was different from the
animals because she was able to speak which was why she was able to alleviate
the man's loneliness.

The third fallacy Grudem commits is that he assumes that the woman was
created to be a helper to the man. In 1 Corinthians 11.8-9, Paul writes that
the woman was made *from* the man and *for* the man, and it is due to these
two verses that *'ezer* is given the definition "helper."[11] But *gunee dia ton andra*
(v. 9) can also be translated "woman because of man," for the woman was
created *because it was not good for the man to be alone*. The woman was not a
helper; the help was the woman created to be with the man. In Genesis 3.6,
the man and woman are found together: "She also gave to her husband with
her ['*imaah*], and he ate." *'Imaah* describes such intimate closeness that is often
used of sexual intimacy (e.g., Gen 30.15). In Genesis 3.12 we find Adam referring to Eve as "the woman whom *You gave to be with me*." Even as Adam tries
to pass the blame, he does not call Eve *'ezer*, as in "the helper you gave me,"
but *'ishshah*, "a woman." Women are never called *'ezer* in the Bible, but the
'ezer "shall be called woman," for the help was not what the woman did, but
who she was.[12]

---

11. The first man recognized God had given the woman as a gift, and similarly God gave
the Sabbath as a gift for humanity (Exod 16.29). Both the woman and the Sabbath are said
to have been created due to a human need, yet both have been ignored, or turned into religious burdens. In the case of the Sabbath, by the first century A.D., the burden had become
so intolerable that Jesus had to remind the Jewish people that "the Sabbath was made for
man, and not man for the Sabbath," (Mark 2.27) for it was meant to be a day of rest and
contemplation, not religious strictures. Similarly Apostle Paul reminded the Corinthians that
the woman was created for the man, to be with him, for God declared the man's loneliness *lo
tow* ("not good").

12. Richard Elliott Friedman offers an alternative translation of the word *'ezer*: "Woman
is usually understood to be created as a suitable "helper" (Hebrew *'ezer*) to man in this
account. The Hebrew root, however, can also mean "strength"... The Hebrew phrase *'ezer*

The Septuagint translates *'ezer kᵃnegᵃdow* with the Greek term *boethoos homoios*. The Perseus online Greek dictionary gives the following definitions.[13]

> boêth-oos – *hasting to the cry for help* or *the call to arms, aiding, helping,* -in Prose, *assisting, auxiliary,*

> homoios – *like, resembling,* in *similar* cases (of persons), *the same, equal in force, a match for one, of things, suiting, according with.*

Boethoos can mean either a person who hastens to help or an assistant. However, *homoios* means someone who is similar.[14] If we assign *boethos* the meaning "assistant" we make also the man an assistant, for what he is, she is. In addition, if *boethos* makes the woman the man's assistant and therefore his subject, Christ is subjected to His church, for in the New Testament Christ is called our *boethos* (Heb 13.6). If we give *boethos* the meaning "to hasten to the cry for help," the woman is the man's equal who, by being another human was able to remove the man's loneliness, which was the help the man needed.

In the Protestant tradition we can trace the "helper" to Luther's German Bible (1545): "Und Gott der HERR sprach: Es ist nicht gut, daß der Mensch allein sei; ich will ihm eine Gehilfin machen, die um ihn sei." *Gehilfe* has the meaning "assistant, helper."[15]

---

kenegdo therefore may very well mean "a corresponding strength." Friedman gives as an example Azariah (*'azar*, 'help' from which *'ezer* is derived) whose alternative name is Uzziah (*'oz*, "strength" derived from *'azah*). He also cites Psalm 46.1 in which the two words are combined: "God is our refuge [*'oz*] and strength [*'ezrah*, fem. of *'ezer*], a very present help in trouble." (Richard Elliott Friedman, *Commentary on the Torah* [San Francisco, CA: Harper Collins, 2001], 19).

13. Perseus Digital Library, hhtp://www.perseus.tufts.edu/hopper/ (accessed June 29, 2009), s.v. "boethoos homoios."

14. The Latin equivalent of *homoios* is *aequālis,* from which the English word "equal" is derived. "Equal, c 1391, from L. *aequalis* "uniform, identical, equal" from *aequus* "level, even, just," of unknown origin. Parallel formation *egal* (from O.Fr, egal) was in use 1380-1600s. *Equalitarian* in reference to the doctrine that all mankind are equal is attested from 1799." (Online Etymology Dictionary, http://www.etymonline.com [accessed June 29, 2009], s.v. "equal").

15. Reverso Dictionary Online, http://dictionary.reverso.net/german-english/ (accessed June 29, 2009), s.v. "Gehilfe."

~

At the end of the second century, Tertullian still understood the loneliness of the man to be the reason for the woman's creation,[16] but by the fourth century, the interpretation of Genesis 2.18 had changed. Ambrose (338-397), the Bishop of Milan, realized the human need for companionship and that the help they provide is mutual, but instead of seeing the woman as a partner and companion, he viewed the woman as the source of men who would be mutually helpful to each other.[17] The eighteenth century theologian Matthew Henry repeated the same sentiment in his Commentary, writing, "God creates a new thing to be a help-meet for man – not so much the woman as the seed of the woman."[18]

Augustine agreed with Ambrose that the woman could not have possibly provided any other help to the man than procreation.

> Now, if the woman was not made for the man to be his helper in begetting children, in what was she to help him? She was not to till the earth with him, for there was not any soil to make the help necessary. If there were any such need a male helper would be better, and the same can be said of the comfort of another's presence if Adam were perhaps weary of solitude. How much more agreeably could two male friends, rather than a man and a woman enjoy companionship and convenience in a life shared together. And if they had to make an arrangement in their common life for one to command and the other to obey, in order to make sure that opposing will would not disrupt the peace of the household, there would be proper rank to assure this, since one would be created first and the other second.[19]

Although Augustine superimposed the ideal Roman society on the Creation account, he was right in questioning what kind of help the woman was supposed to have provided to the man in the garden. Clement of Alexandria thought the help the woman provided was housekeeping,[20] but there was no

---

16. *Five Books Against Marcion,* Book II, Ch. IV.

17. Ambrose, *Three Books on the Duties of the Clergy*, Book I. Ch. XXVIII, 132-138.

18. "Genesis 2.18-20," Matthew Henry's *Commentary on the Whole Bible*: *New Modern Edition.*

19. Torjesen, 220-22.

20. Clement of Alexandria, *The Instructor,* Book III, Ch. XI.

home to manage. Neither was there laundry or meals to prepare, for the two were naked and ate from the trees God had provided. If complementarists are correct in that the woman's role is to be a homemaker, she was never created for the Garden but for the fallen world in which shelter, clothing and food preparation is necessary for survival.[21] Similarly, neither was the man responsible for providing for his family before sin, for there was no land which required farming – only a garden without weeds. Although shelter, clothing and food preparation are necessary in the world after sin, we cannot allow the world *after sin define the world before sin*. A vacation is probably the closest we get to life in the garden, for the only purpose of a vacation is to enjoy the companionship of other people and to participate in leisurely activities, which is probably why we all enjoy it so much.

As he saw the woman, the first man exclaimed, "This is now bone of my bones and flesh of my flesh; she shall be called 'woman,' for she was taken out of man." (Gen 2.23, NIV) Robert Alter, professor of Hebrew and Comparative Literature, explains the linguistic method employed by the writer.

> The first human is given reported speech for the first time only when there is another human to whom to respond. The speech takes the form of verse, a naming-poem, in which each of the two lines begins with the feminine indicative pronoun, *zo't,* "this one," which is also the last Hebrew word of the poem, cinching it in a tight envelope structure.[22]

---

21. Frame writes, "Note also that in 1 Corinthians 11.9 Paul does not base his argument on the word *helper* but on the fact that Eve was made for Adam." Frame believes that the woman "was made after Adam, for the specific purpose of helping him." (Piper and Grudem, Footnote 19, 507). Philosopher Jean Jacques Rousseau would have agreed with him, for he wrote, "The education of women should always be relative to men. To please, to be useful to us,... to educate us when young, and take care of us when grown up, to advise, to console us, to render our lives easy and agreeable: these are the duties of women at all times, and what they should be taught in their infancy... The woman is expressly formed to please the man." (Miriam Gurko, *The Ladies of Seneca Falls, The Birth of the Woman's Rights Movement* (New York: Shocken Books, 1974), 12.

22. Robert Alter, *The Five Books of Moses, A Translation With Commentary* (New York: W. W. Norton & Company, 2004), 22.

The poem could be written in English, "and said the human, this one is now bone of my bones and flesh of my flesh, this one shall be called woman because from the man was she taken, this one." The man recognized that the person who stood in front of him was not like the animals he had just named, but like himself – a human. Yet she was different because she was a female, wherefore he called her 'ishshah, the feminine form of 'yish ("man"), a derivative of 'enowsh ("a mortal").

The phrase "this is now bone of my bones, and flesh of my flesh" is found four times outside of the Creation account.

> And Laban said to him, "Surely you are my bone and my flesh." And he stayed with him for a month. Then Laban said to Jacob, "Because you are my relative, should you therefore serve me for nothing? Tell me, what should your wages be? (Gen 29.14-15)

> Then Abimelech the son of Jerubbaal went to Shechem, to his mother's brothers, and spoke with them and with all the family of the house of his mother's father, saying, "Please speak in the hearing of all the men of Shechem: 'Which is better for you, that all seventy of the sons of Jerubbaal reign over you, or that one reign over you?' Remember that I am your own flesh and bone." (Judg 9.1-2)

> So King David sent to Zadok and Abiathar the priests, saying, "Speak to the elders of Judah, saying, 'Why are you the last to bring the king back to his house, since the words of all Israel have come to the king, to his very house? You are my brethren, you are my bone and my flesh. Why then are you the last to bring back the king? (2 Sam 19.11-12)

> Then all Israel came together to David at Hebron, saying, "Indeed we are your bone and your flesh. (1 Chron 11.1)

Each time the phrase signifies kinship, belonging to the same family. Chrysostom believed the woman's subjection began at the Fall because neither God or the man said anything about subjection to the woman, instead the man said she was "bone of his bones, and flesh of his flesh," which signified her equality with the man.[23] Also Judaism, which shares its Creation account with Christianity, views Genesis 3.16 as the source of the woman's subjection, for "the creation of the woman after the man and from a part of his body need not imply subordination of women to men." Instead, the woman's creation emphasizes the close connection between the man and the woman and is the foundation for marriage.[24]

Ortlund believes God did not create the man from the woman and for the woman, "because, presumably, that would have obscured the very nature of manhood and womanhood that He intended to make clear."[25] But had the woman been created first, and had she given birth to the man, she could not have married the man for he would have been her son. We find the same argument in reverse in Thomas Aquinas's *Summa Theologica*.

> A certain affinity arises from natural generation, and this is an impediment to matrimony. Woman, however, was not produced from man by natural generation, but by the Divine Power alone. Wherefore Eve is not called the daughter of Adam; and so this argument does not prove.[26]

The woman had to be created from the man's side for a man cannot give birth. A woman can, wherefore it would have been unnecessary for the man to have been created from the woman's side. An additional argument against the man's creation from the woman is that the woman does not have the Y chromosome. The man has both the Y and X chromosomes, wherefore the father's genes decide the gender of the child. Had Eve been created first, the second human created from her would have been a woman (XX), not a man (XY).[27] Thus the creation of the woman from the man was necessary and did not introduce subordination, but marriage and interdependence

Ortlund grasps the beauty of the poetry involved in Genesis 2.23 and he

---

23. *Homilies on First Corinthians*, Homily XXVI.
24. *The Jewish Study Bible*, 16, Footnote for vv. 18-24.
25. Piper and Grudem, 102.
26. *Summa Theologica*, First Part, Question 92, Article 2.
27. The supposition that God could have created the man from the woman by adding an X chromosome supernaturally presupposes that the God would defy the laws of nature as He was creating them.

sees the woman as an equal because she is created from the man, for with the woman the man can experience companionship on his own level. But simultaneously he views the man naming the woman as an act of authority, a royal prerogative, since he is naming his helper.[28] Ortlund's reasoning makes the woman the man's slave, since the "naming concept" is adopted from the ungodly Babylonian practice of depriving the slave of his or her previous identity through the imposition of a new name.[29] The biblical practice of name-changing was not an act of authority for names were changed as a sign of a changed situation. Hence Adam named the first woman *Chawah* ("Eve") because she was to become the mother of all living (*chay*) (Gen 3.20). Also Sarai was re-named Sarah as she was to become the mother of Isaac (Gen 17.16).

Grudem suggests that the naming of various people by God and the name giving of children by their parents are examples of an act of authority. However, God owns us as our Creator, and children need parental authority for their own protection. The man does not own the woman nor is she a child, wherefore the comparison fails.[30] Because the woman was not created to be a helper, Ortlund's statement lacks a solid foundation but his belief that Eve understood who she was *by the man's definition*, instead of God's, reveals the true nature of complementarism: the woman is said to be what the man wants her to be – his helper instead of his equal.[31]

---

28. Piper and Grudem, 101-102.

29. Theologians have used the argument indiscriminately as seen in Henry's Commentary, "It is an act of authority to impose names (Dan 1.7), and of subjection to receive them" ("Gen 2.18-20," *Matthew Henry Commentary On the Whole Bible*).

30. *Systematic theology*, 462

31. Piper and Grudem, 103. The man did not define the woman, for God had already defined her before bringing her to the man by calling her "woman" (Gen 2.22). The man simply recognized who she was: a female human being.

CHAPTER 4

Gen 1.26-28

It may seem waste of time to bring forward further arguments,

For truths concerning God gain no strength by repetition;

A single statement suffices to establish them.

Yet it is well for us to know all that has been revealed upon the subject,

For though we are not responsible for the words of Scripture,

Yet we shall have to render an account for the sense we have assigned to them

— HILARY OF POITIERS[1]

~

ORTLUND, WHO RESORTED to a paradox to explain the contradiction between Genesis 1 and 2, must explain the absence of an explicit reference to the man's headship in Genesis 1-3.[2]

> Moses does not explicitly teach male headship in chapter 1; but for that matter, neither does he explicitly teach male-female equality. We see neither the words "male-female equality" nor "male headship" here or anywhere in Genesis 1-3. What Moses does provide is a series of more or less obvious hints as to his doctrine of manhood and woman-

---

1. Hilary of Poitiers, *On the Trinity*, Book IV, 19.

2. Grudem writes, "It is surprising that evangelical feminists can find this requirement [mutual submission] in the New Testament when it is nowhere explicitly stated" (Piper and Grudem, 199). Grudem rejects Ephesians 5.21 due to faulty exegetics, but his words are an apt description of Ortlund's claim that we can find male headship in Genesis 1-3, although it is never explicitly stated.

hood. The burden of Genesis 1.26-28 is male-female equality. That seems obvious – wonderfully obvious![3]

One of these "hints" is the word 'adam, which Ortlund gives the meaning "man."

> But God's naming of the race "man" whispers male headship, which Moses will bring forward boldly in chapter two. God did not name the human race "woman." If "woman" had been the more appropriate and illuminating designation, no doubt God would have used it. He does not even devise a neutral term like "persons." He called us "man," which anticipates the male headship brought out clearly in chapter two, just as "male and female" in verse 27 foreshadows marriage in chapter two.[4]

Ortlund confuses the Hebrew words 'yish and 'adam for the equivalent of the English word "man" is the Hebrew word 'yish, not 'adam, which means "human" (as does the Greek equivalent anthropos). 'Yish becomes aner in Greek, and both are used to distinguish male humans from females in addition to functioning as generic terms for humans in general (e.g., Ps 122.1; James 1.12). Languages which do not use the word man generically do not have words male and female in their vocabulary, but because androcentric languages assimilate women into the word man such defining words are needed to avoid confusion. Thus, Greek uses arsen ("male") and thelus ("female") when a clear distinction is needed, which is also true of Hebrew's zaakaar ("male"), neqebah ("female"), as seen in Genesis 17.23:

> "On that very day Abraham took his son Ishmael and all those born in his household or bought with his money, every male [zakaar] in his household ['yish], and circumcised them, as God told him." (NIV)

Robert Alter, provides another compelling reason why 'adam cannot refer to a male man.

---

3. Piper and Grudem, 98.
4. Ibid.

The term *'adam,* afterward consistently with a definite article, which is used both here [Genesis 1.27] and in the second account of the origins of humankind, is a generic term for human beings, not a proper noun. It also does not automatically suggest maleness, especially not without the prefix *ben,* "son of," and so the traditional rendering "man" is misleading, an exclusively male *'adam* would make nonsense of the last clause of verse 27.[5]

What Alter means by "nonsense" becomes clear when the words in verse 27 are changed into colors: "God created blue... blue and red created he them." Blue cannot contain red and remain a distinct color. Similarly, a man cannot be both male and female and remain distinctly male. But *humanity* can include both male and female and remain a distinct entity of its own, just as the color purple includes both read and blue. Hence the correct English translation is, "God created humanity... male and female created he them."[6]

In the following comparison of 21 languages and 42 translations, *'adam* is translated either "man" or "human."

Man – man and woman (3 translations, 2 languages)

French (La Bible du Semeur, Louis Segond), Portuguese (O Livro)

Man – male and female (17 translations, 4 languages)

Spanish (Reina-Valera 1960, 1995, 1569, Dios Habla Hoy), Italian (La Nuova Diodati, Conferenza Episcopale Italiana), Hungarian, English (NJKV, ASV, Amplified, Darby, Douay-Rheims 1899 American Edition; English Standard

---

5. Alter, 19.

6. Hurley disagrees with Ortlund, "*Man* in 1.26 and 27 is a collective noun (adam = "mankind"). The plural membership of the collectivity is indicated by the phrase "male and female" in verse 27, and then both male and female are given the task appropriate to those created in the image of God (verse 28)" (Piper and Grudem, 227). Also Gregory of Nyssa (A.D. 380) wrote, "What is it then which we understand concerning these matters? In saying that "God created man" the text indicates, by the *indefinite character of the term, all mankind*; for was not Adam here named together with the creation, as the history tells us in what follows? Yet the name given to the man created is not the particular, but the general name: thus we are led by the employment of the general name of our nature to some such view as this—that in the Divine foreknowledge and power all humanity is included in the first creation (Gregory, Bishop of Nyssa, *On the Making of Man,* XVI, 16).

Version, Holman Christian Standar, KJV; NASB, NIV, New Life Version, Young's Literal Translation)

Human – man and woman (14 translations, 13 languages)

German (Luther Bible 1545, Elberfelder), Spanish (Nueva Versión Internacional), Ukrainian, Bulgarian, Haitian Creole Version, Maori, Dutch, Swedish, English (ESV), Norwegian, Danish, Finnish, Icelandic

Human – male and female (8 translations, 5 languages)

Arabic, Albanian, Polish, Russian Synodal version (/man and woman), English (New Century Version, New Living Translation, The message, Today's NIV)

An overwhelming majority of languages – seventeen of the twenty-one considered – favor the translation "human" instead of "man." Androcentric languages tend to choose "man" while the more gender-neutral languages use the word "human." An English translation is found in all except the first category ("man – man and woman"). Thus it is ascertained that the writer of Genesis 1.27 did not use *'adam* in a gender-defining manner but as a reference to the origin of the first human, and consequently all humanity. The first human was called *'adam* because he was made of *'adamah,* the ground, just as the first woman was called *'ishshah* for she was made from *'yish.*[7]

Ortlund needs *'adam* to have the meaning "a man" because of his belief that God called only Adam in Genesis 3.9 and therefore held only him responsible for the Fall of humanity as the leader of the two.[8] However, if *'adam* refers only to the man in 3.9, it should also be true of Genesis 3.21-24.

> Then *the man and his wife* heard the sound of the Lord God as he was walking in the garden in the cool of the day, and they hid from the Lord God among the trees of the garden. But the Lord God called to *the man* [*'adam*], "Where are you?" (Gen. 3.8-9, NIV)

---

7. Everything in the new creation was given a name which revealed the characteristic of the object: God called the day *yowm* ("hot, the warm hours") and night *layil* (from *luwl,* "to fold back"). The earth he called *'erets* ("to be firm"); the sea, *yam* ("to roar"); herb, *'eseb* ("to glisten or to be green"); fruit, *periy* ("to be fruitful, grow"); morning, *boqer* (from *baqar,* "to break forth"), evening, *'ereb* (from *'arab,* "to darken"), creature, *nephesh* (from *naphash,* "to breath"); the bird *'owph* (from *'uwph,* "to fly"); animal, *behemah* ("to be mute").

8. Piper and Grudem, 108.

The LORD God made garments of skin for *the man and his wife* and clothed them. And the LORD God said, *"The man* has now become like one of us, knowing good and evil. He must not be allowed to reach out his hand and take also from the tree of life and eat, and live forever." So the LORD God banished him from the Garden of Eden to work the ground from which he had been taken. After he drove *the man* [*'adam*] *out*, he placed on the east side of the Garden of Eden cherubim and a flaming sword flashing back and forth to guard the way to the tree of life. (Gen 3.21-24, NIV)

Both passages employ the same grammatical construction and concern the same persons, therefore, either only the man was banned from the garden, or the word *'adam* includes both the man and the woman in Genesis 3.9 and 22, as it does in Genesis 1.27. (The male human is called *'yish* in Gen 2.23-24, 3.6 and 3.16, when a clear distinction is needed). Since God called *humanity,* both the man and the woman, in Gen 3.9, He did not hold only the man responsible for the transgression, but both of them.

Ortlund believes the Fall was a role-reversal in which Adam abandoned his headship when he listened to his wife, which led to his "ruination."[9] George W. Knight III agrees with Ortlund for he believes God is rebuking Adam for his "failure to carry out his God-ordained leadership role, not simply a reminder to Adam that he had listened to bad advice from Eve," in Genesis 3.17.[10]

It is obvious from the text of Genesis that Eve encouraged wrong-doing when she gave Adam the fruit. It is equally obvious that she takes the leadership role in that activity and that Adam simply follows

---

9. Ibid., 110. Olofsson writes, "Some theologians have also suggested that the Fall means an upsetting of the God-given hierarchy of creation. Original sin is understood as 'the woman taking over authority from the man, and the man saying and doing nothing to stop it' (Michael Harper, *Equal and Different,* London, 1994). This may well be so. Knowing good and evil in the Old Testament sense means setting one's own standards, like God. Upsetting the God-given order in creation may well be a part of this. *The doctrine of original sin, however, has a wider scope, and this violation of a divine order is rather a symptom than the whole cause*" (Folke T. Olofsson, "God and the Genesis of Gender: The Trustworthy Biblical Design of Man and Woman," *Touchstone Magazine* [Sept. 2001], http://www.cbmw.org/Resources/Articles/God-and-the-Genesis-of-Gender [accessed June 29, 2009]).

10. Piper and Grudem, 529.

her leadership. She allows herself, though, to be drawn into the role of spokesman by the serpent. She does not turn to her husband, from whom she had received God's command (cf. Genesis 2.16-17, where God gives the command to the man before the woman is created, and Genesis 3.2-3, where the woman relays that command), *to ask him about what God has said and meant by his command,* but rather acted unilaterally in opposition to the command that her husband had given to her (Genesis 3.6).[11]

Knight's theology centers the entire Fall scene on the man: the woman is disobeying the commandment given *by the man;* she should have asked *the man* what God had said, wherefore she is opposing *the man,* not God. Knight assumes that the man had given the commandment to the woman, but it is an argument from silence and is not supported by the narrative itself. Contrasted to Genesis 2.16, in which the man is given the commandment, *to'kᵃluw* ("you shall not eat") in Genesis 3.3 is plural, "But of the fruit of the tree which is in the midst of the garden, *God has said, 'You shall not eat it,* nor shall you touch it, lest you die.'" Had God not given the man the commandment as soon as he was placed in the garden, there would have been a moment in time when God did not hold humankind responsible.

Not surprisingly, Grudem disagrees with Knight about the necessity of a wife having to ask her husband what God has said and he gives as an example Peter who, "speaks directly to wives, not to the husbands so that they can tell their wives what he says. Peter assumes that they will hear, ponder, understand, and respond to God's Word themselves."[12] Why would this not have been true of Eve in the garden?

Knight comes to his conclusion also because he reverses the rebellion and dominion found in Genesis 3.6 and 3.16. He views Genesis 3.6 as the woman's rebellion against the man due to her failure to turn to the man and Genesis 3.16 as the woman's rebellion against God, but exactly the opposite is true: the woman did not rebel against the man when the serpent deceived her to take the fruit for it was against God's commandment. Neither does a woman rebel against God when she challenges the man's rule, for it is based on the man's sinful impulse to dominate the woman as she turns to him.

---

11. Ibid.
12. Ibid., 195

It is worth noting that as Adam blamed Eve for giving him the fruit, so has all subsequent generations of men blamed women for the fall of mankind. Even complementarism, which rejects the sole guilt of Eve in principle, nevertheless upholds it in their belief in a role-reversal. Included in the role-reversal is the implicit assumption that had Eve let Adam lead, we would still be in Paradise today, for the woman was deceived; the man was not. How it can be better to sin with one's eyes wide open, and why unintentional sin is forgiven in the Law but intentional is not (Num 15.27-31) is never explained. In fact, it is in this Old Testament concept that we find the reason why the death sentence was given to the man whose disobedience was intentional[13] and why the ultimate sacrifice was promised to the woman who was guilty of unintentional sin. God said, "Because you have..." to both the Serpent and Adam, for they acted willfully, but not to the woman, for she was deceived to disobey.[14] Adam and Eve were equally guilty – although their motivation differed – for guilt is not measured by one's intent; the punishment is. Yet, they would both share the consequences, the woman also being denied access to the tree of life and the man experiencing a distortion in his relationship with the woman, for they are interdependent and do not exist apart from each other.

Much has been said of the woman's influence, contrasted to the man's much vaunted reason, and Eve is often given as a prime example of a woman's negative influence over a man.[15] It is true that those who are powerless must learn to influence those in power, but Eve was not powerless, neither did she use manipulation or any other means to persuade Adam, who was present throughout the entire event. The man took the fruit and ate, knowing fully well that the serpent had lied. God's response to the man's attempt to avoid respon-

---

13. In the law the death penalty was given for murder (Exod 21.12) adultery (Lev 20.10), violating the Sabbath (Exod 35.2), cursing one's parents (Exod 21.17) and blaspheming God (Lev 24.16), all sins which are premeditated acts. A distinction was made between e.g., accidental killing and murder, "Though he was not worthy of death, since he had not hated the victim in time past" (Deut 19.6).

14. Pain associated with childbearing has often been considered a punishment for women ("So God sent pain and suffering to women when their children are born," [1 Tim 2.15, TLB].) But according to Dr. Grantly Dick-Read there is no physiological reason for the pain; instead it is caused by fear and fear was what the first humans experienced in the Garden as a result of sin (Gen 3.10). (*Childbirth Without Fear, Fifth Edition* [New York: Perennial Library, 1985], Introduction, xxiiii.)

15. Eugenia Price, *Woman to Woman* (Grand Rapids, MI: Zondervan, 1959), 14.

sibility in Genesis 3.17 ("Then to Adam He said, 'Because you have heeded the voice of your wife, and have eaten from the tree of which I commanded you, saying, "You shall not eat of it"'") is singular contrasted to Genesis 3.3, for God reminded the man that he had chosen to listen to his wife, instead of Him. The responsibility to choose whether to listen to someone enticing one away from God, or to expose the person, is found later in the Law.

> "If your brother, the son of your mother, your son or your daughter, the wife of your bosom, or your friend who is as your own soul, secretly entices you, saying, 'Let us go and serve other gods,' which you have not known, neither you nor your fathers, of the gods of the people which are all around you, near to you or far off from you, from one end of the earth to the other end of the earth, you shall not consent to him or listen to him, nor shall your eye pity him, nor shall you spare him or conceal him; but you shall surely kill him; your hand shall be first against him to put him to death, and afterward the hand of all the people. (Deut 13.6-9)

A number of explanations to account for the man's inertia have been offered, some more plausible than others. Some suggest that the man wanted to die with his wife, but if the man took the fruit out of love for his wife, as has been suggested, why did he turn around and blame her for giving him the fruit? Perhaps the alternative, that the man had not experienced death wherefore he did not take the commandment seriously, is a more accurate explanation.

Robert Alter provides a superb translation of Genesis 2.25-3.7 in his commentary *The Five Books of Moses.*

> And the two of them were naked, the human and his woman, and they were not ashamed. Now the serpent was most cunning of all the beasts of the field hat the LORD God had made. And he said to the woman, "Though God said, you shall not eat from any tree of the garden – "And the woman said to the serpent, "From the fruit of the garden's trees we may eat, but from the fruit of the tree in the midst of the garden God has said, 'You shall not eat from it and you shall not touch it, lest you die.'" And the serpent said to the woman, "You shall not be doomed to die. For God knows that on the day you eat of it your eyes will be opened and you will become as gods knowing good

and evil." And the woman saw that the tree was good for eating and that it was lust to the eyes and the tree was lovely to look at, and she took of its fruit and ate, and she also gave to her man, and he ate. And the eyes of the two were opened, and they knew they were naked, and they sewed fog leaved and made themselves loincloths. [16]

Alter explains how the words *'arum* ("naked") and *'arumim* ("cunning") are played against each other "in the kind of pun in which the ancient Hebrew writers delighted."[17] The humans and the serpent are portrayed as diametric opposites in the narrative: while the man and woman were innocent and unaware of evil, the serpent was cunning and planning their downfall through deception. The woman did not suspect any evil intent in the serpent's questions for she had never known evil. Alter explains that the woman interrupts the serpent's false statement in mid-sentence, for she recognized the error in the serpent's words. Why the woman adds the word *touch* can be understood as an absolute prohibition. Eating a fruit naturally requires touching it, and therefore the woman may have connected the two into an absolute prohibition: do not even touch the fruit which you are not allowed to eat. Jesus gave a similar absolute prohibition in the Sermon of the Mount: do you not desire with your eyes the one you are not allowed to touch (Matt 5.27-28). This implies that the woman knew what God had said and took it seriously, wherefore the Fall was a result of deception, not a deliberate disobedience.

Traditionally, theology has perceived sexual overtones in the revelation of the nakedness of the first humans. Although clothes provide for modesty in the fallen world, nakedness in itself is amoral. Therefore it is better to connect their newfound revelation of their nakedness to the cunningness of the serpent. The humans had aspired to be like God, but instead of their eyes being opened to their newfound divinity, their eyes were opened to the fact that they were like the cunning serpent, separated from God, wherefore they hid from His presence. It was not a lie that they would be like God and know the difference between good and evil (Gen 3.22);[18] instead, the deception was that they would not die. The humans were mortal, made of the earth and made living beings

---

16. Alter, 24-25.

17. Ibid., 24.

18. God knows everything, including evil, wherefore he can judge between good and evil. By acquiring the knowledge of evil, the humans became godlike.

through the breath of God. Only by participating of the tree of life would they live forever. God prevented them from eating from the tree while having an inclination to do evil by banishing them from the garden but promised a Redeemer who would come to destroy sin and invite the redeemed humanity to eat of the Tree of Life and live forever (Rev 22.14).

~

Not only is the man's authority absent from Genesis 1-3, it is not found in the entire Hebrew Old Testament. But because traditional theology prescribes authority to the man, the concept has found its way into English translations. For example, the creators of the New King James Version added the word *authority* to Numbers 5.19-20. The Hebrew has, "If no man has lain with you and you have not gone aside to uncleanness with another than your husband." The priest was not trying to find out whether the woman had strayed from her husband authority, but whether she had been unfaithful. In Jeremiah 44.19, the NKJV has a similar addition, "And when we burned incense to the queen of heaven and poured out drink offerings to her, did we make cakes for her, to worship her, and pour out drink offerings to her without our husbands' permission?" The original has "without our men," for the women poured the drink offerings to the idol *with* their husbands, not with their permission.

Robertson McQuilkin writes *in Understanding and Applying the Bible,* "Translations, in a sense, are commentaries on the meaning of the text inasmuch as it is impossible to translate without doing some interpreting."[19] While a translator cannot avoid some interpreting, Professor Alter considers explaining the text a common error in modern translations.

> The unacknowledged heresy underlying most modern English translations of the Bible is the use of translations as a vehicle for explaining the Bible instead of representing it in another language, and in the most egregious instances this amounts to explaining away the Bible. This impulse may be attributed not only to a rather reduced sense of the philological enterprise but also to a feeling that the Bible, because

---

19. Robertson McQuilkin, *Understanding and Applying the Bible* (Moody Press, Chicago, 1983), 122-123.

of its canonical status, has to made accessible – indeed, transparent – to all.[20]

A good example of a translation, which explains the text more than it should, is Kenneth Taylor's paraphrase, The Living Bible. Taylor's paraphrase was criticized for being too interpretative, and although it cannot be used to discern the literal meaning of the Bible, it is useful as a description of what the church believes the Bible says. The Living Bible is decidedly androcentric - the woman's entire existence revolves around serving and obeying the man, who should love his wife as a service to himself.[21]

In The Living Bible, kephale ("head") is translated ruler in Colossians 2.10 and leader in Ephesians 5.22-23. Wayne Grudem agrees with Taylor's translation of kephale, for he claims that "Christians throughout history usually have understood the word head in these verses [1 Cor 11, Eph 5] to mean "authority over."[22] However, the evidence Grudem provides is questionable. He considers the Apostolic Fathers to be "extremely valuable for understanding New Testament usage, because of the proximity in time, culture, and subject matter," but he gives only one example, the Shepherd of Hermas, in which the phrase kephalee tou oikou ("head of household") is found (Similitudes 7.3). The phrase is a curious one because it refers to a husband, but the proper Greek terms for the master of the household were oikodespoteo and kurios. Neither is the phrase found in the Bible, as kephale is never connected to oikos ("household"). Hebrew uses ro'sh beeyt for "head of the household," which becomes kephalee tou oikou when translated literally into Greek. However, it is not a proper Greek term and is never found in the Septuagint. Therefore, it is likely that the writer was a Hebrew Christian who did not use the proper idiom when writing the text in Greek.

Grudem writes also that Clement of Alexandria, Tertullian and Cyprian gave kephale the meaning "authority" but he does not quote them for he is relying on

---

20. Alter, xix.

21. That Taylor superimposed the traditional theological interpretation on the text is seen in that many of his paraphrases add concepts not found in the original text. E.g., Taylor translates 1 Cor 11.10, "So a woman should wear a covering on her head as a sign that she is under man's authority, a fact for all the angels to notice and rejoice in." The paraphrase adds the man's authority similarly to Jerome's translation of Genesis 3.16: "Under the man's authority will you be."

22. Piper and Grudem, 425.

a secondary source.[23] We have already noted that Clement of Alexandria gave *kephale* the meaning "ruler" because of his synthesis of Greek philosophy and theology wherefore his example is invalid. And although a superficial reading appears to confirm that Tertullian gave *kephale* the meaning "authority over," the Latin text shows clearly that his intention was not to prove that Christ had authority over the man, but that He was the Creator.

> "Caput viri christus est. Quis Christus? qui non est viri auctor? Caput enim ad auctoritatem posuit, auctoritas autem non alterius erit quam auctoris."[24]

> "The head of every man is Christ. What Christ, if He is not the author of man? The head he has here put for authority; now authority will accrue to none else than the "author."

Tertullian was writing against Marcion whose Gnosticism made a lesser god the author of humanity, but without authority. He used a play on the Latin words *auctor* ("author") and *auctoritas* ("authority") to prove that Christ was the author of the man, and because he was the author, He had authority over the man He had created.[25] Tertullian did not give *caput*, the Latin equivalent of the Greek *kephale*, the meaning "authority over," for he wrote, "The head he has here *put for authority*," signifying that the word itself did not have the meaning. Similarly, in the treatise *Of the Discipline and Advantage of Chastity,* which is attributed to Cyprian on questionable authority, *kephale* in Ephesians 5 refers to a literal head.

> The precepts of chastity, brethren, are ancient. Wherefore do I say ancient? Because they were ordained at the same time as men themselves. For both her own husband belongs to the woman, for the reason that besides him she may know no other; and the woman is given to the man for the purpose that, when that which had been his own had been yielded to him, he should seek for nothing belonging to another. And in such wise it is said, "Two shall be in one flesh," that what had been made one should return together, that a separation

---

23. Ibid., 454.
24. *Against Marcion*, Book V, Ch. VIII.
25. Ibid., Book V, Ch. VII.

without return should not afford any occasion to a stranger. Thence also the apostle declares that the man is the head of the woman, that he might commend chastity in the conjunction of the two. For as the head cannot be suited to the limbs of another, so also one's limbs cannot be suited to the head of another: for one's head matches one's limbs, and one's limbs one's head; and both of them are associated by a natural link in mutual concord, lest, by any discord arising from the separation of the members, the compact of the divine covenant should be broken. Yet he adds, and says: "Because he who loves his wife, loves himself. For no one hates his own flesh; but nourishes and cherishes it, even as Christ the Church." From this passage there is great authority for charity with chastity, if wives are to be loved by their husbands even as Christ loved the Church and wives ought so to love their husbands also as the Church loves Christ.[26]

In an excerpt from Cyprian's treatise, *Unity of the Church, kephale* is given a similar meaning.

As there are many rays of the sun, but one light; and many branches of a tree, but one strength based in its tenacious root; and since from one spring flow many streams, although the multiplicity seems diffused in the liberality of an overflowing abundance, yet the unity is still preserved in the source. Separate a ray of the sun from its body of light, its unity does not allow a division of light; break a branch from a tree, – when broken, it will not be able to bud; cut off the stream from its fountain, and that which is cut off dries up. Thus also the Church, shone over with the light of the Lord, sheds forth her rays over the whole world, yet it is one light which is everywhere diffused, nor is the unity of the body separated. Her fruitful abundance spreads her branches over the whole world. She broadly expands her rivers, liberally flowing, *yet her head is one, her source one*; and she is one mother, plentiful in the results of fruitfulness: from he womb we are born, by her milk we are nourished, by her spirit we are animated. [27]

Neither does Grudem quote any of the later writers, although the largest corpus of what remains from the early church writings comes from the fourth

---

26. Cyprian, *Of the Discipline and Advantage of Chastity*, 5.
27. "Treatise I: *On the Unity of the Church*" *Treatises of Cyprian*, 3-4.

and fifth centuries.[28] Instead of quoting the early church writers, Grudem relies heavily on secular sources, such as the writings of Plato, Plutarch and Philo.

> Although Plato does not use the word *kephale* explicitly to refer to a human ruler or leader, he does say (in the text quoted earlier), that "the head... is the most divine part and the one that reigns over all the parts within us" (Timaeus 44D). This sentence does speak of the head as the ruling part of the body and therefore indicates that a metaphor that spoke of the leader or ruler of a group of people as its "head" would not have been unintelligible to Plato or his hearers.[29]

That a fourth century B.C. philosopher gave *kephale* the implicit meaning "ruler" does not necessitate that a first century A.D. theologian whose outlook on humanity was entirely different gave the word the explicit meaning "leader."

A good example of the effect an underlying philosophy has on the meaning of a word is *ekklesia*. The Athenian *ekklesia* excluded slaves, children, youth, and women, for only freeborn men over twenty-one could be part of the governing assembly of Athens. But the biblical *ekklesia* found in Paul's writings is not a governing assembly formed by male citizens but an assembly of believers who are united by their faith in Christ and in which earthly distinctions are obliterated (Gal 3.28).

Additionally, Paul could not have had Plato's concept in mind when he used *kephale* in Ephesians 5, for Plato's governing *kephale* made the body inferior and sinful, which was decidedly against Paul's theology. Augustine, on the other hand, incorporated Plato's philosophy into his theology and the influence of his previous training is seen in that he gave *kephale* the meaning "ruler" when he wrote about men and women, and "beginning" when he wrote about Christ and the church (see *Appendix A, "Kephale in Early Christian Writings"*).

It is likely that the secondary meaning of *kephale* – "a beginning" – was derived from the primary meaning, "a literal head," for as the body cannot be severed from the head, the object created or born cannot be severed from its

---

28. Hastings, 57.
29. Piper and Grudem, 440.

beginning and source. Augustine thought our union with Christ and other Christians was so crucial that he believed "we would cease to be" if we fell from it.[30] Because the believers are one with Christ, the head and body function as one.

> "Christ is speaking: whether Head speak or whether Body speak; He is speaking that hath said, "Why persecutest thou Me?" He is speaking that hath said, "Inasmuch as ye have done it to one of the least of Mine, to Me ye have done it." The voice then of this Man is known to be of the whole man, of Head and of Body: *that need not often be mentioned, because it is known.* [31]

Christ left the Father to unite Himself as a head to the body, the church (Eph 5.31). But Christ is also our beginning as a creator, just as the Father is the beginning of the Son, as His father.

> "Begetter, the latter the Begotten; the former not of the Son, the latter of the Father: the former *the Beginning of the latter, whence also He is called the Head of Christ,* although Christ likewise is the Beginning, but not of the Father; the latter, moreover, the Image of the former, although in no respect dissimilar, and although absolutely and without difference equal. [32]

A beginning is the starting point and source of the other's existence. Augustine argued that a baptizer could not be the origin of a new Christian, because only Christ is the true source and head of a believer.

> If, then, the baptizer is not his origin and root and head, who is it from whom he receives faith? Where is the origin from which he springs? Where is the root of which he is a shoot? *Where the head which is his starting-point?* Can it be, that when he who is baptized is unaware of the faithlessness of his baptizer, it is then Christ who gives faith, it is then Christ who is the origin and root and head? Alas for human rashness and conceit! Why do you not allow that it is always Christ who gives faith, for the purpose of making a man a Christian

---

30. *Letters of Saint Augustine*, Letter XXX, 2.
31. Augustine, *St. Augustine on the Psalms*, Psalm LXX.
32. *A Treatise on Faith and the Creed*, Ch 9.18.

by giving it? Why do you not allow that Christ is always the origin of the Christian, that the Christian always plants his root in Christ, that Christ is the head of the Christian? ...But unless we admit this, either the Apostle Paul was the head and origin of those whom he had planted, or Apollos the root of those whom he had watered, rather than He who had given them faith in believing; whereas the same Paul says, "I have planted, Apollos watered, but God gave the increase: so then neither is he that planteth anything, nor he that watereth, but God that giveth the increase." Nor was the apostle himself their root, but rather He who says, "I am the vine, ye are the branches." How, too, could he be their head, when he says, that "we, being many, are one body in Christ," and expressly declares in many passages that Christ Himself is the head of the whole body? [33]

The Arian controversy raged in the Church in the fourth century and at the heart of the dispute was the claim that the Son was created by the Father, the ancient equivalent of the Jehovah's Witnesses and Latter Day Saints, a false belief which was refuted with vehemence by the fourth century theologians. Sabellianism on the other hand advocated that the Son was identical to the Father who was unbegotten. The council of Ariminum and Seleucia (A.D. 359) rejected the belief as heresy.

The Creed according to the Council of the East. "If any man says that the Son is incapable of birth and without beginning, saying as though there were two incapable of birth and unborn and without beginning, and *makes two Gods*: let him be anathema. *For the Head, which is the beginning of all things, is the Son; but the Head or beginning of Christ is God*: for so to One who is without beginning and is the beginning of all things, we refer the whole world through Christ. To declare the Son to be incapable of birth is the height of impiety. God would no longer be One: for the nature of the one Unborn God demands that we should confess that God is one. Since therefore God is one, there cannot be two incapable of birth: because God is one (although both the Father is God and the Son of God is God) for the very reason that incapability of birth is the only quality that can belong to one

---

33. Augustine, In answer to the letters of Petilian, the Donatist, Bishop of Certa, Book I, Ch. 4.5.

Person only. The Son is God for the very reason that He derives His birth from that essence which cannot be born. Therefore our holy faith rejects the idea that the Son is incapable of birth in order to predicate one God incapable of birth and consequently one God, and in order to embrace the Only-begotten nature, begotten from the unborn essence, in the one name of the Unborn God. *For the Head of all things is the Son: but the Head of the Son is God.* And to one God through this stepping-stone and by this confession all things are referred, *since the whole world takes its beginning from Him to whom God Himself is the beginning"*[34]

That *kephale* means "origin" and "beginning" is seen in that also Adam is called a "head." Adam was not given authority over all humanity, but he is the origin of all humans.

For so God from the beginning contrived ten thousand ways for implanting her in us. Thus, first, *He granted one head to all, Adam.* For why do we not all spring out of the earth? Why not full grown, as he was? In order that both the birth and the bringings up of children, and the being born of another, *might bind us mutually together.* For this cause neither made He woman out of the earth: and because the thing of the same substance was not equally sufficient to shame us into unanimity, unless we had also the same progenitor, He provided also for this: since, if now, being only separated by place, we consider ourselves alien from one another; much more would this have happened if our race had had two originals. For this cause therefore, as it were from some one head, he bound together the whole body of the human race. And because from the beginning they seemed to be in a manner two, see how he fastens them together again, and gathers them into one by marriage. For, "therefore," saith He, "shall a man leave his father and his mother, and shall cleave unto his wife; and they shall be for one flesh." (Genesis 2.24.) And he said not, "the woman," but, "the man," because the desire too is stronger in him. Yea, and for this cause He made it also stronger, that it might bow the superior party to the absolute sway of this passion, and might subjugate it to the weaker. And since marriage also must needs be introduced, him from whom

---

34. Hilary of Poitiers, *On the Councils, Or the Faith of the Easterns,* XXVI, 59-60.

she sprang He made husband to the woman. For all things in the eye of God are second to love. And if when things had thus begun, the first man straightway became so frantic, and the devil sowed among them so great warfare and envy; what would he not have done, had they not sprung from one root?[35]

Thus we find that Adam was the beginning of humanity to ensure the unity of "one blood" (Acts 17.26). Likewise, God the Father was the beginning of the Son to ensure the unity of the Godhead and to prevent the existence of two Gods.

~

In addition to the fourth century Greek philosopher Plato, Grudem considers the second century Septuagint to be a valuable source for the meaning of *kephale*.

> Though the Septuagint is not perfect as a translation, it was certainly adequate to be used throughout the Greek-speaking world for several hundred years. To some extent it reflected the use of Greek common at the time it was translated, and to some extent (as all widely accepted Bible translations do) it influenced the language of the people who used it. Because of both of these facts, the usage of a word in the Septuagint is *extremely important* for determining the meaning of a word in the New Testament.[36]

If *kephale* truly had the universally accepted meaning "leader" or "authority over" in the second century B.C., we should find it regularly in the Septuagint.

The Hebrew word for "head" is *ro'sh* and it is often translated with words such as "chief," "prince" and "captain," in addition to "head," "beginning" and "to sum up." *Kephale* is used to translate *ro'sh* when the context gives it the most common meaning, a literal head of a literal body. But when *ro'sh* has other meanings, such as "leader" and "chief," the Septuagint overwhelmingly favors words such as *archos* ("leader"), *arche* ("beginning," "ruler") and

---

35. *Homilies on First Corinthians,* Homily XXXIV.
36. Piper and Grudem, 428.

hegeoumai ("leader"). We see this in *archontes oikon patrioon* ("head of their father's house," Josh 22.14), *archontos ethous* ("head of the people," Num 25.15), and *hegoumenoi toon thuloon* ("heads of your tribes," Deut 5.23).

The Book of Numbers offers a crucial insight into the usage of *archos, arche*, and *kephale* in the Septuagint: *Archos* is used to translate *ro'sh* when the text speaks of leaders, captains, and chiefs (Num 1.4; 1.16; 10.4; 13.3; 14.4; 25.15; 30.2; 32.28; 36.1). *Kephale* and *arche* are used when the text speaks of summing up (Num 1.2; 4.2; 5.7; 31.26). *Kephale* and *arche* are found together also in Isa 9.14-15: "Therefore the LORD will cut off head (*kephale*) and tail from Israel, Palm branch and bulrush in one day. The elder and honorable, he is the head (*arche*); the prophet who teaches lies, he is the tail." *Kephale* is used to preserve the literal meaning of the text, but instead of denoting a leader it has the meaning "first" in the sense of a beginning – contrasted to a tail, which is the end – which is also the literal meaning of *arche*. That *kephale* describes the extreme of an object is seen in 2 Chronicles 5.9, *Kephalai toon anathoreoon* ("end of the poles"), yet another literal meaning of *arche*.

In Deuteronomy 28.13-14, being the "head" (*ro'sh, kephale*) refers to the blessings of prosperity and safety from war which follows obedience to God's commandments, and to being the "head" over the enemy, who is the "tail." The blessing is contrasted to the curses which follow disobedience. In Lamentations 1.5, Israel is described as being afflicted by the enemy which is her *ro'sh* (Septuagint, *kephale*). In Judges, *kephale* has a similar military connotation.

> And the people and princes of Gilead said one to another, What man is he that will begin to fight against the children of Ammon? he shall be head [*kephale*] over all the inhabitants of Gilead.... And the elders of Gilead said unto Jephthah, Therefore we turn again to thee now, that thou mayest go with us, and fight against the children of Ammon, and be our head [*kephale*] over all the inhabitants of Gilead. And Jephthah said unto the elders of Gilead, If ye bring me home again to fight against the children of Ammon, and the LORD deliver them before me, shall I be your head [*kephale*]? And the elders of Gilead said unto Jephthah, The LORD be witness between us, if we do not so according to thy words. Then Jephthah went with the elders of Gilead, and the people made him head [*kephale*] and captain over them: and Jephthah uttered all his words before the LORD in Mizpeh. (Judg 10.18; 11.8-11, KJV)

The most important verse in determining the meaning of *kephale* in the Septuagint is 1 Chronicles 29.11: "Yours, O Lord, is the kingdom; you are exalted as head over all" (NIV). The Septuagint translates the text *Basileus kai ethos* ("king over nations").

Kephale is never used of a husband, a head of a household, or God in the Septuagint. Instead it refers to a beginning, summing up and a military leader who is portrayed as a "head." The head leads the group, followed by the tail, but the head can be changed at any time, which is not true of the literal head of a literal body, which is Paul's metaphor in the New Testament.

CHAPTER 5

Eph 1.15-23

God is one, and Christ is one, and His Church is one,
And the faith is one,
And the people is joined into a substantial unity of body
By the cement of concord.
Unity cannot be severed;
Nor can one body be separated by a division of its structure,
Nor torn into pieces, with its entrails wrenched asunder by laceration.
Whatever has proceeded from the womb cannot live and breathe in its
Detached condition, but loses the substance of health.

– CYPRIAN[1]

~

THE HISTORICAL UNDERSTANDING of the church does not agree with Grudem, but he argues further that the context in which *kephale* is found in the New Testament clearly shows the word has connotations of authority.

> This [the context] is especially significant when we realize that a number of the New Testament examples of head have nothing to do with husband-wife relationship in marriage but speak of Christ's universal rule. For example, "he has put all things under his feet and has made him the head over all things for the church" (Ephesians 1.22). Here head is clearly a metaphor, and it occurs in a context dealing with Christ's authority "over all things" and the fact that God the Father" has put all things under his feet." It is hard to avoid

---

1. *The Treatises of Cyprian*, Treatise I, 23.

the sense of "authority over" or "ruler" in this case, since the fact of Christ's universal authority is so clearly mentioned in the very sentence in which the word occurs.[2]

English translations assign the Greek word *pas* the meaning "all things," and although the plural form of *panta* does mean "all things," the "things" are explained by the context. In Ephesians 1.22, the first *pas* refers to the rulers and authorities, the second to the church, i.e., the "things" placed under the feet of Christ are the rulers and authorities, whereas Christ has become the head over all the "things" of the church - all the members of His body. The phrase "to the church" found in the King James Version does not exist in the original. The Greek text has *kai auton ediokeen kefaleen huper panta tee ekklesia heétis estín tó soóma autoú,* which means, "and him gave [to be] head over all the church which is his body." If the word "things" and the phrase "to the church" are removed and *kephale* is given the meaning "ruler," we have, "And him gave to be ruler over all the church, which is his body." The metaphor is lost and we are left with a decapitated body, over which Christ rules. Incidentally, Grudem recognizes that *kephale* must mean an actual head in Colossians 2.19 and Ephesians 4.15 "or else the whole metaphor does not make sense."[3]

Grudem believes also that the immediate context of Ephesians 1.22 is Christ's universal rule because the previous verse has Him seated "far above all rulers and authorities." But Paul explained in Ephesians 4.10, "He who descended is also the One who ascended far above all the heavens, that He might fill all things."

His omnipresence as the Creator was described also by Irenaeus, Bishop of Lyon (A.D. 180).

> He who holds the earth in the hollow of His hand. Who perceives the measure of His right hand? Who knoweth His finger? Or who doth understand His hand, – that hand which measures immensity; that hand which, by its own measure, spreads out the measure of the heavens, and which comprises in its hollow the earth with the abysses; which contains in itself the breadth, and length, and the deep below, and the height above of the whole creation; which is seen, which is

---

2. Piper and Grudem, 425.
3. Ibid., 435.

heard and understood, and which is invisible? And for this reason God is "above all principality, and power, and dominion, and every name that is named," of all things which have been created and established. He it is who fills the heavens, and views the abysses, who is also present with every one of us. For he says, "Am I a God at hand, and not a God afar off?"[4]

The rulers (*arche*) and authorities (*exousia*) mentioned are the apostate angels and heavenly beings, which rebelled and left their abode (Jude 6).[5] Peter wrote about the baptism which saves through the resurrection of Jesus, who has "gone to heaven and is seated at the right hand of God, *angels and authorities [exousia] and powers [dunamis]* having been made subject to Him" (1 Pet 3.22). Paul left us in no doubt about the identity of these beings: the Son created the rulers and authorities (Col 1.16-17); therefore He is the beginning and origin of them (Col 2.10). He disarmed the rulers and authorities through His death on the cross, (Col 2.15) wherefore they were placed involuntarily under his feet as conquered enemies (Eph 1.20-3). God's wisdom (i.e., salvation) is made known to the rulers and authorities by the church (Eph 3.10), which wrestles against them (Eph 6.12), but is safe from harm. In his letter to the Romans Paul reminded his readers that Christ, who died and was raised, is seated at the right hand of God and intercedes for the saints, wherefore nothing can separate them from God's love.

> Yet in all these things we are more than conquerors through Him who loved us. For I am persuaded that neither death nor life, nor angels nor principalities nor powers, nor things present nor things to come, nor height nor depth, nor any other created thing, shall be able to separate us from the love of God which is in Christ Jesus our Lord. (Rom 8.37-39)

---

4. Irenaeus *Against Heresies*, Book IV, XIX. 2.

5. "But what 'rule,' then doth he here say, that Christ 'putteth down?' That of the angels? Far from it. That of the faithful? Neither is it this. What rule then? That of the devils, concerning which he saith, 'Our wrestling is not against flesh and blood, but against the principalities, against the powers, against the world-rulers of this darkness.' (Ephesians chapter 6, verse 12) For now it is not as yet 'put down' perfectly, they working in many places, but then shall they cease" (*Homilies on First Corinthians*, Homily XXXIX).

The larger context of Ephesians 1.22 is the power of God which raised Christ from the dead and seated him at the right hand of God, an event prophesied by David: "The LORD said to my Lord, "Sit at My right hand, till I make Your enemies Your footstool." The LORD shall send the rod of Your strength out of Zion. Rule in the midst of Your enemies!"(Ps 110.1-2). In accordance with the prophecy, Jesus is seated on the right hand of God, "waiting till His enemies are made His footstool" (Heb 10.13), for the enforced submission of all of his enemies is still a future event (Heb 2.5-9). His reign over His enemies will last *until* He "has put all his enemies under His feet" (1 Cor 15.24), death being the last enemy to be destroyed (1 Cor 15.26).

Also Peter wrote about the significance of Christ's exaltation to the right hand of God.

> But Peter and the other apostles answered and said: "We ought to obey God rather than men. The God of our fathers raised up Jesus whom you murdered by hanging on a tree. Him God has exalted to His right hand to be Prince (*archegos*) and Savior, to give repentance to Israel and forgiveness of sins. And we are His witnesses to these things, and so also is the Holy Spirit whom God has given to those who obey Him." (Acts 5.29-32)

At first it seems that Peter is referring to Jesus as a ruler because of the English translation of *archegos*. However, the word reflects His authorship of our salvation as seen in the following verses.

> You killed the author (*archegos*) of life, but God raised him from the dead. We are witnesses of this. (Acts 3.15, NIV)

> In bringing many sons to glory, it was fitting that God, for whom and through whom everything exists, should make the author (*archegos*) of their salvation perfect through suffering. (Heb 2.10, NIV)

> Let us fix our eyes on Jesus, the author (*archegos*) and perfecter of our faith, who for the joy set before him endured the cross, scorning its shame, and sat down at the right hand of the throne of God. (Heb 12.2, NIV)

Although God's enemies are made into a footstool, metaphorically speaking, the church cannot be under the feet of Christ because *the saints are His feet.* As members of His body, we share in the victory, as described in *The Wycliffe Bible Commentary.*

> The word sit is one of the great words in this epistle [Ephesians], indicating the position we have in Christ, as partakers of a finished, accomplished redemption and sharers in a victory.[6]

The subjection of the church to Christ is a voluntary association as a friend, not as a conquered enemy (John 15.15). For although we were His enemies, He did not die to subject us to His rule; He died to bring us back to Himself as His beloved (2 Thess 2.13) and to unite us to Himself (Eph 5.31) without violating our free will.

Grudem recognizes that we are seated with Christ, but He sees it in terms of authority which we share with Christ because he gives *kephale* the meaning "authority over."[7] As already noted, *kephale* must signify a literal head in Ephesians 1.22 for the metaphor to make sense, wherefore our position of being seated with Christ has to do with our salvation: we were seated with Christ when we became members of His body and were raised from death to life (Eph 2.4-10).

Dr. Robert Banks explains in his book *Paul's Idea of a Community* how Paul transformed the secular term *soma* ("body") into a spiritual concept.

> How original is Paul's use of this metaphor? It has no exact parallels in Jewish literature. Although the notion of 'corporate personality' is present in the Hebrew Bible, it was the Greek translation of the Old Testament which introduced the term 'body' into Jewish thought for the first time (e.g. Lev 14.9; Prov 11.17). Yet neither here nor in the literature of the intertestamental period was the term used in any metaphorical sense. The rabbinical speculations on the grossly-inflated size of Adam's body (containing all kind of mankind in embryo) come from a later period and are quite literalistic in character. Gnostic thought recognizes the idea of the saved community as the body of the heavenly redeemed, but only in writings which are later than the New

---

6. *The Wycliffe Bible Commentary*, Electronic Database, Moody Press 1962.
7. Piper and Grudem, 619.

Testament. In any case Paul's initial use of the metaphor, in which the community is represented by the whole body and the emphasis is upon the interdependence of its members, has no parallel in Gnostic sources. In Stoic literature prior to and contemporary with the New Testament, we do find the cosmos (including humanity) depicted as the body of the divine world-soul, and the state as a body in which each member has a different part to play. But then Paul refuses to portray the universe as Christ's body and rejects any idea of the society to which a member belongs having priority over the individual members themselves. For him, the individual and the community are equally objects of concern; neither is given priority over the other. One can only be an individual in a community and a community can only function properly when each individual is playing his own distinctive role within it. He also has a more restricted and, at the same time, more personal community in view than the *polis* – one that is linked to a person and involved in his ongoing personal history. Seneca's reference to the emperor as the 'soul' of the republic and the latter as his 'body' provides a closer parallel to this. But Paul, a good Hebrew here, does not think of soul and body in these dualistic terms and therefore cannot describe the relationship between Christ and the community in this way. While none of these usages yields an exact parallel to his ideas, they do indicate the extent to which the metaphor was 'in the air' in Hellenistic circles. While the term 'body' did not originate with him, Paul was apparently the first to apply it to a community *within* the larger community of the state, and to the *personal* responsibilities of people for one another rather than for more external duties. We see again how a quite 'secular' term is used by Paul to illuminate what Christian community is all about.[8]

The body of Christ is an organic unity of believers who are placed in the body by God (1 Cor 12.18) and given a *charisma* "spiritual gift" by the Spirit for the profit of all (1 Cor 12.7). The work of service given to each member builds the body (Eph 4.16) and each member is needed, for "the eye cannot say to the hand, 'I have no need of you'; nor again the head to the feet, "I have no need of you"" (1 Cor 12.21). The body cares for all of its members:

---

8. Dr. Robert Banks, *Paul's Idea of a Community* (Australia: Paternoster Press, 1980), 69-70.

if one suffers, all suffer (1 Cor 12.26). The members remain connected to the Head and each other by speaking truth to each other (Eph 4.15), as none of the members are severed from the Head by being led astray by false teaching (Col 2.19). God gave some to be "apostles, some prophets, some evangelists, and some pastors and teachers" (Eph 4.11) to perfect the knowledge of the members until they are all unified in faith and knowledge and not deceived by false teachings (Eph 4.13-14). God causes the church to grow, as does the church itself by the work each part does, for the two – the Head and the body – have become one, as pointed out by Augustine.

> "For one man He hath taken to Him, because unity He hath taken to Him.... But they that abide in the bond of Christ and are the members of Him, make in a manner one man, of whom saith the Apostle, "Until we all arrive at the acknowledging of the Son of God, unto a perfect man, unto the measure of the age of the fullness of Christ." (Eph 4.13) Therefore one man is taken to Him, to which the Head is Christ; because "the Head of the man is Christ."[9]

The force which holds the body together is not authority and submission, for "His body, then, which has many members, and all performing different functions, He holds together in the bond of unity and love, which is its true health."[10]

~

Paul was the only New Testament writer who used *kephale* as a metaphor and the word is found seven times in his letters to the Colossians and Ephesians, in addition to 1 Corinthians 11. Grudem recognizes the two letters parallel each other,[11] but in reality, the two letters are more than just twin epistles. They are identical in their content (see *Appendix B: Colossians and Ephesians*). It appears that Paul wrote the same letter twice but from different perspectives, spending

---

9. Augustine, "Commentary on Psalm LXV," St Augustine of Psalms.
10. Augustine, *On Christian Doctrine*, Book I, Ch. 16.
11. Piper and Grudem, 435.

more time on the details on the letter to the Ephesians, which accounts for the differences found in the otherwise identical letters.[12]

In Colossians 1, Paul portrays Christ as the creator of the rulers and authorities. In Ephesians 1, Christ is above them as their victor, and in both chapters the context is our salvation.

> For it pleased the Father that in Him all the fullness should dwell, and by Him to reconcile all things to Himself, by Him, whether things on earth or things in heaven, having made peace through the blood of His cross. And you, who once were alienated and enemies in your mind by wicked works, yet now He has reconciled in the body of His flesh through death, to present you holy, and blameless, and above reproach in His sight – if indeed you continue in the faith, grounded and steadfast, and are not moved away from the hope of the gospel which you heard, which was preached to every creature under heaven, of which I, Paul, became a minister. (Col 1.19-23)

> In Him we have redemption through His blood, the forgiveness of sins, according to the riches of His grace which He made to abound toward us in all wisdom and prudence, having made known to us the mystery of His will, according to His good pleasure which He purposed in Himself, that in the dispensation of the fullness of the times He might gather together in one all things in Christ, both which are in heaven and which are on earth – in Him. (Eph 1.7-10)

Since Paul is describing the same event from a different perspective, we must find the connecting theme. In Ephesians 1.4, Paul describes how God chose the saints for salvation before He created the world, even before the rulers and authorities were created (Col 1.16). In Ephesians 1.9-10, he writes about the mystery, the summing or gathering up of all things (*anakephalaiomai*), whether on Earth or in heaven, in Christ. This summing up is described as a reconciliation in Colossians 1.20, "And by Him to reconcile all things to Himself, by Him, whether things on earth or things in heaven, having made

---

12. In the letter to the Colossians, Paul mentions a letter to the Laodiceans, which the Colossians should read and vice versa (Col 4.16). The Gnostic Marcion thought the letter Paul was referring to was the one commonly called Ephesians, but Tertullian insisted that the proper designation for this other letter was "Ephesians," deciding ultimately that the title was of no consequence (*Five Books Againts Marcion,* Book V, Ch. XVII).

peace through the blood of His cross." In other words, all things have been brought back to the beginning of creation when enmity did not exist, for Christ summed up the enmity in Himself when He died on the cross and removed the handwriting of requirements that was against us. But He did not die for the apostate angels (Heb 2.16), which explains why the rulers and authorities are under the feet of Christ as conquered enemies and the church is seated in Him in the heavenly places (Eph 2.6).

Tertullian described the summing up found in Ephesians 1.10 as a recapitulating of everything into the beginning – Christ – from whom all things proceeded.

> Now, to what god will most suitably belong all those things which relate to "that good pleasure, which *God* hath purposed in the mystery of His will, that in the dispensation of the fullness of times He might *recapitulate*" (if I may so say, according to the exact meaning of the Greek word) "all things in Christ, both which are in heaven and which are on earth," but to Him whose are all things from their beginning, yea the beginning itself too; from whom issue the times and the dispensation of the fullness of times, according to which all things up to the very first are gathered up in Christ? What *beginning*, however, has the other god; that is to say, how can anything proceed from him, who has no work to show? And if there be no beginning, how can there be *times*? If no times, what *fullness* of times can there be? And if no fullness, what *dispensation*? Indeed, what has he ever done on earth, that any long dispensation of times to be fulfilled can be put to his account, for the accomplishment of all things in Christ, even of things in heaven? Nor can we possibly suppose that any things whatever have been at any time done in heaven by any other God than Him by whom, as all men allow, all things have been done on earth.[13]

~

Grudem considers Colossians 2.10 to be a prime example of *kephale* having the meaning "ruler,"[14] but the context is false teaching. Christian Gnosticism

---

13. *Five Books Against Marcion*, Book V, Ch. XVII.
14. Piper and Grudem, 425.

was found in many of the churches of Asia (modern day Turkey), including Colossae.

> Gnosticism developed with particular danger in the Colossian church. The Gnostics held to a dualistic philosophy that made a sharp distinction between spirit as good and matter as evil. According to them, the link between pure spirit and evil matter is a hierarchy. Angels are to receive worship because they have a part in this hierarchy (Col 2.8, 18-19). Salvation is to be achieved mainly by ascetic acts to deny the desires of the material and evil body (vv. 14-17, 20-23) and by a special gnosis or knowledge accessible only to the elite among Christians.[15]

According to Tertullian, Christian Gnosticism was a fusion of Greek philosophy and Christianity.

> These are "the doctrines" of men and "of demons" produced for itching ears of the spirit of this world's wisdom: this the Lord called "foolishness," and "chose the foolish things of the world" to confound even philosophy itself. For (philosophy) it is which is the material of the world's wisdom, the rash interpreter of the nature and the dispensation of God. Indeed heresies are themselves instigated by philosophy. From this source came the Aeons, and I know not what infinite forms, and the trinity of man in the system of Valentinus, who was of Plato's school. From the same source came Marcion's better god, with all his tranquillity; he came of the Stoics. Then, again, the opinion that the soul dies is held by the Epicureans; while the denial of the restoration of the body is taken from the aggregate school of all the philosophers; also, when matter is made equal to God, then you have the teaching of Zeno; and when any doctrine is alleged touching a god of fire, then Heraclitus comes in. The same subject-matter is discussed over and over again by the heretics and the philosophers; the same arguments are involved. Whence comes evil? Why is it permitted? What is the origin of man? and in what way does he come?... Whence spring those "fables and endless genealogies," and "unprofitable questions," and "words which spread like a cancer?" From all these, when the apostle would restrain us, he expressly names *philosophy* as that which

---

15. Earle E. Cairns, *Christianity Through the Centuries*, 3rd Ed. (Grand Rapids, MI: Zondervan, 1996), 71.

he would have us be on our guard against. Writing to the Colossians, he says, "See that no one beguile you through philosophy and vain deceit, after the tradition of men, and contrary to the wisdom of the Holy Ghost."[16]

If Paul argued that Christ was the great Ruler of the rulers and authorities it would not have helped expel the heresy of angels being above humans in a Gnostic hierarchy and therefore worthy of worship. Unless, of course, Paul meant that Christ was above them as the incarnated God, wherefore humanity was elevated above the angels. Grudem does make a distinction between the authority the Son had before His incarnation and after His ascension, which he believes gave the Incarnated God the "glory, honor, and authority that he had never been his before."[17] He explains further that "this welcoming into the presence of God and sitting at God's right hand is a dramatic indication of the completion of Christ's work of redemption," and that it also indicated that "he received authority over the universe." But the Father had already given Him authority to judge because He was the Son of Man (John 5.26-27), as well as authority over all people, that he might give eternal life to all whom the Father had given Him (John 17.2). Christ had all authority over the universe before His ascension, for He drove out demons and cured diseases (Mark 1.34) and gave the power and authority to the disciples to do the likewise (Luke 9.1). In addition, because He told His disciples *before His ascension*, "All authority has been given to Me in heaven and on earth. Go therefore and make disciples of all the nations, baptizing them in the name of the Father and of the Son and of the Holy Spirit" (Matt 28.18-19). As God, Christ has always had and will always have authority over His own creation. As Incarnated God, His death and resurrection ended the dominion of the apostate angles over the fallen humanity (Col 2.13-16), for it was not for His own benefit that Christ was seated on the right hand of God, for as God, what could possibly be added to His perfection?

Christ became a human for the express purpose of delivering us from the fear of death by destroying him who holds the power of death – the devil – through His own death (Heb 2.14). Christ shared in our humanity that He "might become a merciful and faithful high priest in service to God, and that

---

16. *The Prescription Against Heretics*, Ch.VII.
17. *Systematic Theology*, 618.

he might make atonement for the sins of the people" (Heb 2.17, NIV). As a High Priest, He entered into "the inner sanctuary behind the curtain" on our behalf (Heb 6.19), and His priesthood is permanent (Heb 7.24) to ensure the salvation of "those who come to God through Him, because He always lives to intercede for them" (Heb 7.26). Because He was tempted, He is also able to help those who are tempted (Heb 2.18), "for we do not have a High Priest who cannot sympathize with our weakness" (Heb 4.15). After purging us from our sins, Christ became our High Priest when He "sat down at the right hand of the Majesty on high, having become so much better than the angels, as He has by inheritance obtained a more excellent name than they" (Heb 1.3).

Even as the Incarnated Messiah, Christ excelled over the angels because He is God. As He was sent to the world, God the Father said, "Let all the angels of God worship Him" (Heb 1.6), for although he was made little lower than the angels in His humanity (Heb 2.9), Christ is the creator and upholder of all things (Heb. 1.3), the Firstborn of God (Heb 1.5). Angels, on the other hand, are ministering spirits, sent for those who will inherit salvation (Heb 1.14).

Augustine noted that Paul described Christ as both divine and human in Colossians 1.

> According to the form of God, "He is the first-born of every creature, and He is before all things and by him all things consist;" according to the form of a servant, "He is the head of the body, the Church."[18]

Kephale is not connected to the word *soma* (body) in Colossians 2.10, for Paul portrays Christ as the Creator of the angelic beings, not the Head of a body as in Ephesians 1.22. Paul was concerned about the Colossian believers' response to false teaching and he wished the believers to truly understand the mystery of God – that Christ, the Creator of the universe, was *in* them (Col 1.27). And because for they were *in* Christ, in whom are hidden all treasures of wisdom and knowledge, they were complete in Him (Col 2.9) and did not need an additional source of wisdom outside of Christ.

---

18. *On the Trinity*, Book I, Ch.12.

CHAPTER 6

Eph 5.21-33

I long to hear that you have declared an independency. And, by the way, in the new code of laws which I suppose it will be necessary for you to make, I desire you would remember the ladies and be more generous and favorable to them than your ancestors. Do not put such unlimited power into the hands of the husbands. Remember, all men would be tyrants if they could. If particular care and attention is not paid to the ladies, we are determined to foment a rebellion, and will not hold ourselves bound by any laws in which we have no voice or representation. That your sex are naturally tyrannical is a truth so thoroughly established as to admit of no dispute; but such of you as wish to be happy willingly give up – the harsh tide of master for the more tender and endearing one of friend. Why, then, not put it out of the power of the vicious and the lawless to use us with cruelty and indignity with impunity? Men of sense in all ages abhor those customs which treat us only as the (servants) of your sex; regard us then as being placed by Providence under your protection, and in imitation of the Supreme Being make use of that power only for our happiness.

    – ABIGAIL ADAMS TO JOHN ADAMS, MARCH 31, 1776[1]

As to your extraordinary code of laws, I cannot but laugh. We have been told that our struggle has loosened the bonds of government everywhere; that children and apprentices were disobedient; that schools and colleges were grown turbulent; that Indians slighted their guardians, and negroes grew insolent to their masters. But your letter was the first intimation that another tribe, more numerous and powerful than all the rest, were grown discontented. This is rather too coarse a compliment, but you are so saucy, I won't blot it out. Depend upon it, we know better than to repeal our masculine systems.

---

1. "John and Abigail Adams: Abigail Adams' 'Remember the Ladies Letter,'" American Experience, http://www.pbs.org/wgbh/amex/adams/filmmore/ps_ladies.hmtl (accessed June 29, 2009).

Although they are in full force, you know they are little more than theory. We dare not exert our power in its full latitude. We are obliged to go fair and softly, and, in practice, you know we are the subjects. We have only the name of masters, and rather than give up this, which would completely subject us to the despotism of the petticoat, I hope General Washington and all our brave heroes would fight.

— John Adams to Abigail Adams, April 14, 1776

~

Since *KEPHALE* cannot be substituted with "authority over" or "ruler," we must examine Grudem's third suggestion – that the "nuance of 'leader' or 'authority' is never absent, for the person called "head"… is always the person in leadership over the others in view."[2] The "head" is assumed to be the leader because *kephale* is linked to *hypotasso* ("submit"), which is understood to be synonymous with obedience.[3] Although *kephale* is connected to *soma* ("body") in both Ephesians 1.22 and 5.22-23, it is connected to *hypotasso* only in Ephesians 5.22-3. In Ephesians 1.22, *hypotasso* is connected to the rulers and authorities[4] and is followed by *hypo,* for the subjection of the enemies is an involuntary subjection *under* the feet of Christ, as seen also in Hebrews 2.8 and 1 Corinthians 15.27.[5]

One of the definition's Strong's concordance gives *hypotasso* is "put under,"

---

2. Piper and Grudem, 435.

3. Ibid., 196.

4. "Eánoo pásees archeés kaí exousías kaí dunámeoos kaí kurióteetos kaí pantós onómatos onomazoménou ou mónon en toó aioóni toútoo allá kaí en toó méllonti kai panta hypotaxen hupo tous podas autou" (Interlinear Transliterated Bible, Biblesoft, 1994).

5. *Hypotasso* is a combination of *hypo* and *tasso,* the latter having the meaning "to set, to arrange, put in order" (Perseus Digital Library, www.perseus.tufts.edu [accessed June 29, 2009], s.v. "tasso"). In the New Testament *tasso* signifies being set or appointed to a place (Matt 28.16), station (Luke 7.7-8), eternal life (Acts 13.48), a journey (Acts 15.2), activity (Acts 22.10), a day (Acts 28.23), office (Rom 13.1), and ministry (1 Cor 16.15-16). *Hypo* means "under, by, with, into" but when combined with a verb, it either strengthens the verb or creates a new word altogether. Thus, *ballo* ("to throw") becomes *hupoballoo* ("to throw" or put under, to suggest to the mind, to instruct privately"); *grapho* (to "grave" as in writing) becomes *hupogrammos* ("a writing-copy, an example set before one"); *deo* ("to bind") becomes

in which case the antonym should be *hypertasso* ("put over"), but such word does not appear to exist in Greek.[6] If we nevertheless assume *hypotasso* means "put under," what is, for example, a wife put under? Complementarists suggest she is put "under authority," which is why Grudem tries unsuccessfully to give *kephale* the meaning "authority over."

For the same reason, *hypotasso* in Ephesians 5.22-3 is understood to be a military term,[7] but the centurion in Luke 7.8 referred to himself as being "placed under authority" (*hypo exousian tassomenos*), signifying that he *possessed* authority. When he referred to the soldiers under him, he used the word *hypo* ("under"), not *hypotasso*. *Kephale* was not used by the Roman army for those in authority, and therefore *hypotasso* cannot be a military term in Ephesians 5.22-23, for it lacks the corresponding term *exousia* ("authority").

Although marriage is commonly compared to an army, Paul K. Jewett objects to the analogy, for a marriage is not an impersonal relationship between one who commands and one who obeys.

> Men and women are *persons* related as partners in life. Hence neither men nor women by nature are born to command or to obey; both are born to command in some circumstances, to obey in others. And the more personal the relationship between them, the less there is of either; the less personal the relationship between them, the more there is of both. This means, to give a concrete illustration, that at no time can a true marriage be likened to an army, any more than an army can be likened to a marriage. In the military enterprise by reason of its impersonal character, hierarchy is essential. Some men (and women) must command, others must obey, for an army to function. In a true marriage, by contrast, rarely will either party command or obey, and when such occasions do arise one ought not to say the husband should

---

hupodeoo ("to wear [a sandal]"); *dike* ("justice") becomes *hupodikos* ("under judgment, guilty"); meno ("stay") becomes *hupomenoo* ("to remain, persevere").

6. Other examples of combinations with *tasso* are, *paratasso* ("place or post side by side, draw up in battle order, stand side by side in battle"), *diatasso* ("to set in order"), *epidiatassomai* ("to add something that has been ordained"), *protasso* ("to arrange towards"), *katatasso* ("arrange, classify, enlist, rank"), *entasso* ("enroll, enlist, place among"), *suntasso* ("put in order together, put in the same class"), *sunkatatasso* ("arrange or draw up together, range oneself beside"), *enkatatasso* ("arrange or place in"), *prosuntasso* ("arrange beforehand") *metasuntasso* ("alter the arrangement of a treatise").

7. Piper and Grudem, 200.

always give the orders because he is a man while the wife should always obey because she is a woman. Husbands are not to the wives what generals are to privates. So to conceive the husband/wife relationship is to threaten marriage with tyranny on the man's part and artifice on the woman's part.[8]

Because *hypotasso* is understood to mean "obedience" – although the proper word for "obedience" is *hypakouo* – it is commonly assumed that the antonym for *hypotasso* is *epitasso* ("command, enjoin"), but these words are never coupled together in the New Testament. Instead we find *hypotasso* and *antitasso* in the same context three times (Rom 12.16-13.7; James 4.1-10; 1 Pet 5.4-11). Since *hypotasso* is used as an antonym of *antitasso* ("resist, to set one self against") and *anthistemi* ("oppose, stand against"), and appears frequently with *hupenantios* ("set over against, opposite, enemies in battle"),[9] it refers to a friendly ally (contrasted to a hostile enemy).

We find this most explicitly in James 4. The believers had become enemies of God because of their friendship with the world. James reminded them that God resists (*antitasso*) the proud, wherefore if they would acknowledge the error of their ways and resist (*anthistemi*) the devil, whose friend they were being, and submit (*hypotasso*) to God, the devil would flee and God would to draw near, as they drew near to Him (James 4.6-8). In his letter to the Romans Paul wrote, "the carnal mind is enmity (*echthra*) against God, for it is not subject (*hypotasso*) to the law of God, nor indeed can be" (Rom 8.7). Pilate and Herod had previously been at enmity (*echthra*) with each other (Luke 23.12), but became friends (*philos*) after the death of Jesus. Abraham was called God's friend because he was righteous before God, and because he proved his faith by his good works (James 2.22-3) and Jesus calls us, who used to be His enemies (*echthros*), His friends (Rom 5.10; Luke 12.4). Also Chrysostom wrote, "When thou seest any enemy of God wealthy, with armed attendants and many flatterers, be not cast down, but lament, weep, call upon God, that He may enroll him amongst His friends."[10]

---

8. Paul K. Jewett, *Man as Male and Female* (Grand Rapids, MI: William B. Eerdmans Publishing Company, 1975), 132.

9. Perseus Digital Library, www.perseus.tufts.edu (accessed June 29, 2009), s.v. "hupenantios."

10. *Homilies on First Corinthians*, XXXIX.12.

It is equally significant that James called the believers adulterers (James 4.1), for they were metaphorically married to God and committed adultery when they favored another god, a theme commonly found in the Old Testament. Since James 4 is the only passage in the New Testament which describes the subjection of the church to God, mentioned in Ephesians 5.22-3, a connection exists between the two. In Ephesians 5.22-3, Paul guides wives to submit to their own husbands and husbands to love their wives instead of hating (*miseo*) them. *Miseo* describes an intense feeling of hatred which is usually directed towards an enemy in the New Testament. The antonym of *miseo* is *agape*, the love which originates from God, and the husband is directed to love (*agape*) his wife as he loves himself instead of hating her as he would an enemy. The wife should regard her husband as her friend and ally, and remain near in all things. In other words, be devoted to her husband. Although "to be devoted to" is not a literal translation of *hypotasso*, it expresses the meaning of the ancient Greek word in modern English, as seen in 1 Corinthians 16.15-16 where *tasso* is translated "devoted."[11]

Since *hypotasso* does not signify obedience to an authority in Ephesians 5.22-3, *kephale* cannot prescribe authority to the man. Instead, *kephale* and *soma* describe the one flesh unity which is created when the husband cleaves (*proskollao*, lit. "to glue to") to his wife and the two become one flesh. Paul compares the earthly marriage to the mystery of Christ and the church: Christ left His Father to be joined to His bride, the church, just as each husband leaves his mother and father, to become one with his wife. Christ is the Head of the church, "for we are members of His body, of his flesh and bones," (Eph 5.30) just as the first woman was of the man's flesh and bones (Gen 2.23). The great mystery describes the unity which is created when two become one, not the subjection of one to the authority of the other.

In the Roman family, the *patria potestas* (father's authority) was such that a son would have to choose his parents over his wife if there was a dispute,[12] which was equally true of a daughter. Sarah B. Pomeroy describes the authority of the Roman father:

> The laws of guardianship indicate that the powers of the *pater familias* surpassed those of the husband. The *pater familias* decided whether

---

11. In modern speech a praiseworthy wife is not said to be submissive, but devoted.
12. Hamilton, 28.

his daughter would remain in his power, or would be emancipated from his power to that of another man, and if so, who would be her guardian. The guardian was not necessarily a relative, nor was the married daughter inevitably in the power of her husband. The *pater familias* decided whether or not she would be married according to the legal form that would release her from the authority of her father and transfer her to the power (*manus*) of her husband. If the marriage was contracted with *manus,* the bride became part of her husband's family, as though she were his daughter, as far as property rights were concerned.[13]

Contrary to the Roman custom, the Bible has the man leave his parents and be literally glued to his wife. What characterizes this union is not the transferring of power (*manus*) to the husband, but love and respect (Eph 5.33) for love creates respect, just as respect sustains love.[14]

The Bible uses several metaphors to describe the relationship between Christ and the church, but none of the metaphors speak of authority. Instead, as Chrysostom explains, they all describe unity.

> "For other foundation can no man lay than that which is laid." Upon this then let us build, and as a foundation let us cleave to it, as a branch to a vine; and let there be no interval between us and Christ. For if there be any interval, immediately we perish. For the branch by its adherence draw in the fatness, and the building stands because it is cemented together. Since, if it stand apart it perishes, having nothing whereon to support itself. Let us not then merely keep hold of Christ, but let us be cemented to Him, for if we stand apart, we perish. "For they who withdraw themselves far from Thee, shall perish;" so it is said. Let us cleave then unto Him, and let us cleave by our works. "For he that keepeth my commandments, the same abideth in Me"

---

13. Sarah B. Pomeroy, *Goddesses, Whores, Wives and Slaves* (New York: Shocken Books, 1995), 152.

14. Although an adherer to complementarist theology, Gene A. Getz writes, "But for those who take the Word of God seriously, there is little need to continually repeat these exhortations (Eph 5). In fact, couples can actually experience on a day to day basis oneness and unity that leads to consensus and egalitarian benefits" (Getz, *Measure of a Woman,* [Ventura, CA Regal Books, 1977], 130).

And accordingly, there are many images whereby He brings us into union. Thus, if you mark it, He is "the Head," we are "the body:" can there be any empty interval between the head and body? He is "a Foundation," we "a building:" He "a Vine," we "branches:" He "the Bridegroom," we "the bride:" He "the Shepherd," we "the sheep;" He is "the Way," we "they who walk therein." Again, we are "a temple," He "the Indweller:" He "the First-Begotten," we "the brethren:" He "the Heir," we "the heirs together with Him:" He "the Life," we "the living:" He "the Resurrection," we "those who rise again:" He "the Light," we "the enlightened." All these things indicate unity; and they allow no void interval, not even the smallest.[15]

⁓

In Romans 13 *hypotasso* is linked to *exousia,* wherefore "subjection to authority" could be a correct translation. But because *hypotasso* has also the meanings "to associate with, to subjoin, append, to post in the shelter of"[16] and the authorities are set (*tasso*) by God to avenge evil and to keep peace, another possible interpretation is that citizens should associate themselves with the authorities, and not oppose (*antitasso*) them, unless they have become oppressive.

The key to understanding *hypotasso* in this passage is the believer's own conscience.

> "For rulers are not a terror to good works, but to evil. Do you want to be unafraid of the authority? Do what is good, and you will have praise from the same. Do you want to be unafraid of the authority? Do what is good, and you will have praise from the same. For he is God's minister to you for good. But if you do evil, be afraid; for he does not bear the sword in vain; for he is God's minister, an avenger to execute wrath on him who practices evil. Therefore you must be subject, not only because of wrath but also for conscience' sake." (Rom 13.3-5)

---

15. *Homilies on 1 Corinthians,* Chapter 3, Homily VIII.

16. Perseus Digital Library, www.perseus.tufts.edu (accessed June 29, 2009), s.v. "hypotasso."

The fear of punishment should not be a Christian's only motivator for abstaining from evil. Instead, one should voluntarily do good to maintain a good conscience. In his letter, Peter made it clear that subjection to the governing powers entails doing good instead of evil.

> Beloved, I beg you as sojourners and pilgrims, abstain from fleshly lusts which war against the soul, having your conduct honorable among the Gentiles, that when they speak against you as evildoers, they may, by your good works which they observe, glorify God in the day of visitation. Therefore submit yourselves to every ordinance of man for the Lord's sake, whether to the king as supreme, or to governors, as to those who are sent by him for the punishment of evildoers and for the praise of those who do good. For this is the will of God, that by doing good you may put to silence the ignorance of foolish men – as free, yet not using liberty as a cloak for vice, but as bondservants of God. Honor all people. Love the brotherhood. Fear God. Honor the king. (1 Pet 2.11-17)

Peter used the word *eleutheros* ("free"), which was used of freeborn citizens or freedmen, contrasted to slaves, which signified that they were at liberty to choose to do good instead of being forced to do so by the government. *Hypotasso* in Romans 13.3-5 must therefore signify a voluntary subjection to or association with the governing authorities for the sake of civil order which can only be maintained if people follow laws.

Doug Roberts, M.D. writes, "In most situations it is imperative that authority be invested in one individual or the absence of that one will lead to a total breakdown in direction."[17] If one person always yields, harmony is restored quickly. Hence it has also been suggested that *hypotasso* means "to yield," but the proper Greek word for it is *hypeiko*.[18] The belief that without

---

17. Doug Roberts, M.D., *To Adam with Love* (Bible Voice, 1974), 72.

18. "Obey [*peitho*] those who rule [*hegeomai*] over you, and be submissive [*hypeiko*], for they watch out for your souls, as those who must give account" (Heb. 13.17). *Hypeiko* means "to surrender" and "to yield," not "to submit"; *peitho* means also "to trust," "to rely," "to have confidence" and "to be persuaded" as seen in verse 18, "Pray for us; for we are confident (*peitho*) that we have a good conscience, in all things desiring to live honorably." *Hegeomai* means also "to esteem," wherefore the verse could be translated, "Trust those who are highly esteemed among you and surrender to such (instead of fighting against them)." Note that

hierarchy we would by necessity have anarchy is based on the world of sin, not the original sinless creation, for civil governments were instituted because of sin, to control and punish lawbreakers. And although it is undeniable that a leader is often necessary to avoid an impasse, a marriage consists of two people who generally look into the same direction and who share more than an abstract concept of unity which can be broken due to the lack of direction. Perhaps Geoffrey Norman is correct in his assertion that women are more cooperative than men, who are more hierarchical in their thinking due to their innate need to dominate.[19] Since men have traditionally defined theology, hierarchy is perceived as absolutely essential for the health and happiness of all human relationships, including marriage.

Similarly, George A. Kelly writes in the *Catholic Marriage Manual*, "Much of the conflict in modern marriage would disappear if men would assume their responsibilities and women would be content to be heart and homemaker."[20] And although he believes that the man must make the final decisions and the wife should "cheerfully acquiesce in the decision with humility," he writes also that, "even though the husband is the head of the house, the home will run much more smoothly if both partners learn to obey each other." In other words, "a sense of justice contributes to marital harmony because it encourages respect for the other members of the family," and because "a certain amount

---

hegeomai is used three times in Hebrews 13 for the congregation was to remember (v. 7), trust (v. 17) and greet (v. 24) those of high esteem among them.

19. Geoffrey Norman, *Biological Differences Establish Gender Roles, Male/Female Roles*, Auriana Ojeda, Ed. (Chicago, IL: Greenhaven Press, 2005), 21.

20. George A. Kelly, *The Catholic Marriage Manual* (New York City: Random House, 1958), 7. Erich Fromm writes, "One another frequent error must be mentioned here. The illusion, namely, that love means necessarily the absence of conflict. Just as it is customary for people to believe that pain and sadness should be avoided under all circumstances, they believe that love means the absence of any conflict. And they find good reasons for this idea in the fact that the struggles around them seem only to be destructive interchanges which bring no good to either of those concerned. But the reason for this lies in the fact that the "conflicts" of most people are actually attempts to avoid the real conflicts. They are disagreements on minor or superficial matters which by their very nature do not lend themselves to clarification or solution. Real conflicts between two people, those which are experienced on the deep level of inner reality to which they belong, are not destructive. They lead to clarification, they produce a catharsis from which both persons emerge with more knowledge and more strength." (Fromm, 86)

of pain and anguish is inevitably associated with human living, patience and fortitude are necessary characteristics of a struggling couple."[21]

~

In 1 Peter 3.1-2 Peter exhorts the wives married to unbelieving husbands to have a pure conduct with respect, so their husbands may be won without a word since they had disbelieved the words they had heard. As in Ephesians 5.22-23, the word *hypotasso* in 1 Peter 3.1 and 5 can be translated "devoted," for it is the devotion of Sarah that Peter gives as an example. He goes back to the story of Sarah listening in the tent as God speaks to Abraham about the promised heir.

> Then they said to him, "Where is Sarah your wife?" And he said, "Here, in the tent." And He said, "I will certainly return to you according to the time of life, and behold, Sarah your wife shall have a son." (Sarah was listening [shama'] in the tent door which was behind him.) Now Abraham and Sarah were old, well advanced in age; and Sarah had passed the age of childbearing. Therefore Sarah laughed within herself, saying, "After I have grown old, shall I have pleasure, my lord being old also?" And the LORD said to Abraham, "Why did Sarah laugh, saying, 'Shall I surely bear a child, since I am old?' "Is anything too hard for the LORD? At the appointed time I will return to you, according to the time of life, and Sarah shall have a son." But Sarah denied it, saying, "I did not laugh," for she was afraid. And He said, "No, but you did laugh!" (Gen 18.9-15)

Peter condensed the entire story into one sentence: "As Sarah *listened attentively* to Abraham, *calling him lord*, whose daughters you are if you do good and are not *afraid* with any terror" (1 Pet 3.6). The Hebrew word *shama'* is translated with *akouo* ("to listen") in the Septuagint. *Hypakouo*, found in 1 Peter 3.6, is usually translated "to obey," but the general meaning is "to listen attentively." (The New International Version translates *akouo* with "obey" in Acts 4.19, but it is an inaccurate translation.) In Acts 12.13 the servant girl Rhoda answered (*hypakouo*) the door when Peter was knocking and therefore the word can describe an activity as a response to a request or command,

---

21. Kelly, 13.

hence the meaning "to obey." But in Genesis 18.10, Sarah is not responding to a verbal command or a request; she is only listening to a conversation, therefore *hypakouo* in 1 Peter 3.6 should be translated "to listen attentively."

The word *kyrios* ("lord") in 1 Peter 3.6 has caused a lot of trouble in theology, for it has been used to make the man the woman's lord – literally – although the word has the meaning "lord" only when applied to God. When the word *kyrios* is used of humans in the New Testament, it is invariably translated "sir," which is a term of respect (Matt 21.29-30; 27.62-63; John 4.11, 49; 5.7; 12.21; 20.15). John used *kyria,* the feminine form of *kyrios,* in his second letter for in the Greek-speaking world it was a "courteous form of address in letters."[22]

In the Old Testament, we find the word *'adown* used by people of various relationships. In Genesis 19.2, Lot calls the angels *'adown* and Abraham is called *'adown* by his neighbors while he is the one bowing down (Gen 23.6). Rebecca called Abraham's servant *'adown* by the well (Gen 24.18), and Rachel called her father *'adown* after her marriage to Jacob (Gen 31.35), who calls Esau *'adown* when making peace with him (Gen 32.4). Joseph's brothers called Joseph *'adown* in Egypt (Gen 42.10) and Aaron called Moses *'adown* when beseeching for their sister who had become leprous (Num 12.11). The chief fathers of the tribe of Manasseh called Moses *'adown* when discussing legal matters (Num 36.1-4), Ruth calls Boaz *'adown* before they were married (Ruth 2.13), and Hannah called Eli the priest *'adown* in the sanctuary (1 Sam 1.15).

From the remains of Mari, a city which flourished during Abraham's time, more than twenty thousand letters have been found by Andre Parrot. One of these letters provides further information of the usage of the term *lord* during the era of the Patriarchs.

> The city of Nahor (Gen 24.10) is mentioned quite frequently in the Mari letters. One letter from Nahor is sent by a lady of that town to the king, and reads as follows: To my lord say: Thus Inib-shaarim, thy maidservant. How long must I remain in Nahor? Peace is established, and the road is unobstructed. Let my lord write, and let me

---

22. Adolf Deissmann, *Light from the Ancient East,* 168 (referring to 2 John 1 and 5); quoted by Ute E. Eisen, *Women officeholders in Early Christianity* (Collegeville, MN: The Liturgical Press, 2000), 90.

be brought, that I may see the face of my lord from whom I am separated. Further, let my lord send me an answer to my tablet. [23]

Similarly, as previously stated, Hannah called Eli the priest "lord" and herself his maidservant (1 Sam 1.15-18), and Ruth addressed Boaz in the same manner before they were married (Ruth 2.13). It was clearly a cultural custom, similar to our "sir," and did not include obedience.

Chrysostom considered Abraham and Sarah's relationship to be one of mutual respect and affection.

> Wherefore both his wife commanded this [to accept Hagar], and he obeyed, yet not even thus for pleasure's sake. But "behold," it will be said, "how he cast Hagar out again at her bidding." Well, this is what I want to point out, *that both he obeyed her in all things, and she him.*[24]

Sarah is usually reprimanded for lack of faith in giving Hagar to Abraham. Grudem writes, "Genesis 16.2 is a classic example of role reversal leading to *disobedience* to God, for in this verse Abraham gives in to Sarah's urging and has a son by Hagar."[25] However, God did not mention Sarah the first time He promised Abraham an heir; the son was said to come from Abraham's body (Gen 15.4). According to the marriage laws of the era of the biblical patriarchs, it was a wife's duty to provide a surrogate mother in case of infertility. In an Assyrian marriage contract dating from the 19th century B.C., the wife was given two years to give birth to an offspring, after which she was under obligation to buy a slave woman for her husband,[26] who would later dispose of the slave. In the marriage laws of Nuzu, the son born of such an arrangement was not to be expelled, which explains why Abraham was reluctant to send Ishmael away [27] and complied only after God intervened (Gen 21.12).

God never rebukes Sarah and Abraham for the birth of Ishmael. In Genesis

---

23. Merrill F. Unger, *Archeology and the Old Testament* (Grand Rapids, MI: Zondervan, 1954), 124.

24. *Homilies on First Corinthians 11*, XXIV.

25. Piper and Grudem, 196.

26. Sue Poorman Richards and Lawrence O. Richards, *Women of the Bible* (Nashville, TN: Nelson Reference & Electronic, 2003), 217.

27. Ibid., 122-123.

17 God reaffirms His covenant with Abraham and adds that it is Sarah who will be the mother of his heir, but that He will bless Ishmael and make him the father of twelve tribes and a great nation (Gen 17.15-23). After the death of Sarah, Abraham re-married and had six more sons with Keturah (Gen 25.1-2) for Isaac was not to be his only son. Although their descendants would experience conflict, Ishmael and Isaac were not enemies, for they came together to bury their father Abraham after his death (Gen 25.9).

Why did Peter use Abraham and Sarah as an example of a marriage which Christian women married to unbelieving husbands should emulate considering Abraham was not an unbeliever, but the epitome of faith (Rom 4.16)? In Genesis 18.9-15, Sarah is the focus of the narrative. The sheer impossibility that she would have a child caused Sarah to laugh to herself, just as Abraham had earlier when God promised him an heir through his wife Sarah (Gen 17.17). God exposed her thoughts as evidence that nothing is too hard for Him and Sarah believed in God's promise as seen in the letter to the Hebrews, where she is commended for her faith in the promise of God (Heb 11.11).[28]

Similarly, in 1 Peter 3.1-6, Hebrew Christian married women are the focus of the text and the impossibility of the conversion of the unbelieving husbands was a reality for many. Because the husbands had already heard the gospel, and rejected it, Peter wanted the women to demonstrate the gospel through pure living and remember Sarah, who despite her husband's shortcomings was respectful towards him, calling him 'adown in her thoughts. Sarah exhibited an inner attitude of love and devotion despite the disappointment of her infertility and the reality of Abraham's old age. She did not win Abraham's love and affection through outwardly beauty, but through her own devotion towards him. As in the modern world, the women of antiquity attempted to please their husbands and win their affection by wearing worldly apparel, braided hair, and gold, but Peter exhorted them to rather exhibit the inner person who is gentle and quiet, for thus the women of old, such as Sarah,

---

28. Also Elizabeth, who was barren, and Mary, who was a virgin, were reminded of God's power, "And the angel answered and said to her, "The Holy Spirit will come upon you, and the power of the Highest will overshadow you; therefore, also, that Holy One who is to be born will be called the Son of God. Now indeed, Elizabeth your relative has also conceived a son in her old age; and this is now the sixth month for her who was called barren. For with God nothing will be impossible" (Luke 1.35-37).

used to adorn themselves.[29] With this Paul agreed for he wanted the women of Ephesus to adorn themselves with reverence and sobriety and not with braided hair and gold (1 Tim 2.9).[30]

Slaves and wives are often lumped together in an effort to prove that Christianity did not abolish social distinctions, but an important distinction between slaves and wives has been overlooked: in 1 Timothy 6.1-2 slaves are admonished not to despise believing masters but rather serve them because they are beloved brothers and sisters; in 1 Peter 3.1 Peter writes to the wives that they should be devoted to their unbelieving husbands. This distinction is possible only if the church taught the equality of masters and slaves, and husbands and wives, for the slaves would naturally have lowered their guard if they considered themselves equal to their masters and the wives would not have been inclined to exhibit a heartfelt devotion to husbands who were not believers, especially if the husbands made their lives difficult. Peter reminded the slaves to serve even the harsh masters well, for if they suffered they were following in the footsteps of Christ who suffered without a cause. It is important to note that the slaves were treated harshly by their unbelieving masters (2.19); within the community, the believers should love as brothers and be tenderhearted (3.8-9). Neither did Peter accept domestic violence, "Husbands, likewise, dwell with them with understanding, giving honor to the wife, as to the weaker vessel, and as being heirs together of the grace of life, that your

---

29. Clement of Alexandria wrote, "But there are circumstances in which this strictness may relaxed. For allowance must sometimes be made in favour of those women who have not been fortunate in falling in with chaste husbands, and adorn themselves in order to please their husbands. But let desire for the admiration of their husbands alone be proposed as their aim. I would not have them to devote themselves to personal display, but to attract their husbands by chaste love for them—a powerful and legitimate charm. But since they wish their wives to be unhappy in mind, let the latter, if they would be chaste, make it their aim to allay by degrees the irrational impulses and passions of their husbands. And they are to be gently drawn to simplicity, by gradually accustoming them to sobriety. For decency is not produced by the imposition of what is burdensome, but by the abstraction of excess" (*The Instructor*, Book III, Ch. XI).

30. Neither Paul nor Peter condemned external beautification. Rather, they were against the practice of Roman women to spend their days before the mirror, for freed from domestic labor they had little else to do to adorn themselves.

prayers may not be hindered."[31] Peter reminded all believers that they should continue to do good, even if they suffered for righteousness sake and not be afraid of threats (3.13-14). Presumably some of the unbelieving husbands were harsh, since domestic violence was common and accepted, but Peter wanted the wives to continue to do good and not be afraid with any terror (3.6). Sarah was afraid when God exposed her thoughts but she had no reason to fear, for God was not against her but for her, wanting to bless her with a child. Peter's words to the married women were that of comfort and reassurance, in the likeness of Paul's, "What then shall we say to these things? If God is for us, who can be against us?" (Rom 8.31)

~

On the Council for Biblical Manhood and Womanhood's Web site, Grudem challenges egalitarians to provide an example in which *hypotasso* is being applied "to relationships between persons and where it does not carry the sense of being subject to an authority."[32] We have already found this to be true in Ephesians 5.21-33, James 4.4-10, and 1 Pet 3.1-6, and we find additional examples from the writings of the Apostolic Fathers. Clement of Rome, who is believed by many to be the Clement mentioned by Paul in Philippians 4.3, is an early witness to the mutual subjection of all believers.

> Let us take our body for an example. The head is nothing without the feet, and the feet are nothing without the head; yea, the very smallest members of our body are necessary and useful to the whole body. But all work (lit. all breathe together) harmoniously together, and are under *one common rule (lit. use one subjection)* for the preservation of the whole body. Let our whole body, then, be preserved in, Christ Jesus; and let every *one be subject to his neighbour,* according

---

31. Although *skeuos* ("vessel") can refer to the whole human being, (Rom 9.22; 2 Tim 2.20), it refers also to the body, which was originally made of the earth, and which contains the soul (2 Cor 4.7; 1 Thess 4.4). The woman's "vessel" is weaker because her physical strength is lesser than the man's.

32. Wayne Grudem, "The Myth of Mutual Submission as an Interpretation of Eph 5.21, *Biblical Foundations for Manhood and Womanhood,* http://www.cbmw.org.

to the special gift (lit. according as he has been placed in his *charism*) bestowed upon him.[33]

Polycarp was the disciple of John the Apostle, and in his letter love, humility, and good works are all part of mutual subjection.

> Stand fast, therefore, in these things, and follow the example of the Lord, being firm and unchangeable in the faith, loving the brotherhood, and being attached to one another, joined together in the truth, exhibiting the meekness of the Lord in your intercourse with one another, and despising no one. When you can do good, defer it not, because "alms delivers from death." *Be all of you subject one to another* having your conduct blameless among the Gentiles, that ye may both receive praise for your good works, and the Lord may not be blasphemed through you. But woe to him by whom the name of the Lord is blasphemed! Teach, therefore, sobriety to all, and manifest it also in your own conduct.[34]

The disciple of Polycarp, Irenaeus, wrote in his only surviving work, *Against Heresies*, "Submission to God is eternal rest, so that they who shun the light have a place worthy of their flight; and those who fly from eternal rest, have a habitation in accordance with their fleeing."[35] Also Origen connected submission with salvation in the beginning of the third century.

> What, then, is this "putting under" by which all things must be made subject to Christ? I am of opinion that it is this very subjection by which we also wish to be subject to Him, by which the apostles also were subject, and all the saints who have been followers of Christ. For the name "subjection," by which we are subject to Christ, indicates that the salvation which proceeds from Him belongs to His subjects, agreeably to the declaration of David, "Shall not my soul be subject unto God? From Him cometh my salvation."[36]

---

33. Clement of Rome, *The First Epistle of Clement to the Corinthians*, Ch. XXXVII-III.

34. Polycarp, *The Epistle of Polycarp to the Philippians,* Ch. X.

35. *Against Heresies,* Book IV, Ch. XXXIX.

36. Origen, *Origen de Principiis,* Book I, Ch. VI.

Complementarists acknowledge that Ephesians 5.21 must mean mutual submission because of the word *allelon* ("one another"), but because they give *hypotasso* the meaning "yield to authority," Piper and Grudem must create a mutual submission which is experienced in different ways.

> But even if Paul means complete reciprocity (wives submit to husbands and husbands submit to wives), this does not mean that husbands and wives should submit to each other *in the same way*. The key is to remember that the relationship between Christ and the church is the pattern for the relationship between husband and wife. Are Christ and the church mutually submitted? They aren't if submission means that Christ yields to the authority of the church. But they are if submission means that Christ submitted himself to suffering and death for the good of the church. That, however, is not how the church submits to Christ. The church submits to Christ by affirming His authority and following his lead. So mutual submission does not mean submitting to each other *in the same way*. Therefore, mutual submission does not compromise Christ's headship over the church and it should not compromise the headship of a godly husband. [37]

Since *hypotasso* does not mean "yield to authority," Piper and Grudem's argument is invalid, but there is also another fallacy in their argument: the members of the church show their devotion to Christ by willingly sacrificing themselves due to their love for Christ (2 Tim 2.12), which is the devotion and love Christ showed to the church when He willingly died to make the church holy and blameless (Eph 1.4; 5.27).

Complementarists point also to the fact that the Bible tells wives to submit and husbands to love as evidence that Ephesians 5.21 cannot teach mutual submission (*hypotassomenoi allelois*).[38] Although it is true that the Bible doesn't explicitly tell wives to love (*agape*) their husbands,[39] the New Testament tells believers to love each other (*agapate alleleous*).[40] Since the husband is also a brother, a wife should love her husband just as he loves her, for the instructions given to the married cannot conflict with the rest of the Bible. If a wife ought

---

37. Piper and Grudem, 62-63.
38. Piper and Grudem, 199.
39. In Titus 2.4 Paul uses *philoandros* and *philoteknos*. Not *agape*.
40. See John 13; Romans 12; 1 Thessalonians 4.9; 1 Peter 1.22; 1 and 2 John.

to love her husband, the husband ought to be devoted to his wife, especially since it is explicitly mentioned in Ephesians 5.21.

Because Ephesians 5 does not mention authority, Knight makes the husband's love the means of his authority over the wife.

> Paul's direct command to the husbands is to "love your wives, just as Christ loved the church and gave himself up for her..." (verse 25). This is clearly how the apostle demands that the husband exercise his leadership in everything as the head over his wife. He is to love her "just as" (*kathos*) Christ loved the church [41]

But it is not possible for Ephesians 5.1-2 says, "Therefore be imitators of God as dear children. *And walk [peripateo] in love, as Christ also has loved us and given Himself for us,*[42] an offering and a sacrifice to God for a sweet-smelling aroma." Are all Christians called to exercise authority over the other members of the body?

Paul mentions love three times in Ephesians 5.

> Husbands, love your wives, just as Christ also loved the church and gave Himself for her... So husbands ought to love their own wives as their own bodies; he who loves his wife loves himself... Nevertheless let each one of you in particular so love his own wife as himself (Eph 5.25, 28, 33a).

If the husband's love for his wife is the means for his leadership, is he to exercise authority over himself since he should love his wife as he loves himself, and by loving his wife he loves himself? Knight's attempt to find authority in the text is in vain, for Christlike love is about sacrificing oneself for the benefit of a friend (John 15.13); no hierarchy of authority and subjection exists within friendship.

Mutual submission is taught also in 1 Peter 5.5-6. Modern English translations do not convey the meaning, for *allelon* ("one another") is connected

---

41. Piper and Grudem, 171.

42. A better translation of *peripateo* is "to live." The New International Version translates the verse accurately: "Live a life of love."

to *tapeinophrosune* ("humility of mind") instead of *hypotasso* as seen in the NIV, "All of you, clothe yourselves with humility toward one another." But how does one clothe oneself *toward* another? Not surprisingly, the post-Reformation translations do not follow the Vulgate which connects the humility of mind with "one another" while modern English translations do [43] for the modern church shares its affinity towards a powerful clergy with the patristic church, while the Post-Reformation churches attempted to bring more equality between the clergy and the laity after a millennium of powerful and corrupt bishops by emphasizing the mutual submission of the two.

Clement of Rome agreed with the post-Reformation Bible translators.

> For God," saith [the Scripture], "resisteth the proud, but giveth grace to the humble." Let us cleave, then, to those to whom grace has been given by God. *Let us clothe ourselves with concord and humility*, ever exercising self-control, standing far off from all whispering and evil-speaking, being justified by our works, and not our words.[44]

Clement appears to translate *hypotasso* with "cleave," and he considers clothing oneself with humility to be personal, not "toward one another." First Peter 5.5-6 makes eminently more sense if *hypotasso* is connected to *allelon* ("be subject to another") and *tapeinophrosune* to each believer's relationship towards God ("Be clothed with humility, for God resists the proud, but gives grace to the humble"), for the believers are directed to submit to another *and* to humble themselves under the mighty hand of God, so He might exalt them in due time.

~

It has also been suggested that the husband is the head and the wife the heart of the family, and therefore, as the human head leads the rest of the body, the husband ought to lead his wife. But in reality, the head and heart function

---

43. Tyndale (1526), Miles Coverdale (1535), The Bishop's Bible (1568), Geneva Bible (1587), The King James Version (1611) and Wesley's New Testament (1755) all have "be subject to one another." The Vulgate translates the text, "Similiter adulescentes subditi estote senioribus omnes autem invicem humilitatem insinuate quia dues superbis resistit humilibus autem dat gratiam."

44. *The First Epistle of Clement to the Corinthians,* Ch. XXX.

in unison, both performing vital functions without which the human body would not survive. The heart is responsible for the circulatory system without which the brain and the limbs would die due to lack of oxygen and which functions independently from the nervous system, regulated by the brain.[45] On the other hand, if the brain dies, the nervous system ceases to function and the body will not be able to move, although the heart still beats, keeping the body alive. In complementarist theology, the man's prior existence gives him authority, but an attempt to make the man the leading head using the human body as an analogy fails for the heart begins to beat in the embryo before the brain is fully developed because the brain is dependent of the oxygen the heart disperses into the bloodstream and can therefore not exist prior to the heart. The wife is not an extension of the husband as the body is of the head, neither does she lack the rational faculty, wherefore the head-body metaphor, as applied to marriage, describes two independent entities which co-operate harmoniously to keep their marriage alive without one leading the other.

Just as in 1 Corinthians 11, the beginning of Ephesians 5 is connected to the end; verse 33 speaks of love and respect which corresponds to the head and body metaphor of verses 22-24. Christ is portrayed as a husband who leaves His Father to become one flesh with His wife (v. 31). Through His death, Christ washed the church from all impurity, "that He might present her to Himself a glorious church, not having spot or wrinkle or any such thing, but that she should be holy and without blemish" (v. 27). The washing is described also in the letter to Titus.

> For we ourselves were also once foolish, disobedient, deceived, serving various lusts and pleasures, living in malice and envy, hateful and hating one another. But when the kindness and the love of God our Savior toward man appeared, not by works of righteousness which we have done, but according to His mercy He saved us, through the washing of regeneration and renewing of the Holy Spirit, whom He poured out on us abundantly through Jesus Christ our Savior, that having been justified by His grace we should become heirs according to the hope of eternal life. (Titus 3.3-7)

The analogy does not compare the husband with Christ as far as His work as

---

45. "Human Body Organ Systems," *Get Body Smart*, http://www.getbodysmart.com/ap/systems/tutorial.html (accessed June 29, 2009).

the Messiah is concerned, for a husband cannot save his wife anymore than he can save himself. Instead, *kephale* and *hypotasso* describe the insoluble unity of the head and body, for as the head cannot be severed from the body, neither can the church be separated from Christ, for He promised to never forsake, nor leave us (Heb 13.5).[46]

---

46. One of the more inexplicable aspects of complementarism is that a man has authority over his wife although he does not have it over her body (1 Cor 7.4) as if it were possible to separate the body from the mind. That a wife has authority over the husband's body is often forgotten; on the Internet a woman was convinced by a preacher that rebellion against a husband's sexual advances is equivalent to witchcraft for wives should "give their husbands what they want when they want it." (www.jesus-is-lord.com)

CHAPTER 7

Phil 2.1-4

The truth about marriage is that it is a way not of avoiding any of the painful trials

And subtractions of life, but rather of confronting them, of exposing, and tackling them most intimately, most humanly.

It is a way to meet suffering personally, head in, with the peculiar directness,

The reckless candidness characteristic only of love.

It is a way of living life with no other strategy or defense or protection than that of love.

And so it is the gradual unfolding of an amazing process of interpersonal consecration,

A process in which all the pain locked up in two lonely,

self-centered lives is no longer hidden or suppressed

(as it tends to be everywhere else in life),

But rather released,

Released so that in the hands of love it might be used as the raw material for sanctification.

Marriage is a way not to evade suffering, but to suffer purposefully.

– MIKE MASON[1]

～

IN HIS ESSAY *A Vision of Biblical Complementarity*, John Piper outlines the different roles for men and women: the man was created to lead, provide and protect and the woman to affirm, receive and nurture. Piper creates the roles

---

1. Mike Mason, *The Mystery of Marriage, As Iron Sharpens Iron* (Colorado Springs, CO: Multnomah Press, 1985), 142.

using the head-body metaphor in Ephesians 5 as an analogy; as the human head is the source of guidance, food and alertness for the body, so is the man to the woman.[2] While Piper calls it an impossibility for women never to influence or guide men,[3] he explains that a woman can lead, provide, and protect if a) a man is not present, b) a man is present, but unwilling to perform the role, c) a man is present who is willing to perform the role but is unable or a woman is in a position or rank above him, in which case the woman must assume a correct demeanor and accept culturally accepted courtesies (such as opening of the door) in order to affirm the unique role of man as a leader and protector.[4] Because women should influence men in a way that does not compromise the leadership of men, some roles are not open to women.

> Some roles would involve kinds of leadership and expectations of authority and forms of strength as to make it unfitting for a woman to fill the role.... To the degree that a woman's influence over a man is personal and directive it will generally offend a man's good, God-given sense of responsibility and leadership, and thus controvert God's created order.[5]

Piper explains further that a woman may pray for a man, but not be a drill sergeant, since the non-directive influence is about petitioning and persuasion, not giving commands. The closeness of the relationship between a man and woman is the most important indicator of the appropriateness of the directive influence: a woman can be in a position of authority and give directions only if they are non-personal in nature – authority in marriage is out of the question.[6]

Piper's view on teaching follows the same guidelines: since it is impossible for women never to teach men, they are allowed to do so in the church if it does not dishonor the calling of men to bear the primary responsibility to teach and lead, it is allowed by the elders, does not make the woman a de facto spiritual shepherd over men and is not a "strong or forceful pressing of men's consciences on the basis of divine authority."[7]

---

2. Piper and Grudem, 63.
3. Ibid., 50.
4. Ibid., 50-51.
5. Ibid., 51.
6. Ibid., 52.
7. Ibid., 69-70.

Piper considers it to be an order of creation for the man to be responsible for providing for the family and the woman to care for the children.

> The point of this Genesis text is not to define limits for what else the man and the woman might do. But it does suggest that any role reversal at these basic levels of childcare and breadwinning labor will be contrary to the original intention of God, and contrary to the way he made us male and female for our ordained roles. Supporting the family is primarily the responsibility of the husband. Caring for the children is primarily the responsibility of the wife.[8]

Piper does, however, recognize that men cannot always provide for and protect the family due to various circumstances. If a man is unable to physically perform his role, he retains his masculinity by *sensing* his responsibility to lead, provide and protect and by accepting it as given by God. A man who does not sense or affirm his responsibility to lead, provide and protect, is immature and incomplete in his masculinity.[9] If a woman has to perform the role assigned to the man, she must avoid a role-reversal by having a proper feminine demeanor. The key to retaining proper femininity is for the woman to have the right *disposition*: she must *sense* that the role would properly be done by a man if one was available or willing.[10] What is important is not what roles men and women *actually* perform, but how they, as men and women, relate to the roles they *should* and *would* perform if they lived in a perfect world, as originally created by God, without sin, sickness and death. In a later chapter, Piper concludes that "headship does not prescribe the details of who does precisely what activity."[11] But one is tempted to ask why the roles are necessary if they do not define precise activity – unless, of course, their sole function is to exclude women from leadership.[12]

---

8. Ibid., 43.

9. Ibid., 36.

10. Ibid., 46.

11. Ibid., 64.

12. Elliot believes the essence of femininity is receiving, which defines the woman's role as subordinated to the man, "Femininity receives. It says, "May it be to me as you have said." It takes what God gives – a special place, a special honor, a special function, and glory, different from that of masculinity, meant to be a help. In other words, it is for us women to receive the given as Mary did, not to insist on the non-given, as Eve did" (Piper and Grudem, 398). But also masculinity receives by saying, "O My Father, if this cup cannot pass away from

In his essay *The Family and the Church*, George W. Knight III believes one of the effects of the gospel is the "wonderful by-product" of equality, which is presently being replaced by secularization as women are removing themselves from distinctive roles and men are becoming increasingly abusive or passive.[13] Since near equality was gained by women at the twentieth century and only through hard work and enduring patience, it is likely that Knight's historical vision is limited to the 1950's when women were "equal but different." The tendency to view one's childhood as the Lost Paradise to which one must return is not limited to Christianity. Evolutionist Steven E. Rhoads is a case in point: he grew up in the '50s and he advocates for a return to the era in his book *Taking Sex Differences Seriously,* for he believes that it allowed us to live according to the innate characteristics we possess as a result of evolutionary development. Others, such as evolutionists Rosalind Barnett and Caryl Rivers, see through this tendency, "In the absence of any verifiable facts about the inclinations, behaviors, or strategies of our remote ancestors, many evolutionary psychologists have decided to portray them as idealized 1950s American family: breadwinning, dominant males and domestically oriented, passive females."[14]

Not surprisingly, Rhoads agrees with, and even admires, complementarism.

> If marriage means bringing together one person with a taste for asser-
> tion and another with a taste for generosity, we should not be surprised
> to find that the former is, in some sense, the head of the family. This
> doesn't mean that he rules like an absolute dictator. Indeed, it's still
> quite common to hear of small, feminine women who have their
> strong, masculine husbands "wrapped around their little fingers."
> Happy women usually rule indirectly. They can rule because their
> husbands love and want to please them. They can also rule because, as
> psychological studies have demonstrated, women can read men better
> than men can read women. What matters, then, is only that men be
> the ostensible heads of the households. In such cases, both parties
> emerge happy. One way to get men to dominate less and be open to
> their wives' influence is to create what Brad Wilcox calls "soft patri-

---

Me unless I drink it, Your will be done" (Matt 26.42). It receives as Jesus did, not power and prestige, but humble servanthood. It does not insist on the non-given, a higher position on a manmade hierarchy, but accepts the given - the equality of men and women.

13. Piper and Grudem, 346.

14. Rosalind Barnett and Caryl Rivers, *Same Difference*, (New York: Basic Books, 2004), 51.

archs." Such figures can be found in conservative Protestant churches, which urge husbands to be "servant leaders" who attend to their wives' need for communication and affection as well as to the family's needs for economic wherewithal and moral leadership. While the emotional work of marriage may not be inherently pleasurable or come naturally to men, it can become central to their lives if it is seen as a duty or as intrinsic to a mission. (Men hate to iron, but even a Marine, who typically loves risk-taking and excitement, can take to ironing his dress uniform with attentive skill.)[15]

Knight believes Paul "exalts the home and women's duties in it and encourages women to be 'busy at home' while the husband assumes his responsibility as a breadwinner."[16] He believes further that the "division of duties in the home and household must take seriously the respective roles of the woman and the man," the wife influencing and advising the husband, who is the head with the responsibility to make decisions. [17] Both Rhoads and Knight agree that although a woman may work, preferably part-time, housework is her responsibility.[18] Knight can resort to the Bible for a few select verses which out of context excuses the man from housework, but Rhoads does not have such a handy resource and must therefore claim women "like housework more than men do,"[19] and that the difference has a biological basis, although in a far more honest evaluation he concludes that men want "their women to be babes" while "they do not want to bothered with much housework."[20] Rhoads believes that marriages in which the domestic work is distributed evenly are more likely to divorce than marriages in which the labor is "somewhat unfair to the wife."[21] And although he believes the reason to be that "a man who believes that his wife does more than her share notices and appreciates what she does," he provides a more likely answer in his observation that men seek divorce if the woman

---

15. Steven E. Rhoads, *Taking Sex Differences Seriously* (San Francisco, CA: Encounter Books, 2004), 262.

16. Piper and Grudem, 348.

17. Ibid., 349-351.

18. Ibid., 348; Rhoads, 259.

19. Rhoads, 256.

20. Ibid., 258.

21. Ibid., 260.

fails to perform her domestic duties according to his expectations,[22] which can be linked to his earlier observation that men do not want to bothered with much housework. Rhoads admits that not all women like housework, and even those who do, prefer to do other things. He is also candid about the fact that most women complain that men do not do enough around the house, and he concludes that husbands show that "they love their wives" and "appreciate the importance of their work" when they clean up after themselves.[23]

Knight's headship gives the man the right of veto, but Rhoads is more concerned about how the man feels, than the actual state of affairs; a belief which closely mirrors Piper's reasoning that the man must "sense" his leadership if unable to perform it.

> Wives doubtful about whether grant titular household leadership to husbands should realize they may not have to give up much more than the title. Some studies have shown that husbands overestimate their decision-making power, while wives underestimate theirs. Yet an early study "found that the most satisfied husbands were those who believed they had the greater decision-making power even when there was no independent evidence of it."[24]

Rhoads believes that our innate characteristics were created during the 99 percent of the human existence called "environment of evolutionary adaptation" and that we are "more suited for the life in the EEA than to life in the

---

22. Ibid., 61.

23. Ibid., 260. Evolutionary biology can only describe the very human dislike towards chores which are considered menial and the man's success in relegating these to the woman, who in turn hands them over to a servant – if she is able to. It is important to note that men, due to their desire to dominate, will devote their time only to the tasks society considers important. If it is music, men will produce musical works which endure for centuries; if it is art, frescos and status will grace the most important buildings of the era; if it is literature, the literary works created will endure for thousands of years; if its warfare, men will die valiantly on the battle-field; if it is money, men will work from dawn to dusk to acquire more. Modern fathers are very much involved in raising their children, and consider it natural, instead of leaving it solely to the mother because the Century of the Child succeeded in making childrearing important. Women should not demean housework if they wish their husbands do their equal share. Instead, cleaning and laundry must be made as important for the average man as ironing his dress uniform is for the Marine.

24. Ibid., 263.

present."[25] Incidentally, it was during the '50s that the myth of the Man the Hunter, the primeval man born in Africa, was created to fill the need for an anti-racist, universal message of brotherhood for a world torn apart by conflict.[26] Evolutionists held that the man's hunting had made us humans to begin with, and because men hunted, and presumably dominated the other carnivores in the Stone Age, the modern man should possess the primary positions in the modern "jungle."[27] But as Barnett and Rivers point out in *Same Difference*, there is no evidence for the existence of Man the Hunter. Instead, the extant evidence points to nomadic tribes that moved frequently, both men and women scavenging and being killed by humans and animals alike, as paleontologist Richard Leakey explains, "There is absolutely no evidence that we became human through hunting. Up until recent times, there's no record at all of human aggression. If you can't find it in the prehistoric record, why claim it's there?"[28]

Evolutionists maintain that the present is the key to the past and biologists believe the man desires to dominate because the evolutionary process gave the man a higher testosterone level,[29] wherefore Rhoads argues women should realize that the man's dominion is a natural impulse which should not be suppressed. But Rhoads cannot remain consistent for testosterone causes the man also to be promiscuous. Rhoads believes that women should suppress the male tendency to chase every skirt for "men can and will change their behavior in response to what they think women require for sex" – i.e., marriage. The reason for Rhoads's sudden change of heart lies in the fact that "men seem to gain the most from marriage, although almost all studies conclude that women gain some."[30] If women require a ring before sharing their bed, men will have a motivation to "turn their lust into love."[31] But no such motivation exists in the area of dominion for the change of behavior would mean housework which provides added benefits only to the woman.

The man's impulse to dominate is linked to his desire for access to women

25. Ibid., 27.
26. Barnett and Rivers, 129.
27. Ibid., 130.
28. Ibid., 132.
29. Rhoads, 28.
30. Ibid., 92.
31. Rhoads, 95.

and to gain it he seeks "high status through dominance over other men," for women, who in turn are trapped in a perpetual beauty pageant, are presumed to be attracted to powerful and wealthy men.[32] Thus dominance is a means to an end, for the man who appears "competitive and cocky" will have a better change to climb the male hierarchy and attract women by "indicating his ability to protect."[33] Erich Fromm considers this approach to love a peculiar part of the western society which focuses on being loved rather than loving; in order to be lovable and to find a suitable partner, men seek success, power and wealth, and women work hard to make themselves attractive, reducing love to "a mixture between being popular and having sex appeal."[34]

The man's search for dominion does not end at the altar, for Rhoads claims also that male dominion is beneficial for marriage, but his true reasoning is the man's unwillingness to lose his status among other men,[35] for dominance creates a "pleasurable testosterone high" while being dominated causes "a testosterone low," which accounts for the fact that men "hate to be dominated."[36] The man should dominate in the financial realm in the home and Piper affirms Rhoads's conclusion that the man's self-esteem will be lowered if his wife earns more, for he believes that "a man will feel his manhood compromised if he through sloth, folly or lack of discipline, becomes dependent over the long haul on his wife's income."[37] Although Rhoads is convinced that women who earn more than their husbands risk their marriages, other researchers disagree with him.

> Today, more than 40 percent of white, college-educated married women earn more than their husbands. According to evolutionary theory, these couples should be highly divorce prone. But a 1999 nationally representative sample of 4,405 couples found that divorce is more likely when a woman has no earnings than when she brings home a paycheck. In particular, the marriage of a woman with no earnings was more than twice as likely to dissolve than that of a woman who earned up to $ 18,000. The traditional homemaker – who stays by the hearth and wastes no energy on earning money – is commonly

---

32. Ibid., 27, 150.
33. Ibid., 157.
34. Fromm, 1-2.
35. Rhoads, 66.
36. Ibid., 151.
37. Piper and Grudem, 42.

thought to have the most stable marriage. But having an income of her own in fact protects a woman's marriage.[38]

Rhoads believes also that a marriage is happy if the spouses do not need to negotiate or compromise, although negotiating is needed, and even desirable, in all human relationships.[39] Although Rhoads is convinced that men must dominate in the financial realm, all husbands do not resent having a wife who earns more, but rather the ones who hold traditional opinions about breadwinning.[40] Similarly, the men who hold traditional opinions about dominion are unhappy if the marriage is a partnership.[41]

Both complementarism and Rhoads's Ultra-Darwinism portray feminism as intrinsically evil and glorify the 1950's with a tangible nostalgia. But they do not mention segregation or the Civil Rights Movement, McCarthyism or the effect World War II and the atom bomb had on the people who were trying to re-build their lives. They focus solely on how white, middleclass men and women related to each other in suburbia during the post-war decades and ignore the reasons the experiment failed. Consequently, they prescribe the cause as a remedy for the modern social problems instead of looking for new solutions which would provide real answers.

While theologians emphasize the importance of authority and subjection, marriage counselors – who must solve the problems created by the rigid roles – stress servanthood, mutual love, and respect. Dr. Larry Crabb writes, "With its insistence on living by rigid rules and functioning within narrow roles, moralistic Christianity has done real damage. And nowhere has the damage been greater than in marriage."[42] Role-play has never enhanced a marriage; instead it causes people to hide behind the ready-made masks which are easy to put on, but difficult to remove.

---

38. Barnett and Rivers, 80.
39. Rhoads, 74.
40. Barnett and Rivers, 81.
41. Ibid., 93.
42. Dr. Larry Crabb, *Men and Women, Enjoying the Difference* (Nashville, TN: Zondervan, 1991), 32.

Too often, marriage becomes the mere attachment of mask to mask, rather than the union of one whole person with another whole person. In such marriages, the masks of Mother, Father, Provider or Cook come to be regarded as the major portion of the person. Living beyond the limits of the mask is discouraged as threatening to the very basis of the marriage. For many people, life stagnates inside the mask – becomes suffocating, uncreative, non-spontaneous. In some marriages, the death mask might as well be made right after the honeymoon, because there is no more growth – ever.[43]

As L. Richard Lessor points out, if a marriage is not growing, it is dying,[44] and a long-term self-and partner-deception leads more often than not to the divorce court in a desperate attempt to find who one was before the mask.[45]

Although complementarists believe God designed men and women with specific innate characteristics and that these characteristics are the foundation of the different roles, the brain, which makes us who we are, can have both male and female characteristics.

The degree of feminization or masculinization – the "gender" of the brain – varies widely from woman to woman and from man to man. At one extreme of the spectrum is the traditional male brain; at the other, the traditional female brain. Yet the masculinization or feminization of brain regions may vary from one area to another *even within one brain*. So, it's possible that you could have both the mood circuits of a traditional female brain and the visuospatial, map-reading capabilities of the traditional male brain. You might "throw like a boy," for instance, but "talk like a girl."[46]

Dr. Schulz points out that a traditional female brain no longer exists due to the complexity of the modern world, which has molded and rebuilt the female

---

43. Lessor, 37.

44. Ibid., 117.

45. Ibid., 38; The need to return to the time before the mask may explain why many middle-aged people who married young, experience a midlife crisis and have an irresistible desire to be young and free again.

46. Mona Lisa Schulz, M.D., *The New Feminine Brain, Developing Your Intuitive Genius.* (New York: Simon and Schuster, 2006), 23.

brain. This change was made possible by the larger amount of connections in the female brain, which can increase and change in response to a new and more challenging environment. Hormones are responsible for the changes, wherefore "repeated changes in hormone levels through the menstrual cycle, pregnancy, childbirth, and menopause may help the female brain develop its characteristic extensive pathways between cells."[47] Though the male brain is anatomically more stable, with less connections between the left and right hemisphere, a man can be pressured to remain in the left side by the society if rigid roles prevent the man from expressing emotions and the man learns to "stuff his feelings."[48] Although emotionality and irrationality is often associated with femininity, testosterone causes impulsivity,[49] which coupled with pent up emotions, results often in violent and irrational behavior. Regardless of conventional wisdom, both men and women need to use the left and the right side of their brain to remain healthy.[50]

> Neither man nor woman can live by one brain alone. You don't want to trap yourself in the comfort of your left brain's more tidy, pleasant, socially ordered environment. If your right brain's emotions and intuition don't have equal input into decisions and actions, they initiate biochemical and hormonal events that trigger physical and emotional problems: Chronic depression, anxiety, panic, dementia, heart disease, immune system dysfunction, and cancer are the products of an overly dominant left brain, a silenced right brain, and censored intuition.[51]

---

47. Ibid., 22.

48. Ibid., 28.

49. Ibid., 40. Sheila E. Rothman describes the nineteenth century belief in the debilitating effect of menstruation, "Physicians and advice books cautioned women who might think themselves as exceptional, with special talents or robust health, that they too were prone to the perils of femininity. Every woman, for example, experienced 'the temporary insanity of her menstruation.' During their monthly periods, as one physician explained, women were 'more prone than men to commit any unusual or outrageous act,' and that fact alone ought to keep them at home [away from the professional life]" (Rothman, *Woman's Proper Place,* [New York, Basic Books, 1978], 25). The belief that menstruation causes mental instability has proven to be tremendously resilient both to facts and actual experience.

50. Intuition is often considered exclusively female, while reason is assigned to the man, but Dr. Schulz writes, "Let's be clear: Traditional men *do* get intuitive information. They may not talk about it; their right-brain or body intuition may simply be shunted directly into making choices or taking action with little discussion" (Schulz, 42).

51. Schulz, 47.

The brain may determine who we are, but Barnett and Rivers argue also that the so called innate characteristics are in reality situation related – i.e., how one behaves dependents on who has the power and what role one is expected to play.[52]

> We are all surprisingly flexibly in our speech, speaking differently in different situations. We don't talk to our kids in the same way we talk to our bosses. That commonsense observation is supported by a study in which women were told they were going to be judged on their leadership ability. In this case, they spoke up as much as the men. But when women were told that they were going to meet attractive men who preferred women who let them take the lead, they altered their behavior to be more stereotypically feminine. We're aware of what others expect from us regarding appropriate sex-role behavior and we tend to react accordingly.[53]

That one rejects gender based roles does not necessitate that one rejects roles *per se*, for human society needs roles to remain cohesive, as observed by Elizabeth Janeway.

> Role behavior has another use: it is a device for learning. We have noted Talcott Parsons' theory that the family is a center for teaching children their own social roles and, beyond this, the place of such roles in the structure of society. School and community together continue the process, for a great deal of education is not factual, but emotional and behavioral.... So every individual finds the world structured and explained by other people's experience. It has been imagined for him in the shape of his native culture by those who lived before him. He may disagree with these findings, but at least he has a body of knowledge to argue against and a place to begin.[54]

The trouble begins when the roles become too rigid and cannot be modified as society changes, for the individual's response will cease to meet the expectations of society. Janeway concludes that "the value of a particular role, in a

---

52. Barnett and Rivers, 10-11.
53. Ibid., 106.
54. Elizabeth Janeway, *Man's World, Woman's Place*, (New York: William Morrow and Company, Inc, 1971), 81.

particular time, is quite a separate thing, then, from the value of role-playing in general. Role-playing is a complex activity necessary to society and useful in many ways to the individual."[55]

Complementarists insist that egalitarianism causes divorce among other social evils,[56] but L. Richard Lessor observed that the industrial age demands a large portion of one's time and energy and allows only for "left-over" time for caring for one's marriage.[57] The situation is worsened when the husband is overworked and the wife is under-stimulated and bored, for neither is emotionally capable to sustain the marriage.

The complementarist model assumes that everyone is by nature adequately prepared as they enter marriage and that the wife must only accept the husband's authority cheerfully for the marriage to work, but such a simplistic approach ignores the reality of human development. According to Lessor, every person must grow from dependence to independence via counterdependence to enable interdependence which is essential for healthy human relationships. But all people exhibit also the patterns of a *Child*, a *Parent,* and an *Adult* which co-exist harmoniously in a mature person. The *Child* is spontaneous and playful, and responds to the *Parent*, one's own or another's, either by complying or by rebelling. The *Parent* dictates ("you should/n't") and the *Adult* reasons, gathers information and decides in case of an internal *Child-Parent* conflict. In a marriage, one of the spouses may be momentarily a *Child* in need of a *Parent* response, either in the form of emotional affirmation or correction. If he or she gets a *Child* response, sparks will inevitably fly. Similarly, if one of the spouses is an *Adult* who wishes to discuss and the other is

---

55. Ibid., 82.

56. The Catholic Encyclopedia boldly claims that "the freedom enjoyed by married woman during the [Roman] empire had as a sole result that divorce increased enormously and prostitution was considered a matter of course. After marriage had lost its religious character the women exceeded the men in license, and thus lost even the influence they had possessed in the early, austerely moral Rome." (The Catholic Encyclopedia, New Advent, www.newadvent.com [accessed June 29, 2009], Cf. Donaldson, *"Woman, Her Position and Influence in Ancient Greece and Rome and among the Early Christians"*). On the contrary, both Greeks and Romans regarded chastity as strictly for women; men were never under the obligation to remain faithful, prostitution was commonplace both in Plato's Greece and Caesar's Republican Rome and female adultery was punished often with death.

57. Lessor, 8.

a dictating *Parent* or a rebellious *Child*, the discussion will quickly degenerate into an argument. Lessor came to the conclusion that "indeed, a good case could be made for the argument that a sizable majority of American marriages are locked in a struggle to emerge from the counterdependent *Parent-Child* conflict."[58] A healthy marriage is formed when both spouses have had a change to mature, realize their need for relationships and seek interdependency, not dominion or dependency.[59]

Dr. Larry Crabb describes the need for interdependency from the perspective of self-centeredness, commonly found in dependent and counter-dependent people.

> Before we can begin to talk about putting marriages together, before we can properly discuss the differences between men and women and how they can be enjoyed, before we can recover from our wound, we must deal with our common problem of self-centeredness in a way that transforms us more and more into other-centered people.[60]

Self-centeredness makes us forget the impact of little things: a thoughtless word, a broken promise, a forgotten anniversary – until we are at the receiving end. Dennis Rainey, the author of *Staying Close*, agrees that "selfishness is possibly the most dangerous threat to oneness that any marriage can face"[61] for it leads to isolation, which he considers to be the main reason marriages fail. To prevent the drift towards isolation Rainey recommends an "Oneness Marriage" formed "by a husband and wife who are crafting intimacy, trust, and understanding with one another."[62] To attain oneness and intimacy each spouse must give up his or her will and practice mutual dependence and be accountable to each other by "giving the other person the freedom to make honest observations and evaluations about you," for "each partner is fallible

---

58. Ibid., 35. If the husband is a counterdependent *Child* and the wife is an interdependent *Adult*, submission to the rebellious demands of the husband will hardly enhance and solidify the marriage or help the man to grow towards interdependence. On the other hand, if the husband is an interdependent *Adult* and the wife is counterdependent *Child*, the wife will use manipulation to advance her own interests which will hinder her personal growth as it enables her to avoid personal responsibility.

59. Ibid., *In the Middle of Marriage*, 19-29.

60. Crabb, *Men and Women, Enjoying the Difference*, 28.

61. Dennis Rainey, *Staying Close* (Dallas, TX: Word Publishing, 1989), 59.

62. Ibid., 7, 30.

and quite capable of using faulty judgment."[63] Yet, Rainey believes husbands and wives have different responsibilities,[64] the man being called to lead in accordance to Ephesians 5, but he does not view leading as "male dominance, where the man lords it over the woman and demands her total obedience to every wish and command." Instead, a loving leader cares enough for his wife to willingly serve her, for "according to the New Testament, being head of your wife doesn't mean being her master, but her servant." Although the "servant-leader" sounds contradictory to men who believe a leader should be served by others, Rainey is convinced that husbands are included in the model of servanthood Jesus left us when he washed the disciple's feet (John 13.1-17) and when He became a servant through His incarnation (Phil 2.7).[65]

Although Rainey upholds the traditional spheres, he rejects the 50/50 plan which says "you do your part, and I'll do my part," for men and women enter marriage with certain expectations and it is often impossible to determine exactly what "your part" and "my part" include – and exclude. Consequently, "each is left to scrutinize the other's performance from his or her own jaded perspective."[66] The problem in finding the halfway becomes evident in a situation in which a wife expects her husband to help with the household chores and the man believes his only duty is to bring home a paycheck which entitles him to spend his evenings before the TV. To solve the problem, Rainey suggests that couples adopt a 100/100 plan, "which calls for a total change of mind and heart, a total commitment to God and one another," i.e., the spouses should serve one and forsake selfishness which leads to isolation. But because Rainey maintains the traditional division of labor in the home, his advice does not provide a solid foundation on which couples who cannot – or will not – adhere to traditional roles can base their 100/100 plan.

John M. Gottman, Ph.D., was one of the first psychologists to begin a scientific research to find what truly makes marriages fail or succeed in the 1980s. He observed that conventional wisdom was often wrong, e.g., conflict and fighting, which had traditionally been considered pathological, proved to be one of the healthiest things a couple could do for their relationship. This

---

63. Ibid., 97.
64. Ibid., 122.
65. Ibid., 146-7.
66. Ibid., 50-51.

proved to be true especially in the early stages of the marriage for they "help couples weed out actions and ways of dealing with each other that can harm the marriage in the long run."[67] Gottman observed that "a lasting marriage results from a couple's ability to resolve the conflicts that are inevitable in any relationship."[68] He found three different styles of problem solving.

> In a *validating marriage* couples compromise often and calmly work out their problems to mutual satisfaction as they arise. In a *conflict-avoiding marriage* couples agree to disagree, rarely confronting their differences head-on. And finally, in a *volatile marriage* conflicts erupt often, resulting in passionate disputes.[69]

Regardless of the style of conflict solving, the marriage must have "at least five times as many positive as negative moments together if your marriage is to be stable."[70] If the negative moments exceed the positive, the couple begins the downward spiral which begins with criticism, followed by contempt and defensiveness, and finally withdrawal. The last stage is the most destructive for it hinders communication which is a vital component of a stable marriage. Without communication the couple will eventually become isolated from each other, which leads more often than not to divorce.

When we compare Gottman's model to the first conflict human beings experiences the similarity is striking: Adam denied any responsibility and criticized Eve for giving him the fruit, and God for giving him Eve, who in turn blamed the serpent. According to Gottman complaining is one of the best things a couple can do for it allows the couple to deal with their problems instead of suppressing them. But the crucial difference between complaining and criticism is that whereas complaining is about airing grievances, criticism is an attack or an accusation which will quickly lead to contempt on both sides. Unless the couple is able to use repair mechanisms, such as certain mutually agreeable

---

67. John Gottman, Ph. D., with Nan Silver, *Why Marriages Succeed or Fail... And How You Can Make Yours Last* (New York: A Fireside Book, 1994), 67.

68. Ibid., 28.

69. Ibid.

70. Ibid., 29.

actions and phrases which communicate their willingness to reconcile, they will become engulfed in negativity which will lead to withdrawal and divorce.[71]

Dr. Emerson Eggerichs's book *Love and Respect* is based on Gottman's research and as far as he remains faithful to the principles of gender differences in communication, the gestures of reconciliation and the breaking of the cycle of negativity (which Eggerichs calls "the Crazy Cycle"), all is well, but as soon as he begins to incorporate complementarian theology into his concept, the trouble begins. Firstly, he perpetuates the belief that Eve conversed with the Serpent by herself and that Adam was later influenced by Eve to disobey God, which he couples with the age-old conviction that women have intuition while men are analytical.[72] Both beliefs are erroneous, for as already noted, Adam was with Eve as she spoke to the serpent and both men and women must use intuition and reason to remain healthy. Secondly, Eggerichs believes "the passage that spells out biblical hierarchy is Ephesians 5.22-24."[73] He gives *hypotasso* the definition "to rank under or place under," wherefore he believes that the wife is to place herself under the man's protection, while the husband's responsibility is to "place himself over the female and protect her." In case of a conflict, the "wife is called upon to defer to her husband, trusting God to guide him to make a decision out of love for her as the responsible head of the

---

71. Ibid., 73, 85, 99. Perhaps it is the *volatile couple* which has given egalitarianism a bad name for from the perspective of the *validating couple* the *volatile couple's* marriage seems unhealthy. The *volatile couple* see themselves as equals more than the other types. "They are independent sorts who believe that marriage should emphasize and strengthen individuality." (42) The danger the *volatile couple* faces is that their honesty, openness about their feelings and constant bickering can cause too much negativity which may ruin their marriage if they are not careful to ensure they have more positive than negative moments. The standardized Christian couple fits the description of the *validating couple* in which the responsibilities are divided into separate spheres, the wife being responsible for the home and children and the husband being the final decision maker. The man views "himself as analytical, dominant and assertive," the woman herself as "nurturing, warm, and expressive." Although they usually enjoy a stable marriage, the *validating couple's* greatest challenge is to hinder their marriage from becoming a passionless arrangement, a friendship instead of a romance. Both conflict solving styles produce equally stable marriages for they fit the temperament of the couples.

72. Dr. Emerson Eggerichs, *Love and Respect* (Brentwood, TN: Integrity Publishers, 2004), 230-231.

73. Ibid., 206.

marriage."[74] Also this belief is erroneous for it is based on the false translations of *kephale* and *hypotasso*, as discussed in the previous chapter.

Because a biblical hierarchy based on Ephesians 5.22-24 cannot be reconciled with Ephesians 5.21, Eggerichs attempts to avoid a contradiction by applying Grudem's concept of differentiating between the submission the husband owes the wife and the one owed by the wife to the husband.

> What, then, did Paul mean when he said Christians should submit to one another? For husbands and wives I believe the answer is found in Love and Respect. If husband and wife have a conflict over how to spend money, for example, the husband "submits" to his wife be meeting her need to feel that he loves her in spite of the conflict. He submits to her need for love (see Ephesians 5.21, 25). On the other side, the wife "submits" to her husband during a conflict by meeting her husband's need to feel that she respects him in spite of the unresolved issued. She submits to his need for respect (see Ephesians 5.21-22, 33).[75]

But if *hypotasso* means "to rank under or place under" how can the word be applied to the man in his relationship to the woman if it is his responsibility to place himself "over her"? How can the man be "over the woman" and "under the woman" in a hierarchy at the same time? And how does one place oneself under someone's need?

As we noted earlier, evolutionist Rhoads believes the evolutionary process gave the man a higher testosterone level, wherefore the man's dominion is a natural impulse which should not be suppressed. Eggerichs agrees with Rhoads's overall principle although he finds a divine origin behind the impulse.

> What your husband wants is your acknowledgment that he is the leader, the one in authority. This is not to grind you under or treat you as an inferior. It is only to say that because God has made your husband responsible (review Ephesians 5.25-33), he needs the authority to carry out that responsibility. No smoothly running organization can have two heads. To set up a marriage with two equals at the head is to se it up for failure. That is one of the big reasons that people are

---

74. Ibid., 207, 218.
75. Ibid., 218.

divorcing right and left today. In essence, these marriages do not have anyone who is in charge. God knew someone had to be in charge, and that is why Scripture clearly teaches that, in order for things to work, the wife is called upon to defer to her husband.[76]

But is a hierarchy necessary to avoid the dissolution of a marriage? Gottman found that the greatest causes of conflict are "how frequently the couple has sex and who does more housework."[77]Although Eggerichs does not discuss housework in detail, he believes that, "Sex is symbolic of his [the husband's] deeper need – respect… When a wife refuses, that symbolizes to him that she does not care about him and does not respect him and his needs…. The rule that never changes is: you can't get what you need by depriving your partner of what your partner needs."[78] Gottman could not have agreed more with Eggerich's statement.

> Housework may seem like a trivial concern compared to sexuality, but women see it as a major issue affecting their sex life, as well as the overall quality of their marriage. I've interviewed newlywed men who told me with pride, "I'm not going to wash the dishes, no way. That's a woman's job." Two years later, the same guys asked me, "Why don't my wife and I have sex anymore?" They just don't understand how demeaning their attitude about housework is toward their wives. Treating your wife as a servant will inevitably affect the more intimate, fragile parts of a relationship. Being the sole person in a marriage to clean the toilet is definitely not an aphrodisiac![79]

Gottman continues, "The message you send your wife when you do so little around the house is lack of respect for her." Eggerichs places so much emphasis on the man's need for respect that he misses Gottman's point that *both men and women need love and respect equally.* Instead Eggerich believes that "women want love far more than respect and men want respect far more than love." [80] He also concluded that "women are locked in love" wherefore they have no

---

76. Ibid., 221.
77. Gottman, 154.
78. Eggerichs, 250.
79. Gottman, 155.
80. Eggerichs, 48.

trouble loving their husbands. But if the instruction for the man to love his wife in Ephesians 5 is necessary because love is not natural for a man, why is the instruction for the man to treat his wife with honor necessary in 1 Peter 3 if he naturally honors and respects her, just as the wife naturally loves him?

Elizabeth Janeway observes that divorce is a peculiarly American way of solving marital problems.

> Even during the nineteenth century, however, the American pattern began to diverge from this earlier European arrangement and to become what it is today. Here it's usual for marriages that turn bad to be followed not simply be extramarital affairs, but by divorce and remarriage between lovers. For us, it is not adultery that supports marriage, or prostitution, but divorce; and this situation began to develop a long time ago. In 1886, to take a representative "high Victorian" year, when there were just over seven hundred divorces in Great Britain (the European country most similar in culture to ours, where the divorce scandal involving Sir Charles Dilke was shaking society), there were more than twenty-five thousand in the United States. Divorce rates have been rising lately (though even the 1969 rate did not quite reach that of 1946, when hasty war marriages were breaking up all over), but the rise has not been spectacular enough to change the long-term trend.... The *plausibility* of divorce has been taken for granted at least since the twenties. The right to end a marriage for personal, emotional reasons, then, is very much a part of our approach to the relationship; and since we see marriage as specializing in emotional rewards, this is not surprising.[81]

Also Betty Friedan noticed an increase in divorce rates in the beginning of the 1960s, when men were still "in charge."

> Four years ago, I interviewed a number of wives on a certain pseudo-rural road in a fashionable suburb. They had everything they wanted: lovely houses, a number of children, attentive husbands. Today, on that same road, there are growing spate of dream-houses in which, for various and sometimes unaccountable reasons, the wives now live alone

---

81. Janeway, 222.

with the children, while the husbands – doctors, lawyers, account-chiefs – have moved to the city. Divorce in America, according to sociologists, is in almost every instance *sought by the husband*, even if the wife ostensibly gets it. There are of course, many reasons for divorce, but chief of them seems to be the growing aversion and hostility that men have for the feminine millstones hanging around their necks, a hostility that is not always directed at their wives, but at their mothers, the women they work with – in fact, women in general.[82]

~

A society in which also women are able to support themselves financially and obtain a divorce tends to have a higher divorce rate, and we find that the financial dependence of women insured the endurance of marriages in the nineteenth century, but at what cost? Victoria Woodhull (1838-1927) mentioned in a speech that she knew "hundreds of wives who confess privately that they would not live another day with their husbands if they had any another method of support."[83] Women living in the Victorian Era, which can be compared to modern Saudi Arabia as far as legislation is concerned, had no other choice but to accept their husband's habitual infidelity and often violent behavior for the law placed them under the husband's absolute authority.[84] If

---

82. Betty Friedan, *The Feminine Mystique* (New York: W.W. Norton & Co. 1963), 272-273. Another surprise is that the fifties social experiment promoted sexual permissiveness. Friedan describes a psychologist's study of American newspapers which revealed that there was an "enormous increase in explicit references to sexual desires and expressions between January 1950 and January 1960, the decade of the feminine mystique. More than 2, 5 times as many references were found, while men's magazines reached new heights in their excesses and magazines for homosexuals became available. The fifties preoccupation with sex was the result of the sex-education which was geared towards convincing women that they could find fulfillment only through marriage and motherhood (i.e. through sex). The advent of the single girl in the sixties caused people to drop marriage and children from the equation while continuing the urgent search for happiness through sex.

83. Barbara Goldsmith, *Other Powers* (New York: Harper Perennial, 1998), 151.

84. As in the nineteenth century Anglo-Saxon world, a Saudi woman is a legal minor and she is denied custody of her children in case her husband divorces her. "In Saudi Arabia divorce is simple – if you are a man. He merely recites 'I divorce you,' three times, in the presence of witnesses, and the thing is done. A woman, however, must struggle through the byzantine procedures at a religious court, and her only hope for divorce is on the grounds of manifestly un-Islamic behavior. (Adultery and beatings don't count.)" (Carmen bin Laden, *Inside the Kingdom, My Life in Saudi Arabia*, [New York: Warner Books], 88, 102, 152).

financial dependency insured the stability of nineteenth century American marriages, the fear of the husband insures the Saudi marriage – unless, of course, the husband decides to end it.[85]

Already the Romans believed that marriages would endure if wives were under their husband's authority.

> What does emerge from this investigation is the concept that when "wives had no other refuge," as Dionysius puts it, or when they were totally under the authority of their husbands, as envisioned by Cato [the Censor], marriages were more enduring. This power of husbands over their wives – if, in fact, it had been prevalent in early Rome – was idealized and became as element in the marriage propaganda or Stoics and Augustan authors, both concerned with promoting marriage among their contemporaries. [86]

But the Roman society allowed also male infidelity and domestic violence – and the church did not always object.

> A married man committing lewdness with a single woman, is severely punished as guilty of fornication, but we have no canon to treat such a man as an adulterer; but the wife must co-habit with such a one: But if the wife be lewd, she is divorced, and he that retains her is [thought] impious; such is the custom, but the reason of it does not appear.[87]

Gregory Nazianzen rejected such partiality as hypocrisy caused by unequal legislation, created by those who benefited from it.[88]

> The question which you have put seems to me to do honour to chastity, and to demand a kind reply. Chastity, in respect of which I see that the majority of men are ill-disposed, and that their laws are unequal and irregular. For what was the reason why they restrained

---

85. bin Laden, 67.

86. Pomeroy, 154.

87. Basil, *First Canonical Epistle of Our Holy Father Basil, Archbishop of Caesarea in Cappadocia*, Canon XXI.

88. The modern Catholic Church rejects unequal legislation in morality, "On account of the moral equality of the sexes the moral law for man and woman must also be the same. To assume a lax morality for the man and a rigid one for the woman is an oppressive injustice even from the point of view of common sense ("The Catholic Encyclopedia," www.newadvent.com).

the woman, but indulged the man, and that a woman who practises evil against her husband's bed is an adulteress, and the penalties of the law for this are very severe; but if the husband commits fornication against his wife, he has no account to give? I do not accept this legislation; I do not approve this custom. They who made the Law were men, and therefore their legislation is hard on women, since they have placed children also under the authority of their fathers, while leaving the weaker sex uncared for. God doth not so; but saith Honour thy father and thy mother, which is the first commandment with promise; that it may be well with thee; and, He that curseth father or mother, let him die the death. Similarly He gave honour to good and punishment to evil. And, The blessing of a father strengtheneth the houses of children, but the curse of a mother uprooteth the foundations. See the equality of the legislation. There is one Maker of man and woman; one debt is owed by children to both their parents. How then dost thou demand Chastity, while thou dost not thyself observe it? How dost thou demand that which thou dost not give? How, though thou art equally a body, dost thou legislate unequally? If thou enquire into the worse – The Woman Sinned, and so did Adam. The serpent deceived them both; and one was not found to be the stronger and the other the weaker. But dost thou consider the better? Christ saves both by His Passion. Was He made flesh for the Man? So He was also for the woman. Did He die for the Man? The Woman also is saved by His death. He is called of the seed of David; and so perhaps you think the Man is honoured; but He is born of a Virgin, and this is on the Woman's side. They two, He says, shall be one Flesh; so let the one flesh have equal honour." And Paul legislates for chastity by His example. How, and in what way? This Sacrament is great, he says, But I speak concerning Christ and the Church. It is well for the wife to reverence Christ through her husband: and it is well for the husband not to dishonor the Church through his wife. Let the wife, he says, see that she reverence her husband, for so she does Christ; but also he bids the husband cherish his wife, for so Christ does the Church.[89]

---

89. Gregory Nazianzen, "Oration XXXVII," *Orations*, VI-VII.

John Stuart Mill observed that marriage had to be the only option for women in the nineteenth century lest they would have refused to marry the men who were willing to see them only as servants.

> If they mean what they say, their opinion must evidently be that men do not render the married conditions so desirable to women, as to induce them to accept it for its own recommendations. It is not a sign of one's thinking the boon one offers very attractive, when one allows only Hobson's choice, "that or none." And here, I believe, is the clue to the feelings of those men, who have a real antipathy to the equal freedom of women. I believe they are afraid, not lest women should be unwilling to marry, for I do not think that any one in reality has that apprehension; but lets they should insist that marriage should be on equal conditions; lest all women of spirit and capacity should prefer doing almost anything else, not in their own eyes degrading, rather than marry, when marrying is giving themselves a master, and a master too of all their earthly possessions.[90]

In the preface of his book *Evangelical Feminism*, Grudem acknowledges that the women's rights movement has brought needed reform in the area of husband's authority over the wife. However, Grudem and Piper also express the belief that stressing headship and submission does not cause abuse because of the complementarist commitment to "sacrificial headship" and "thoughtful submission which does not make the husband an absolute lord."[91] Yet, the editor of the *Priscilla Papers,* William David Spencer, reported that a resent study showed "that the rate of abuse among Christians was no less than that in the general population – even though it was often cleverly concealed."[92] John Stuart Mill remarked astutely that people – unless they are thinkers – are ready to believe that a law or practice does not produce evils, because they have not personally experienced the evil, and if generally approved of probably do good and that it is wrong to object to them.[93]

The fear of being cuckolded has caused men to hide women behind walls and veils, often without education and more often than we would like to think

---

90. Mill, 51.
91. Piper and Grudem, 62.
92. *Priscilla Papers* Volume 23, Number 1, [Winter 2009], 2.
93. Mill, 83.

of under the constant threat of physical harm. According to Betty Friedan, "Anthropologists know that in any society that denies women full humanity and full participation in the mainstream, in that society, sex is an obsession or a repression, and in that society, violence breeds. "[94] The twin effect of Genesis 3.16 is strengthened by the natural reproductive hormones, for the man's desire for dominance is linked to testosterone and the woman's desire for protection to estrogen. Rhoads quotes Naomi Wolf who after becoming a mother described how she felt a "childlike surge of need for repetitive, utterly simple affirmations that I was – that we, the baby and I, were – not going to be abandoned."[95] Wolf was convinced that the increased levels of estrogen and oxytocin caused the change in her. Rhoads cites also Helen Fisher who "believes that the female taste for egalitarian, harmonious connections is associated with estrogen." This belief is further strengthened by the fact that in many cultures women assume more leadership roles after menopause "as estrogen no longer masks the dominance-motivating effects of testosterone."[96] Not only do men desire to dominate because of testosterone and serotonin, it also causes aggression, which often results in violence.[97] Sin exaggerates these two natural inclinations as it causes men to seek dominance, often through violence, and women to accept the dominance through a submissive demeanor as an increase in estrogen causes them to seek protection from men during motherhood. But the submissive demeanor has also been created artificially, for achievement, social standing and power changes the level of estrogen and testosterone in the body.[98] Consequently, the enforced subjection, and the deprivation of education and opportunity, has lowered the testosterone level in women, while it has increased it in dominating men.[99]

---

94. Betty Friedan, *It Changed My Life*, (Boston, MA: Harvard University Press, 1998), 193.

95. Rhoads, 205.

96. Ibid., 154.

97. Ibid., 141.

98. Mona Lisa Schulz MD, Ph.D. describes studies in which the testosterone level of male monkeys went up, as they achieved more dominance, and down, as their power declined (Schulz, 33).

99. Dr. Schulz writes, "As more women enter very competitive traditional male fields such as law enforcement, firefighting, and the military services, stress causes testosterone levels to rise. As a result, women are helped hormonally to acquire new visuospatial skills, such as the ability to use weapons and tools and read a map, whether of a war zone or

Since most Christians are complementarian, if the husband's authority does not cause domestic violence, what does? Paul K. Jewett concluded, "[I]n a sinful world it is unrealistic to suppose that half the human race could be made to depend on the other half without the one abusing, the other suffering the abuse of, such a relationship."[100] A behavior cannot be separated from its corresponding belief as Jesus pointed out in the Sermon of the Mount.

> Or how can you say to your brother, 'Brother, let me remove the speck that is in your eye,' when you yourself do not see the plank that is in your own eye? Hypocrite! First remove the plank from your own eye, and then you will see clearly to remove the speck that is in your brother's eye. For good tree does not bear bad fruit, nor does a bad tree bear good fruit. For every tree is known by its own fruit. For men do not gather figs from thorns, nor do they gather grapes from a bramble bush. (Luke 6.42-44)

Difference has been used as a justification to exclude women, black people, Jews, Catholics, Italians, Native Americans and the Irish from full participation in the American society. As a result, these people groups have created their own institutions, philosophies and protest movements, often rejecting the belief in innate differences. Both feminism and black power have been criticized for being too extreme, but their critics forget often that it is impossible to reject a false image without first re-creating the self-respect needed to forge a new identity. For an oppressed and suppressed people group such as the black people, black power created the necessary psychological realization that being black does not make one a lesser human being.[101] Similarly, women found courage and support through feminism to challenge the image of femi-

---

Greater Los Angeles. In fact, women are helped hormonally to adapt to virtually any career and pursuit in a man's world that they want" (Schulz, 39). X chromosome controls the body's sensitivity to testosterone and androgens, and since women have two X chromosomes, "they are doubly sensitive to even small amounts of testosterone during development" (Schulz, 51).

100. Jewett, 129-130.

101. Columbus Salley and Ronald Behm explained that, "Black Power is the bold assertion of the fact that the humanity of blacks is a non-negotiable, indisputable, non-compromising reality" (Salley and Behm, *Your God Is Too White* [Chicago, IL: InterVarsity Press, 1970], 65).

ninity created by sexism. But neither black power nor feminism is the accurate expression of what it means to be a woman or a black person; instead they function as a bridge between yesterday's discriminating practices and tomorrow's integrated society in which difference is not a threat.

The aberrant roles are a rebellion against the old roles, as seen that they appear as society changes.

> [Dr.] Lifton's study of China since the Second World War and the Communist take-over indicates "a sudden emergence in often exaggerated form of psychological tendencies previously suppressed by social custom." He believes that this "release phenomenon," producing a proliferation of deviant types, follows unexpected social upsets. In other words, when aberrant roles are commonly seen, we may take it as a hint to look for profound social change. More and more individuals are finding it impossible to fit into the old sanctioned patterns.[102]

If society as a whole does not realize the meaning and function of the protest movements and aberrant roles, it will waste the opportunity to create a new identity for all, and end up with two mutually hostile camps which will wage war until one side wins and everyone loses.

Men and women are different, but the difference is in *how* men and women perform functions, not their inability to perform a function other than childbearing and tasks related to superior physical strength. If men and women were physically or mentally unable to perform specific tasks, we should find uniform evidence of it across the globe, but anthropologist Margaret Mead describes the flexibility which characterizes the assignment of different roles in societies around the world.

> Now it is boys who are thought of as infinitely vulnerable and in need of special cherishing care, now it is girls. In some societies it is girls for whom parents must collect a dowry or make husband-catching magic, in other the parental worry is over the difficulty of marrying of the boys. Some peoples thing of women as too weak to work out of doors, others regard women as the appropriate bearers of heavy burdens, "because their heads are stronger than men's." The periodicities of female reproductive functions have appealed to some peoples as

---

102. Janeway, 120.

making women the natural sources of magical or religious power, to other as directly antithetical to those powers; some religions, including our European traditional religions, have assigned women an inferior role in the religious hierarchy, others have built their whole symbolic relationship with the supernatural world upon male imitations of the natural functions of women. In some cultures women are regarded as sieves through whom the best-guarded secrets will shift; in others it is the men who are gossips. Whether we deal with small matters or with large, with the frivolities of ornament and cosmetics or the sanctities of man's place in the universe, we find this great variety of way, often flatly contradictory one to the other, in which the roles of the two sexes have been patterned.[103]

Mead mentions that although the patterning is always found, the only aspect in which women differ from men is childbearing. In all other aspects, "they are simply human beings with varying gifts, no one of which can be exclusively assigned to either sex."

In secular thinking, complementarity in marriage refers to character traits which complement each other, such as cautious-adventurous, extrovert-introvert, punctual-procrastinator etc. The opposites may attract at first and ultimately provide balance, but they can also become a major source of irritation and frustration as Judith Viorst points out, "[S]ome of us, sooner or later, may come to resent, resist, or outright loath qualities we initially embraced, a dramatic change of heart that is yet another of the shocks of married life."[104] Theological complementarity in marriage, although portrayed as the pairing of the complementary elements of male and female, is the twin of the complementarity and role play of a mother and child found in anthropology.

Or she [the mother] may treat the child as one who is different from herself, who receives while she gives, with the emphasis upon difference between the mother's behaviour and that of the child as she cherishes and shelters and above all feeds a weak, dependent creature. This patterning of the relationship may be called complementary, as each of the pair is seen as playing a different role, and the two roles

---

103. Margaret Mead, *Male and Female: A Study of the Sexes in a Changed World* (New York: William Morrow, 1949), 7-8.

104. Judith Viorst, *Grown-Up Marriage*, (New York: The Free Press, 2003), 41.

are conceived as complementing each other... To the extent that the child's whole individuality is emphasized, there is symmetry; to the extent that its weakness and helplessness are emphasized, there is complementary behaviour; and to the extent that the mother gives not only her breast, but milk, there is the beginning of reciprocity. But cultures differ greatly as to which they emphasize most.[105]

The theological namesake follows the same concept, for the physically stronger man cherishes, shelters, and feeds the weak, dependent woman just as she cares for and feeds the weak, dependent child. But whereas the child is naturally weak and dependent of the parent, the woman must be made weak and dependent of the man artificially.

The egalitarian approach to marriage rejects rigid gender roles and the artificial dependency of the woman without disregarding the natural differences which exists between men and women, as explained by Don S. Browning in *Equality and the Family*.

This view does not mean, as some believe, that husband and wife must become identical and suppress the distinctiveness of being male and female. It means instead that husbands and wives must live by a strenuous love ethic of regarding the other with equal seriousness to themselves just as they expect their partner to regard them. Within such an ethic they should work together to determine their responsibilities and privileges in light of respective talents, inclinations, and realistic constraints.[106]

105. Mead, 64-65.

106. Don S. Browning, *Equality and the Family, A Fundamental, Practical Theology of Children, Mothers, and Fathers in Modern Societies* (Grand Rapids, MI: Wm. B. Eerdmans Publishing Co, 2007), 307-308.

CHAPTER 8

1 Cor 15.20-28

Faith is profitable, therefore, when her brow is bright with a fair crown of good works.

This faith—that I may set the matter forth shortly—

Is contained in the following principles, Which cannot be overthrown.

If the Son had His origin in nothing, He is not Son;

If He is a creature, He is not the Creator;

If He was made, He did not make all things;

If He needs to learn, He hath no foreknowledge;

If He is a receiver, He is not perfect;

If He progress, He is not God.

If He is unlike (the Father) He is not the (Father's) image;

If He is Son by grace, He is not such by nature;

If He have no part in the Godhead, He hath it in Him to sin.

"There is none good, but Godhead."

— AMBROSE[1]

~

KEPHALE IS GIVEN the meaning "authority over" in 1 Corinthians 11.3 in order to create a hierarchy in which the man rules over the woman. But although complementarism models the woman's subjection after the Son's assumed subjection to the Father, in the early church, as the inferiority of the woman was incorporated into theology, the subjection of the woman became the model for the subjection of the Son in the many heresies that challenged

---

1. Ambrose, *Exposition of the Christian Faith*, Book II, Introduction, 14.

the church. Thus we find that in Arian theology, Christ owes thank to humans for He was believed to have been made for them.

> First, the Son appears rather to have been for us brought to be, than we for Him; for we were not created for Him, but He is made for us; so that He owes thanks to us, not we to Him, *as the woman to the man.* 'For the man,' says Scripture, 'was not created for the woman, but the woman for the man.' Therefore, as 'the man is the image and glory of God, and the woman the glory of the man,' so we are made God's image and to His glory; but the Son is our image, and exists for our glory. And we were brought into being that we might be; but God's Word was made, as you must hold, *not that He might be; but as an instrument for our need,* so that not we from Him, but He is constituted from our need.[2]

The early church theologians of the patristic era refused to make the Son subject to the Father although they subjected the woman to the man. Chrysostom, for example, explicitly refuted the heresy of the Son's inferiority and subjection, which was modeled after the subjection of the woman.

> "But the head of the woman is the man; and the head of Christ is God." Here the heretics rush upon us with a certain declaration of inferiority, which out of these words they contrive against the Son. But they stumble against themselves. For if "the man be the head of the woman," and the head be of the same substance with the body, and "the head of Christ is God," the Son is of the same substance with the Father. "Nay," say they, "it is not His being of another substance which we intend to show from hence, but that He is under subjection." What then are we to say to this? In the first place, when any thing lowly is said of him conjoined as He is with the Flesh, there is no disparagement of the Godhead in what is said, the Economy admitting the expression. However, tell me how thou intendest to prove this from the passage? "Why, as the man governs the wife, saith he, "so also the Father, Christ." Therefore also as Christ governs the man, so likewise the Father, the Son. "For the head of every man," we read, "is Christ." *And who could ever admit this?*[3]

---

2. Athanasius, *Four Discourses Against the Arians,* Discourse II, Ch. XVII, 30.
3. *Homilies on First Corinthians,* XXVI.

Chrysostom argued that it was impossible for *kephale* to mean "authority over," for had Paul meant to speak of rule and subjection he would have used the example of a slave and a master instead of marriage. Neither did Chrysostom agree with those who found a similarity between 1 Corinthians 11 and Ephesians 5, for if we were to understand *kephale* in the same way in both, "extreme absurdity will result." Therefore he argued that we should reject "these particulars," and "accept the notion of a perfect union, and the first principle," and even here recognize that which is "too high for us and suitable to the Godhead, for both the union is surer and the beginning more honorable."

Gregory of Nazianzen called the subjection of the Son to the Father "a new theology," indicating that it was not part of the apostolic tradition.

> For as these low earthly minds make the Son subject to the Father, so again is the rank of the Spirit made inferior to that of the Son, until both God and created life are insulted by the new Theology. No, my friends, there is nothing servile in the Trinity, nothing created, nothing accidental, as I have heard one of the wise say.[4]

Yet, Thomas R. Schreiner maintains in his essay *Head Coverings, Prophecies and the Trinity* that there is subordination within the Trinity, because "the Son has a different function or role from the Father," and because "the Son willingly submits Himself to the Father's authority."[5] This subordination to authority is seen in that the "Father commands and sends; the Son obeys and comes into the world to die for our sins." [6] Schreiner attempts to prove the subordination of the Son from 1 Corinthians 15.28, but by doing so He contradicts himself, "It is clear that this subjection of the Son to the Father is *after his earthly ministry*, so how anyone can say that there is no hint of a difference or order or role within the Trinity is difficult to see."[7] But if the subjection of the Son begins *after* his earthly ministry, how could the Son have been subject to the Father *before* his incarnation? Because complementarists give *kephale* the meaning "authority over" in 1 Corinthians 11.3, they create a triple subjection of the Son, which resembles the twofold of the woman found

---

4. "Oration XL, The Oration on Holy Baptism," *Orations*, XLII.
5. Piper and Grudem, 128.
6. *Ibid.,* 129.
7. Ibid.

in the *Summa,* for if the Son was subject to the Father from the beginning, his subjection became less voluntary after His incarnation and will become even less voluntary after He delivers the kingdom to the Father. But such a concept is not only absurd, it is impossible, for how can the Son be forced into subjection? Tertullian rejected the subjection of the Son due to the impossibility of the proposition.

> Since therefore he [Marcion] is obliged to acknowledge that the God whom he does not deny is the great Supreme, it is inadmissible that he should predicate of the Supreme Being such a diminution as should subject Him to another Supreme Being, for He causes (to be Supreme), if He becomes subject to any. Besides, it is not the characteristic of God to cease from any attribute of His divinity – say, from His supremacy.[8]

Basil argued in his comment on John 5.19 that the Son would be lower than the humans He created if He is subject to the Father's authority.

> If freedom of action is better than subjection to control, and a man is free, while the Son of God is subject to control, then the man is better than the Son. This is absurd. And if he who is subject to control cannot create free beings (for he cannot of his own will confer on others what he does not possess himself), then the Saviour, since He made us free, cannot Himself be under the control of any. If the Son could do nothing of Himself, and could only act at the bidding of the Father, He is neither good nor bad. He was not responsible for anything that was done. Consider the absurdity of the position that men should be free agents both of good and evil, while the Son, who is God, should be able to do nothing of His own authority![9]

The belief that the Son was under the Father's authority because the Son was sent by the Father was already taught in the fourth century but was refuted decidedly by Ambrose.

> Who is it Who says: The Lord God hath sent Me and His Spirit, except He Who came from the Father that He might save sinners?

---

8. *Five Books Against Marcion,* Book I, IV.
9. Basil, *On John V. 19. The Son Can Do Nothing of Himself.*

And, as you hear, the Spirit sent Him, lest when you hear that the Son sends the Spirit, you should believe the Spirit to be of inferior power. So both the Father and the Spirit sent the Son; the Father sent Him, for it is written: "But the Paraclete, the Holy Spirit, Whom the Father will send in My Name." The Son sent Him, for He said: "But when the Paraclete is come, Whom I will send unto you from the Father, even the Spirit of Truth." If, then, the Son and the Spirit send each other, as the Father sends, *there is no inferiority of subjection, but a community of power.* [10]

Although complementarists reject the concept of inferiority, and rightly so, in the fourth century subjection was synonymous with inferiority as seen in that the virgin was considered equal to the man contrasted to the inferior, subjected married woman.[11]

The sending of the Son, mentioned by Schreiner, signifies the unity of will and purpose within the Trinity, for had the Son come of His own accord and spoken His own words, He would have severed Himself from the unity of the Godhead. Because He was sent by the Father and the Spirit, spoke the words of the Father, and performed miracles through the Spirit (Luke 4.1, 14-18), a unity of will is retained in the Godhead. The Son, sent by the Father and the Spirit, came to the world to glorify the Father and to speak the words, which the Father had given Him. The Spirit, sent by the Father and the Son, glorifies the Son because He speaks the words given by the Son, which are also the words of the Father, because all that is the Father's, belongs also to the Son (John 16.5-15). Although the Trinity expresses itself in various ways, there is a unity of purpose: the Father brings us to Himself through the work of the Son (John 6.39); the Son brings us to Himself through the work of the Spirit and the Father (John 6.37; 15.26). The sending of the Son had nothing to do with the Father's authority; it had everything to do with our salvation, "For God did not send His Son into the world to condemn the world, but that the world through Him might be saved"(John 3.17).

---

10. Ambrose, *Three Books on the Holy Spirit*, Book III, Ch. I, 7-8.

11. Although complementarists deny the ontological inferiority of the woman (Piper and Grudem, 256), they are not able to avoid making the woman inferior to the man in some respect. D.A. Carson considers prophesy inferior in authority to teaching and since women are not allowed to teach (1 Tim 2), they are inferior in authority to the man, and thus a sense of inferiority is retained (Piper and Grudem, 153).

Obedience and subjection does not exist within the Godhead, for the Son became obedient in His humanity, not His divinity.

> Who, in the days of His flesh, when He had offered up prayers and supplications, with vehement cries and tears to Him who was able to save Him from death, and was heard because of His godly fear, though He was a Son, yet He *learned obedience* by the things which He suffered. And having been perfected, He became the author of eternal salvation to all who obey Him. (Heb 5.7-9)

The Son *learned* obedience in the Garden of Gethsemane as He asked the Father to spare His life, yet accepted the Father's will and willingly died (Matt 26.36-46). It is important to note that the Son did not need to learn obedience for Himself, for He always did that which was pleasing to the Father, but that His willing obedience was an example for us to follow, as explained by Gregory of Nazianzen.

> For in His character of the Word He was neither obedient nor disobedient. For such expressions belong to servants, and inferiors, and the one applies to the better sort of them, while the other belongs to those who deserve punishment. But, in the character of the Form of a Servant, He condescends to His fellow servants, nay, to His servants, and takes upon Him a strange form, bearing all me and mine in Himself, that in Himself He may exhaust the bad, as fire does wax, or as the sun does the mists of earth; and that I may partake of His nature by the blending. Thus He honours obedience by His action, and proves it experimentally by His Passion. For to possess the disposition is not enough, just as it would not be enough for us, unless we also proved it by our acts; for action is the proof of disposition.[12]

Ambrose stated in his work *Exposition of the Christian Faith,* "If the one name and right of God belong to both the Father and the Son, since the Son of God is also true God, and a King eternal, the Son of God is not made subject in His Godhead."[13] Similarly to Chrysostom, Ambrose refused to use

---

12. Gregory Nazianzen, "Oration XXX. The Fourth Theological Oration, " *Orations,* V-VI.

13. *Three Books on the Holy Spirit*, Book V, XIII-XIV.

the subjection of the woman to the man as a model for the subjection of the Son for he considered it to be "impious to compare a man to the Father, or a woman to the Son of God." Ambrose further emphasized that the subjection of the Son is a future event.

> We see, then, that the Scripture states that He is not yet made subject, but that this is to come: Therefore now the Son is not made subject to God the Father. In what, then, do ye say that the Son will be made subject? If in His Godhead, He is not disobedient, for He is not at variance with the Father; *nor is He made subject, for He is not a servant,* but the only Son of His own proper Father. Lastly, when He created heaven, and formed the earth, He exercised both power and love. There is therefore no subjection as that of a servant in the Godhead of Christ. But if there is no subjection then the will is free.[14]

Complementarists agree that the Son is not a servant, but they maintain that He is subject to the Father as an equal, and has been so from the beginning. Ambrose refuted the concept because the subjection of the Son exists in time.

> For if He were made subject through His nature, He would always remain in subjection; but since He is said to be made subject in time, that subjection must be part of an assumed office and not of an everlasting weakness: especially as the eternal Power of God cannot change His state for a time, neither can the right of ruling fall to the Father in time. For if the Son ever will be changed in such wise as to be made subject in His Godhead, then also must God the Father, if ever He shall gain more power, and have the Son in subjection to Himself in His Godhead, be considered now in the meantime inferior according to your explanation.[15]

Basil agreed with Ambrose, for he wrote, "If the Son is subjected to the Father in the Godhead, then He must have been subjected from the beginning, from whence He was God. But if He was not subjected, but shall be subjected, it is in the manhood, as for us, not in the Godhead, as for Himself."

---

14. Ibid.
15. Ibid.

Ambrose asked further, "If the Son pleases the Father in all things, why should He be made subject, Who was not made subject before?"[16] The reason for Ambrose's question was that an equal could be subjected involuntary as a result of displeasing or harming behavior. A conquered enemy, for example, if not killed, became the conqueror's slave. The concept is clearly found in Chrysostom's theology, for he wrote the woman was involuntarily subjected to the man, "when she made an ill use of her privilege and she who had been made a helper was found to be an ensnarer and ruined all."[17] Because the man, who was deemed innocent, was ruined by the woman, the subjection was to prevent the man from destroying the woman because of the "resentment caused by her sin."

Ambrose concluded that because "the Father, the Son, and the Holy Spirit are of one Nature," the Father cannot be in subjection to Himself, and therefore the Son cannot be subject to the Father in His divinity, "lest it should seem that through the unity of the Godhead the Father also is in subjection to the Son." It was not the fullness of the Godhead but "our weakness that was brought into subjection," through the cross, and therefore the Son "will become subject to the Father in the participation of our nature." The flesh is in a state of enmity and cannot be subject to God (Rom 8.7), but the same flesh "is made subject through the Passion of Christ." Therefore, as the body of Christ is completed and raised to be with the Head, the Son will subject Himself with His body – all the saints – to God. The enmity caused by sin will cease and God will be all in all for all eternity.

The Son is said to become subject to the Father after He delivers the Kingdom to the Father (1 Cor 15.24). Hilary of Poitiers wrote that the Son cannot cease to possess the Kingdom after delivering it to the Father, for it would mean that the Father "lost all, when He delivered all the to Son" (Luke 10.22), and it would also have included all authority (Matt 28.18). Since "the Father did not cease to possess that which he delivered, neither does the Son surrender that which He delivers." The delivering is therefore about the dispensation, not the Kingdom itself.

---

16. Basil, *On John V. 19. The Son Can Do Nothing of Himself.*
17. Ambrose, *Exposition of the Christian Faith,* Book V, XXVI.

> When all things are subjected to Him, says He, then must He be
> subjected to Him, Who subjects all things to Himself; and by this
> 'then' he means to denote the temporal Dispensation. For if we put
> any other construction on the subjection, Christ, though then to be
> subjected, is not subjected now, and thus we make Him an insolent
> and impious rebel, whom the necessity of time, breaking as it were
> and subduing His profane and overweening pride, will reduce to a
> tardy obedience.[18]

Hilary pointed out that throughout the New Testament, when one person of the Trinity is spoken of the same is also true of the others. Thus we find that although the Father places all things under the feet of the Son, also the Son subjects all things under His own feet (Phil 3.21) for, "through the birth the nature of God is abiding in the Son, and does that which He Himself [God] does."

Gregory of Nazianzen asked rhetorically whether the Son would cease to be a King and be removed from Heaven after His enemies were destroyed, and He delivered the Kingdom to the Father. Since it is impossible for the Son to cease from being a King, Gregory wrote that the mistake of those who would subject the Son was that they misunderstood the word *until*. The Son would cease to reign over His enemies and to bring more people unto subjection to God for "what need is there to work submission is us when we have already submitted?" The Son took the disobedience of humanity upon Himself and therefore, "as long then as I am disobedient and rebellious, both by denial of God and by my passions, so long Christ also is called disobedient on my account." The Son will become subject when His Body, i.e., all believers, are perfected at the resurrection of the just. Because the context of the subjecting of all things to the Son in Philippians 3.21 is resurrection, Hilary made the following observation.

> The Apostle tells us also of the special reward attained by this subjection
> which is made perfect by the subjection of belief: Who shall fashion
> anew the body of our humiliation, that it may be conformed to the
> body of His glory, according to the works of His power, whereby He
> is able to subject all things to Himself. *There is then another subjection,*

---

18. Hilary of Poitiers, Book XI, 30.

which consists in a transition from one nature to another, for our nature ceases, so far as its present character is concerned, and is subjected to Him, into Whose form it passes. But by 'ceasing' is implied not an end of being, but a promotion into something higher. Thus our nature by being merged into the image of the other nature which it receives, becomes subjected through the imposition of a new form.[19]

The enemies subjected under his feet will be destroyed, the last being death, but the saints will live forever in glorified bodies, for "as we have borne the image of the man of dust, we shall also bear the image of the heavenly Man" (1 Cor 15.49). Also Irenaeus wrote that, "being in subjection to God is continuance in immortality, and immortality is the glory of the uncreated One."[20]

The delivering of the kingdom is therefore connected to the abolishing of death, and the transformation of our bodies.

Thus it is as King that He shall deliver up the Kingdom, and if any ask Who it is that delivers up the Kingdom, let him hear, Christ is risen from the dead, the firstfruits of them that sleep; since by man came death, by man came also the resurrection of the dead. All that is said on the point before us concerns the Mystery of the body, since Christ is the firstfruits of the dead. Let us gather also from the words of the Apostle by what Mystery Christ rose from the dead: Remember that Christ hath risen from the dead, of the seed of David. Here he teaches that the death and resurrection are due only to the Dispensation by which Christ was flesh.[21]

Hilary was careful not to remove the Son from the Godhead by making only the Father all in all, and he safeguarded the divinity of the Son by viewing the subjection as a translation of the body for the Son to once again become God only.[22]

---

19. Ibid., Book XI, 35.
20. *Against Heresies,* Book IV, Chapter XXXVII.
21. Hilary of Poitiers, Book XI, 39.
22. Hilary of Poitiers, Book XI, 40. The belief that only the Father will be all in all is found for example in the spurious Ignatian letter to the Tarsians "And that He Himself is not God over all, and the Father, but His Son... Wherefore it is one [Person] who put all things under, and who is all in all, and another [Person] to whom they were subdued, who also Himself, along with all other things, becomes subject [to the former]" (Ignatius, Ch V.).

Also Augustine argued against the subjection of the Son in His divinity and maintained that the future subjection is related to His assumed humanity.

> For we shall then contemplate God, the Father and the Son and the Holy Spirit, when the Mediator between God and men, the man Christ Jesus, shall have delivered up the kingdom to God, even the Father, so as no longer to make intercession for us, as our Mediator and Priest, Son of God and Son of man; but that He Himself too, in so far as He is a Priest that has taken the form of a servant for us, shall be put under Him who has put all things under Him, and under whom He has put all things: so that, in so far as He is God He with Him will have put us under Himself; *in so far as He is a Priest, He with us will be put under Him.* And therefore as the [incarnate] Son is both God and man, it is rather to be said that the manhood in the Son is another substance [from the Son], than that the Son in the Father [is another substance from the Father].[23]

Augustine emphasized further that a clear distinction exists between the humanity and divinity of Christ.

> For, because He Himself, being the first-begotten of the dead, made a passage to the kingdom of God to life eternal for His Church, to which He is so the Head as to make the body also immortal, therefore He was "created in the beginning of the ways" of God in His work. For, according to the form of God, He is the beginning, that also speaketh unto us, in which "beginning" God created the heaven and the earth; but according to the form of a servant, "He is a bridegroom coming out of His chamber." According to the form of God, "He is the first-born of every creature, and He is before all things and by him all things consist;" according to the form of a servant, "He is the head of the body, the Church." According to the form of God, "He is the Lord of glory." From which it is evident that He Himself glorifies His saints: for, "Whom He did predestinate, them He also called; and whom He called, them He also justified; and whom He justified, them He also glorified." Of Him accordingly it is said, that He justifieth the ungodly; of Him it is said, that He is just and a justifier. If, therefore, He has also glorified those whom He has justified, He

---

23. *On the Trinity,* Book I, Ch. 10.

who justifies, Himself also glorifies; who is, as I have said, the Lord of glory. Yet, according to the form of a servant, He replied to His disciples, when inquiring about their own glorification: "To sit on my right hand and on my left is not mine to give, but [it shall be given to them] for whom it is prepared by my Father."[24]

As a High Priest, Christ prays for us, but "as He is equal with the Father, He with the Father grants." After the resurrection, the saints will no longer need His intercessory prayer, for sin and death will be no more.

Augustine agreed with Hilary in that "what is said of each [of the persons in the Trinity] is also said of all, on account of the indivisible working of the one and same substance." Therefore, in His humanity the Son affirmed that it is impossible for a human to perform the works He did on his own, wherefore the works were the Father's. Yet, "take care you understand also, that if 'all things which the Father hath are mine,' then this certainly is mine also, and I with the Father have prepared these things."

~

Gregory of Nyssa (335-394) vehemently denied the subjection of Spirit, which was suggested by Eunomius.[25] After describing in great detail the divinity and power of the Spirit, Gregory of Nyssa wonders, "How is it then that Eunomius goes so far as to define that He also is one of the things that came into being by the Son, condemned to eternal subjection." Eunomius described the Spirit as being "once for all made subject," but Gregory could not quite make out what kind of subjection he was referring to, considering the word has many meanings in the Bible. Gregory wondered whether he meant "the subjection of irrational creatures, or of captives, or of servants, or of children who are kept in order, or of those who are saved by subjection." The subjection of humans to God is salvation for by the subjection eternal perdition is prevented, but, asked Gregory, is the Spirit, which gives life, in need of subjection to obtain life? If we would take "the plain and unambiguous meaning of the word subjection," is the Spirit subject to the Son and the Father? Or as the Son is subject to the Father? But since the latter would place both the Son and the Spirit on a lower

---

24. Ibid., Book I, Ch. 12.
25. Gregory of Nyssa, *Against Eunomius*, Book II, Ch. 14, 16.

rank, the comparison fails, according to Gregory. And because the Sprit is not subject as the animals are to humans, Gregory concluded that He has to be of the rebellious ranks, "forced by a superior Force to bend to a Conqueror." Since it is impossible for God to rebellious, the Spirit cannot be subject to the Father and the Son. Thus also the subjection of the Son is disproven, for the Spirit cannot be greater than the Son.

CHAPTER 9

1 Cor 11.1-16

And here, I think there is a view of the matter more close to nature, by which we may learn something of the more refined doctrines. For since the most beautiful and supreme good of all is the Divinity Itself, to which incline all things that have a tendency towards what is beautiful and good, we therefore say that the mind, as being in the image of the most beautiful, itself also remains in beauty and goodness so long as it partakes as far as is possible in its likeness to the archetype; but if it were at all to depart from this it is deprived of that beauty in which it was. And as we said that the mind was adorned by the likeness of the archetypal beauty, being formed as though it were a mirror to receive the figure of that which it expresses, we consider that the nature which is governed by it is attached to the mind in the same relation, and that it too is adorned by the beauty that the mind gives, being, so to say, a mirror of the mirror; and that by it is swayed and sustained the material element of that existence in which the nature is contemplated.

– Gregory of Nyssa[1]

~

THE TWOFOLD SUBJECTION of Thomas Aquinas altered the translation and interpretation of 1 Corinthians perhaps more than any other chapter in the Bible; consequently it is considered one of the most difficult chapters to interpret. Thomas R. Schreiner writes in his essay *Head Coverings, Prophecies and the Trinity,* "The difficulties with this text could lead one to say that it should not be used to establish any doctrine or teaching on the role relation-

---

1. Gregory of Nyssa, *On the Making of Man,* Ch. XII.

ship of men and women."[2] Although he is correct in rejecting the proposition that we should not use the chapter, he rejects also the interpretation of the chapter which removes the inherent difficulties.

As the woman's subjection as a created order was challenged, 1 Corinthians 11 was re-interpreted to reflect the change, or, rather, the return to the theology of the early church. Instead of rule and submission, the text was viewed as teaching the interdependency of men and women based on their equality as a created order. Because 1 Corinthians 11 is one of the cornerstones of complementarian theology, the re-interpretation has not been accepted largely due to the false interpretation of the word *kephale* found in verse 3.

> Another argument used for the translation "source" in 1 Corinthians 11.3 is that Paul says woman came from man in verse 11.8, and this obviously suggests the idea of source. Surely this understanding of verse 8 is correct, but verse 8 does not explicate the meaning of head in verse 3. Instead, Paul uses this argument from source to prove that woman is the glory of man.[3]

Schreiner neglects the connection of *eikoon* ("image") and *kephale* ("head") in verse 7 because he gives *kephale* the incorrect meaning "authority over." "A beginning" and "a first principle," the meanings Chrysostom gave *kephale* in his homily are synonymous to an archetype of which the other person is an image, "for images are the forms of their archetypes."[4] According to Origen, "The true God, then, is 'The God,' and those who are formed after Him are gods, images, as it were, of Him the prototype. But the archetypal image, again, of all these images is the Word of God, who was in the beginning, and who by being with God is at all times God."[5] Gregory of Nyssa explained, "[T]hen all the Cause beyond, which is God over all, is found through Our Lord, Who is the Cause of all things; nor, indeed, is it possible to gain an exact knowledge of the Archetypal Good, except as it appears in the (visible) image of that invisible."[6] In other words, the archetype is the source of the image, which possesses the characteristics of its source.

---

2. Piper and Grudem, 125.
3. Ibid., 130.
4. Alexander, *Of the Manichaeans*, Chapter XXIII.
5. Origen, *Commentary on the Gospel of John*, Book II, 2.
6. *Against Eunomius*, Book I Ch. 36.

According to Gregory of Nazianzen, the same attributes that are found in the archetype must also be found in the image.[7] However, the image is not an identical copy of the archetype, as described by Theodoret (d. 458) in a dialogue between Eranistes and Orthodoxus.

> *Eran.* – The type must have the character of the archetype.
>
> *Orth.* – Is man called an image of God?
>
> *Eran.* – Man is not an image of God, but was made in the image of God.
>
> *Orth.* – Listen then to the Apostle. He says: "For a man indeed ought not to cover his head, forasmuch as he is the image and glory of God."
>
> *Eran.* – Granted, then, that he is an image of God.
>
> *Orth.* – According to your argument then he must needs have plainly preserved the characters of the archetype, and have been uncreate, uncompounded, and infinite. He ought in like manner to have been able to create out of the non existent, he ought to have fashioned all things by his word and without labour, in addition to this to have been free from sickness, sorrow, anger, and sin, to have been immortal and incorruptible and to possess all the qualities of the archetype.
>
> *Eran.* – Man is not an image of God in every respect.
>
> *Orth.* – Though truly an image in the qualities in which you would grant him to be so, you will find that he is separated by a wide interval from the reality.
>
> *Eran.* – Agreed.
>
> *Orth.* – Consider now too this point. The divine Apostle calls the Son the image of the Father; for he says "Who is the image of the invisible God?"
>
> *Eran.* – What then; has not the Son all the qualities of the Father?
>
> *Orth.* – He is not Father. He is not uncaused. He is not unbegotten.
>
> *Eran.* – If He were He would not be Son.

---

7. *"Oration XXXVII," Orations,* XXII, 3-4.

> *Orth.* – Then does not what I said hold good; the image has not
> all the qualities of the archetype?
> *Eran.* – True [8]

A copy is called a "shadow" in the New Testament (Heb 8.5). For example, the Law was a shadow of Christ, whom Paul portrays as the body or true substance (Col 2.17). A shadow is the opposite of an image (Heb 10.1) for whereas the copy is temporary and is destroyed when the substance is provided (Heb 10.9) an image co-exists with the archetype, its source. Thus, as the image of the Father, the Son is similar to the Father in essence and power, but He is not the identical to the Father, for He is not unbegotten. The man is in the image of God in the inner person, but he is enclosed in a body, whereas God is a spirit. The woman is also in the image of God in the inner person for she is a human being, but her body is in the image of the first man, wherefore it is different from his.[9]

1 Corinthians 11.7 caused many patristic theologians to consider only the man as having been created in the image of God. For example, Tertullian believed that each woman was an Eve and therefore thoroughly subjected to men who were solely created in the image of God.[10] Augustine reconciled the apparent contradiction between Genesis 1 and 1 Corinthians 11 by affirming that the man is always in the image of God, while a woman is in the image of God only together with her husband.[11] Also the medieval doctor Thomas Aquinas, who studied Augustine, believed the woman was not in the image of God in the same way as the man. He considered both men and women to be in the image of God in their intellectual nature, but because God is the beginning of man and the man is the beginning of the woman, the image of God is not found in the woman in the same way as it is in the man.[12] His exact meaning is somewhat obscure, but his belief that the woman lacked the man's

---

8. Theodoret, "Dialogue II: The Unconfounded, Eranistes and Orthodoxus," *Dialogues.*

9. "And Adam lived one hundred and thirty years, and begot a son in *his own* likeness, after *his* image, and named him Seth" (Gen 5.3). All humans are in the image of the man of dust because they all find their origin in the first man (1 Cor 15.49); all humans differ, none is an exact copy of his or her parents.

10. *On the Apparel of Women,* Book I, Ch. I; *On the veiling of virgins,* Chapter X.

11. Augustine, *Of the Work of Monks.*

12. *Summa Theologica,* First Part, Question 93, Article 4.

reason became the foundation of his twofold subjection, wherefore he did not assign equal intellectual powers to the woman.

John M. Frame affirms that God is not male or female in his essay *Men and Women in the Image of God* wherefore both the man and the woman are created in the image of God. But because God is described overwhelmingly as male in the Bible, and "lordship in Scripture always connotes authority," we should think of God as Lord and not use feminine terms.[13] Yet, Frame believes also that the woman images God through her subjection because Christ became a servant, but he denies that God is subject the way the woman is to the man because the woman does not have authority, which God does. Frame does not feel he needs to explain the contradiction of God not being male yet having primarily male qualities, for in his androcentric theology the male human defines God.

The progression of God becoming male begins when the woman is prevented from using her entire mental faculty, either in theory or practice, and she becomes a bridge between humanity and the animal kingdom, as occurred in early evolutionary biology.[14] When the woman is returned to full humanity, the man in his turn becomes divine,[15] and as the man becomes divine, the divine becomes male. It is not necessary or even possible to limit God into an image which belongs to the created order, for although God is called a Father in the Bible, He calls Himself also a Mother (Isa 66.13).[16] God's fatherly care and motherly tender mercy are both part of His perfection. After all, God created humans in His *own* image.

Schreiner believes the word *glory* found in verse 7 could be translated "honor." And accordingly, the woman "honors the man by wearing a head covering, thereby showing that the man is the head, i.e. authority… If woman

---

13. Piper and Grudem, 229.

14. Rosenberg, 9.

15. "Suppose a woman feels God is leading her definitely opposite to what her husband has commanded. Whom should she obey? The Scriptures say a woman must ignore her "feelings" about the will of God, and do what her husband says. *She is to obey her husband as if he were God Himself.* She can be certain of God's will, when her husband speaks, as if God had spoken audibly from Heaven!" (Elizabeth Rice Handfrod, *Me? Obey Him?* (Murfreesboro, TN: Sword of the Lord Publishers, 1972), 28.

16. Also Apostle Paul called himself both a father (1 Cor 4.15) and a tender mother (1 Thess 2.7).

was created for man's sake, i.e. to help him in the tasks God gave him, then it follows that the woman should *honor* man."[17] However, Schreiner's concept sounds eerily similar to the decree found in the book of Esther where the man is called a ruler (Heb., *sarar)* whom the wife ought to honor.

> When the king's decree which he will make is proclaimed throughout all his empire (for it is great), all wives will honor their husbands, both great and small." And the reply pleased the king and the princes, and the king did according to the word of Memucan, as a result of an ungodly kings. Then he sent letters to all the king's provinces, to each province in its own script, and to every people in their own language, that each man should be master in his own house, and speak in the language of his own people. (Esther 1.20-22)

Both Matthew Henry ("It is the interest of states and kingdoms to provide that good order be kept in private families") and Adam Clarke ("Both God's law and common sense taught this from the foundation of the world") believed the decree was in harmony with the rest of the Bible, although it was issued by an ungodly ruler who did not know God.

Image and glory are found together in 1 Corinthians 11.7 and therefore *kephale* is also connected to glory (*doxa*), for an image is the glory of its origin and always found with the source, as explained by Basil.

> For whenever we are contemplating the majesty of the nature of the Only Begotten, and the excellence of His dignity, we bear witness that the glory is *with* the Father; while on the other hand, whenever we bethink us of His bestowal on us of good gifts, and of our access to, and admission into, the household of God we confess that this grace is effected for us *through* Him and *by* Him. It follows that the one phrase "with whom" is the proper one to be used in the ascription of glory, while the other, *"through* whom," is specially appropriate in giving of thanks.... But we do not rest only on the fact that such is the tradition of the Fathers; for they too followed the sense of Scrip-

---

17. Piper and Grudem, 133. Grudem disagrees for he writes that it is the wife who ought to be honored by the husband according to 1 Pet 3.7, for "it is appropriate that those who are 'feminine,' those who give characteristic expression to 'womanhood,' should receive special honor, for this is what God has directed" (Piper and Grudem, 208).

ture, and started from the evidence which, a few sentences back, I deduced from Scripture and laid before you. For "the brightness" is always thought of with "the glory," "the image" with the archetype, and the Son always and everywhere together with the Father; nor does even the close connection of the names, much less the nature of the things, admit of separation.[18]

Hebrews 13 describes Jesus as the brightness of God's glory, and as the rays cannot be separated from the sun, neither can He from the Father. He is also "the image of the invisible God" (Col 1.15), and always with God (John 1.1-2). Humans were created in the image of God, to be with God, and were severed from the fellowship because of sin; similarly the woman was created to be with the man, and is therefore the man's glory and it is only because of sin that women and men have been separated into different spheres.[19]

Basil argued further that glory is an inherent part of the origin and cannot be separated from it, "For the glory is inseparable from the Godhead."[20] Also Paul wrote that glory cannot remain if an attribute in the object is changed, "Professing to be wise, they became fools, and changed the glory of the incorruptible God into an image made like corruptible man – and birds and four-footed animals and creeping things" (Rom 1.22-23). Justin Martyr is an early witness of connecting the origin of the person with glory, for he called the Son the glory of the Begetter.[21] Also Tertullian called Christ the glory of the woman, presumably because He was born of Mary,[22] and Hilary of Poiters believed that oneness is attained by shared glory.[23]

Schreiner recognizes that Paul was concerned about women and men changing their outward appearance, but he believes men wore the veils which the women

18. Basil, *The Book of Saint Basil on the Spirit*, Ch. VII, 16.

19. The inferiority of women caused theologians to lose the connection between *doxa* and *kephale*, for, as Gregory Nazianzen put it, "the lowering of those who are from Him is no glory to the source." ("Oration XL, The Oration on Holy Baptism," *Orations*, XLIII).

20. Basil, On John XVII. 5.

21. Justin, *Dialogue of Justin, Philosopher and Martyr, with Trypho, a Jew*, Ch. LXI.

22. Tertullian, *The Chaplet* or *De Corona*, Ch. XIV.

23. *On the Trinity*, Book VIII, 11-12.

had discarded, which made them appear feminine.[24] The face covering veil appears in the Early Church Writings with Clement of Alexandria and Tertullian (end of second century). Clement of Alexandria's wrote in the *Instructor*, "It is a wicked thing for beauty to be a snare to men,"[25] wherefore he prescribed a face covering veil. Although Tertullian claimed apostolic authority for the veil – "So, too, did the Corinthians themselves understand him. In fact, at this day the Corinthians do veil their virgins. What the apostles taught, their disciples approve"[26] – no evidence of women wearing face-covering veils in first century Corinth exists.[27] Because Augustine associated women with sinful flesh, he believed the veiling of women was a symbol of the curbing of the lust of the body to allow the mind to advance to higher things because "too great a progression towards inferior things is dangerous to that rational cognition that is conversant with things corporeal and temporal."[28] But had Paul truly prescribed a face-covering veil, he could have made it clear by using the phrase *kaluma epi prosoopon,* found in 2 Corinthians 3.13, instead of *katakalypto.*

Tertullian admitted that he could not find a commandment in the Old Testament for women to veil themselves and had to therefore resort to custom.

> If I nowhere find a law, it follows that tradition has given the fashion in question to custom, to find subsequently (its authorization in) the apostle's sanction, from the true interpretation of reason. This instances, therefore, will make it sufficiently plain that you can vindicate the keeping of even unwritten tradition established by custom; the proper witness for tradition when demonstrated by long-continued observance.[29]

---

24. Piper and Grudem, 130. Although men cover their heads in Judaism with a *Tallit* (prayer shawl) it is a sign of one's humility before God, not a sign of subjection within a human relationship.

25. *The Instructor,* Book II, Ch XI.

26. *On The Veiling of Virgins,* VIII.

27. Nancy A. Carter, "Paul and Corinthians Women's Head Coverings," Global Ministries of the United Methodist Church, http://gbgm-umc.org/UMW/corinthians/veils.stm. (accessed June 29, 2009).

28. Augustine, *On the Trinity,* In Fifteen Books, Book XII, Ch. 7.

29. *The Chaplet,* or *De Corona,* Ch. IV.

It appears that married women already wore veils in North-Africa by the end of the second century but that virgins were exempted wherefore Tertullian argued for the veiling of the virgins, not only because they were women, but also because of his belief that it was because of women that the angels had sinned.

> So perilous a face, then, ought to be shaded, which has cast stumbling-stones even so far as heaven: that, when standing in the presence of God, at whose bar it stands accused of the driving of the angels from their (native) confines, it may blush before the other angels as well; and may repress that former evil liberty of its head, – (a liberty) now to be exhibited not even before human eyes. [30]

Tertullian considered any kind of "glory," i.e., recognition, to be unlawful for women since they were in a state of probation because of Eve's sin, and their lot was "humility of every kind" and modesty. Therefore he objected to the practice of allowing virgins to carry a mark of honor, an unveiled head, when they should have remembered their shame. According to Tertullian, men prayed rightly to God with their heads uncovered, for freed from sin they had nothing to be ashamed of.[31]

Chrysostom agreed with Tertullian, "Being covered is a mark of subjection and authority, for it induces her to look down and be ashamed and preserve entire her proper virtue."[32] But he thought also that Paul was referring to the custom of men covering their heads when praying and prophesying and letting their hair grow long, which were both Grecian customs,[33] and that the Corinthians themselves thought long hair was a sign of piety.[34] He wrote further that a man should not wear a veil when he prays but that long hair is discouraged at all times, while a woman ought to be covered with a veil at all times. Yet, he also equated the covering with long hair.

---

30. *On the Veiling of Virgins,* VII.
31. *The Apology,* Ch XXX.
32. *Homilies on First* Corinthians, Homily XXVI.
33. Ibid.
34. *Homilies on Matthew,* Homily LXXXVI.

Wherefore, as touching the woman, he said, "But if she be not veiled, let her also be shorn;" so likewise touching the man, "If he have long hair, it is a dishonor unto him." He said not, "if he be covered" but, "if he have long hair," Wherefore also he said at the beginning, "Every man praying or prophesying, having any thing on his head, dishonors his head." He said not, "covered," but "having any thing on his head;" signifying that even though he pray with the head bare, yet if he have long hair, *he is like to one covered.* "For the hair," says he, "is given for a covering."[35]

And because Paul did not write "let her have long hair" but "let her be covered," he "affirm[ed] the covering and the hair to be one." Chrysostom had to naturally answer the question how the woman could be considered shaved if she discarded the veil considering her long hair was a covering, and he reconciled the problem by concluding that the woman's long hair was a lesson given by nature so she might learn to veil herself.

A question found in Islam mirrors closely 1 Corinthians 11.13, "Is the woman's prayer worthless when her hair is not covered?"[36] The Christians practice of veiling women began in the second-century Northern Africa. Similarly, the Muslim practice of *hijab* ("veil") had spread throughout the Middle-East and Northern-Africa by the sixteenth century. As with the Bible, the Koran does not command women to wear veils. The *hijab* was given in a specific circumstance which involved the Prophet and his new wife Zaynab, and separated *two men*, not a man and a woman.

The "descent of the *hijab*" had a double perspective form the beginning. There was a concrete aspect: the Prophet drew a tangible curtain between himself and Anas Ibn Malik. There was also an abstract aspect: the descent of the verse, from Heaven to earth, from God to the Prophet, who recited it. The Prophet drew a real curtain between himself and the only man in his house who was still there after the departure of the other guests, and at the same time he recited the

---

35. *First Corinthians*, Homily XXVI.

36. Fatima Mernissi, *The Veil and the Male Elite*, [New York: Basic Books, 1987], 99. In Islam the covering is a veil, but the Koran was written in Arabic, six centuries after the Bible was written and four centuries after Christians begun to veil women in Africa, a habit which eventually spread to other regions as well.

verse which was inspired in him on the spot by God.... This dimension of the *hijab* as a delimitation of areas is strongly affirmed in some versions, where it is said that "the *hijab* descended," the *sitr* (curtain) referring to a physical curtain, and the *hijab* to the Koranic verse.[37]

Both in Christianity and in Islam, the veiling of women became a norm because of the perceived need for the protection of female modesty and the prevention of sexual immorality. In the words of the influential bishop Ambrose:

> Let custom itself teach us. A woman covers her face with a veil for this reason, that in public her modesty may be safe, That her face may not easily meet the gaze of a youth, let her be covered with the nuptial veil, so that not even in chance meetings she might be exposed to the wounding of another or of herself, though the wound of either were indeed hers. But if she cover her head with a veil that she may not accidentally see or be seen (for when the head is veiled the face is hidden), how much more ought she to cover herself with the veil of modesty, so as even in public to have her own secret place.[38]

The veil became also the symbol of the woman's exclusion from the closeness with God the man enjoyed, which further excluded her from representing God in ecclesiastical leadership.[39]

It was common for both men and women, including the emperor, to wear veils in worship in the Greco-Roman world, but the assumption that Paul forbade men from wearing veils during Christian worship does not explain why women would have discarded the veil.[40] Another possible explanation is found in the Hermaphrodite which appeared in the Hellenistic Greece and which "embodied wholeness, transcending the imperfection of belonging to

---

37. Ibid, 100.

38. Ambrose, *Two Books Concerning Repentance*, Book I, Ch. XIV, 69.

39. A derogative practice is often called a symbol of respect, as seen in Saudi Arabia where the *abaya,* which literally hides the woman underneath the black folds, is considered a symbol of respect for women, although the true reason is the obsession with sexual mores which dictate that a woman may never be seen by a man who is in a position to marry her (bin Laden, 55, 71).

40. "Paul and Corinthian Women's Head Coverings."

one sex or the other." It was a departure from the Classical period in which the male was clearly the superior being "and to taint him with the characteristics of 'the inferior' would have been a lessening of perfection."[41] In the case of the Hermaphrodite, the man did not lessen his perfection by having also female qualities such as long flowing hair, but increased his perfection by attaining wholeness.

Yet another possible scenario is found in the habit of cutting of the women's hair to erase the distinction of sex in accordance with Galatians 3.28. The Synod of Gangra of the fourth century condemned women who "from pretended asceticism shall cut off her hair, which God gave her as the reminder of her subjection, thus annulling as it were the ordinance of subjection."[42] In the Synodical Letter we read of the group in Gangra who was loyal to one Eustathius and who condemned marriage wherefore women forsook their husbands, and husbands their wives. They wore strange apparel "to the destruction of the common custom of dress"; the women wore men's clothing, "thinking to be justified" because of it and "under a pretext of piety" cut off their hair. Also Hermias Sozomen wrote in his *Ecclesiastical History*, comprising years A.D. 323-425 that, "women, under the pretext of religion, cut off their hair, and behaved otherwise than is fitting to a woman, by arraying themselves in men's apparel."[43] The Apocryphal figure Thecla[44] is said to have told Apostle Paul she would cut her hair in order to follow him, and later she is described as having sown her tunic to resemble a man's cloak.[45] Also Jerome wrote about virgins who, "change their garb and assume the mien of men, being ashamed of being what they were born to be – women. They cut off their hair and are

---

41. Pomeroy, 146.

42. The Synod of Gangra, Canon XVII.

43. Hermias Sozomen, *Ecclesiastical History,* Book III, XIV.

44. A comment written in 1870 found in adjunction of *Acts of Paul and Thecla,* states, "Acts of Paul and Thecla.—This book is of undoubted antiquity. There seems reason to accept the account of it given by Tertullian, that it was written by an Asiatic presbyter in glorification of St. Paul who, however, unquestionably occupies only a secondary place in it, and in support of the heretical opinion that women may teach and baptize." But how could it be possible for anyone to *glorify* Paul and *attribute heresy* to his name at the same time? It is more likely that Paul was known for having allowed women to teach and that Tertullian disliked it enough to defame the presbyter who wrote the apocrypha to discredit the literary work, for in his theology women did not even belong in the laity.

45. *Acts of Paul and Thecla.*

not ashamed to look like eunuchs. Some clothe themselves in goat's hair, and, putting on hoods, think to become children again by making themselves look like so many owls."[46]

Did Paul refer to a veil or long hair, and was the cover a sign of subjection? If Paul truly referred to a veil, he would not have used *katakalypto* ("to cover down"), for the proper Greek word is *kaluma*. *Katakalypto* describes a cover, but it is not necessarily an external one, for it can also be produced by the object itself. A similar word is found in eucalyptus (*eu* and *kalypto*) the tree which received its name from its flower bud, which is completely covered; hence the name "well covered."[47] In verse four Paul wrote, "Every man who prays or prophesies down (*kata*) his head having shames his head." What Paul was objecting to was for the man having *something* down his head, as also Chrysostom noted ("He said not, 'covered,' but 'having any thing on his head'").

In the early centuries hair was said to cover the head, or body, as seen in the writings of Lactantius.

> But where there is reason and the hand, that is not so necessary as a *covering of hair*. To such an extent are all things most befittingly arranged, each in its own class, that nothing can be conceived more unbecoming than a quadruped which is naked, or a man that is covered. [48]

He added further that, "though nakedness itself on the part of man tends in a wonderful manner to beauty, yet it was not adapted to his head." Therefore, the human head is clothed with hair and "all the back part of the head [is] covered."

Although he prescribed a veil, Tertullian recognized that the text spoke about the length of hair, "Hence let the world, the rival of God, see to it, if it asserts that *close-cut hair* is graceful to a virgin in like manner as that *flowing*

46. Jerome, "Letter XXII: To Eustochium," 27-28.

47. *The New Webster Encyclopedic Dictionary of the English Language*, The International Edition (Grolier, New York, c. 1968) 301.

48. Lactantius, *On the Workmanship of God, or the Formation of Man*, A Treatise Addressed to His Pupil Demetrianus, Ch. VII.

hair is to be a boy."[49] The same is also found in the writings of Ambrose who called the woman's long hair a natural veil.[50] But the most explicit reference to long hair is found in a letter from Epiphanius, Bishop of Salamis, to John, Bishop of Jerusalem.

> Paul, too, the "chosen vessel," who in his preaching has fully main-
> tained the doctrine of the gospel, instructs us that man is made in the
> image and after the likeness of God. "A man," he says, *"ought not to*
> *wear long hair,* forasmuch as he is the image and glory of God.""[51]

The letter was written originally in Greek in A.D. 394, but it was trans-lated into Latin by Jerome at the writer's request.[52] Also Jerome understood *katakalypto* to refer to long hair:

> Vos ipsi iudicate decet mulierem non velatem orare Deum. Nec ipsa
> natura docet vos quod vir quidem si comom nutriat ignominia est
> illi. Mulier vero comom nutriat Gloria est illi quoniam capilli pro
> velamine ei dati sunt."

The English translation of the Vulgate, Douay-Rheims, translates the above:

> You yourselves judge. Doth it become a woman to pray unto God
> uncovered? Doth not even nature itself teach that a man indeed, of
> he nourish his hair, it is a shame unto him? But if a woman nourish
> her hair it is a glory to her; for her hair is given to her for a covering.
> (1 Cor 11.14-15)

Jerome clearly equated being covered with the woman's long hair which she should nourish and not cut off.

In the Old Testament, Ezekiel 44.20 distinguishes between a shaved head, well trimmed hair and long hair. Therefore we can conclude that Paul writes

---

49. *On the Veiling of Virgins*, VII.

50. *Three Books on the duties of the Clergy*, Book I, Ch. XLVI.

51. Epiphanius, "Letter LI," *Epihanius, Bishop of Salamis, in Cyprus, to John, Bishop of Jerusalem*, 6.

52. *The Nicene and Post-Nicene Fathers Second Series Vol. VI.* Jerome: Letters and Select Works. (Logos Research Systems: Oak Harbor 1997, Schaff, Philip).

that it if a woman does not have long hair (*akatakalypto*) it is *as if* her head were shaved.

> But every woman who prays or prophesies with her head uncovered (*akatakalypto*) dishonors her head, for that is one and the same *as if* her head were shaved (*xurao*). For if a woman is not covered (*katakalypto*), let her also be shorn (*keiro*). But if it is shameful for a woman to be shorn (*keiro*) or shaved (*xurao*), let her be covered. (1 Cor 11.5-6)

In other words, if the woman cuts her hair short, she might as well shave off the rest; but if it is shameful for a woman to be shaved, let her be covered, i.e., have long hair.

In Protestantism women have worn head covers of some sort until very recently because 1 Corinthians 11.10 has been understood to prescribe a veil as a symbol of the man's authority.[53] However, the Greek text – "*Diá toúto ofeílei hee guneé exousían échein epí teés kefaleés diá toús angélous*" – does not speak of a symbol, or of the man's authority. In the four other instances in which *exousían échein epi* is found in the Bible, *the authority always belongs to the person in question* (Matt 9.6; Luke 19.17; Rev 11.6; 1 Cor 7.37). The same is found in the eight passages in which *exousían échoon* is used (Matt 7.29: Mark 3.14-15, John 10.18; 19.10; Acts 9.14; Rom 9.21; 2 Thess 3.9; Heb 13.10). Since the grammatical construction always gives authority to the person in question, 1 Corinthians 11 cannot be used to argue for the woman's subjection to the man's authority.[54]

1 Corinthians 11 is structured chiastically, i.e. the first statement corresponds to the last, the second to the second last, etc. The literary structure focuses the reader's attention to the center of the argument as the key to its

---

53. *The Bible, An American Translation* translates *katakalypto* with "veil" and 1 Corinthians 11.10, "That is why she ought to wear upon her head something to symbolize her subjection, out of respect to the angels, if to nobody else" (*The Bible, An American Translation*, New Testament trans. by Edgar J. Goodspeed [The University of Chicago Press, 1931]).

54. In a fragment of the writings of Clement of Alexandria, an enigmatic statement is found, "And he said that women were punished on account of their hair and ornaments by a power placed over those things, which also gave strength to Samson by his hair, and punishes those who by the ornament of their hair are urged on to fornication."

interpretation, while the arguments leading to and from the central argument explain and reinforce it. The central argument in 1 Corinthians 11.2-16 is verse 10, "For this cause ought the woman to have power on her head because of the angels" (KJV). Complementarism uses 1 Corinthians 11.3 to explain the meaning of verse 10, but as seen above, it leads to the erroneous conclusion that the woman ought to wear a symbol of the man's authority on her head.

Due to the chiastic structure, the corresponding statement to verse 3 is found in verses 14-15.

a) Now I praise you, brethren, that you remember me in all things and keep the traditions just as I delivered them to you. (v. 2)…. But if anyone seems to be contentious, we have no such custom, nor do the churches of God. (vv. 16)

b) But I want you to know that the head of every man is Christ, the head of woman is man, and the head of Christ is God. (v. 3)… Does not even nature itself teach you that if a man has long hair, it is a dishonor to him? But if a woman has long hair, it is a glory to her; for her hair is given to her for a covering. (vv. 14-15)

c) Every man praying or prophesying, having his head covered, dishonors his head. But every woman who prays or prophesies with her head uncovered dishonors her head, for that is one and the same as if her head were shaved. For if a woman is not covered, let her also be shorn. But if it is shameful for a woman to be shorn or shaved, let her be covered (vv. 4-6)… Judge among yourselves. Is it proper for a woman to pray to God with her head uncovered? (v. 13)

d) For a man indeed ought not to cover his head, since he is the image and glory of God; but woman is the glory of man. For man is not from woman, but woman from man. Nor was man created for the woman, but woman for the man. (vv. 7-9)… Nevertheless, neither is man independent of woman, nor woman independent of man, in the Lord. For as woman came from man, even so man also comes through woman; but all things are from God. (vv. 11-12)

e) For this cause the woman ought to have power on her head because of the angels (KJV). (v. 10)

1 Corinthians 11.14 states, "Does not even nature [*physis*] itself teach you that if a man has long hair, it is a dishonor to him?" In the 14 occasions in which *physis* is used in the New Testament (Rom 1.26; 2.14, 27; 11.21, 24; 1 Cor 11.14; Gal 2.15; 4.8; Eph 2.3; Jas 3.7; 2 Pet 1.4) the word refers to a quality the object was created – or born – with and which is part of its original perfection. Hence the significance of *physis* in verse 14 is that God created the man to be *by nature* a man and the woman to be *by nature* a woman and a change which affects this basic division goes against God's original plan.

Why did Paul write that the woman should have authority over herself? A likely explanation is that in Corinth the influence of philosophy was felt in all aspects of life. Paul had already addressed the issue by reminding the believers that their faith should not be based on human wisdom but in the power of God (1 Cor 2.5). Aristotle was well known for having taught that the woman's reason was without authority wherefore she had to be under the man's rule. Paul may have countered this belief by his affirmation that the woman's reason was not without authority, for she was created from the man; and what the man was, the woman was. The likelihood of this being the correct explanation is strengthened by the simple fact that Thomas Aquinas made the woman subject from creation by reinstituting Aristotle's belief that the woman lacked the man's reason, and therefore authority over herself.

It has been suggested that the woman dishonors the man, her head, if she prays without a head covering, but the Greek word for "dishonor" in verses 4-5 is *kataischuno,* a combination of the words *kata* ("down") and *aischunomai* ("to feel shame for oneself"). *Aischunomai* is used five times (Luke 16.3; 2 Cor 10.8; Phil 1.20; 1 Pet 4.16; 1 John 2.28) in the New Testament and the contexts deal with speech, hope, activity, confidence and suffering; the person in question is always the one who is the object of the shame. *Kataischuno* is used thirteen times in the New Testament and translated in the NIV "humiliated" (Luke 13.17; 1 Cor 11.22), "disappointed" (Rom 5.5), "put to shame" (Rom 9.33; 10.11; 1 Cor 1.27; 1 Pet 2.6), "to be ashamed" (2 Cor 9.4;

1 Pet 3.16), "embarrassed" (2 Cor 7.14), and "dishonor" (1 Cor 11.4-5). In the context nearest to 1 Corinthians 11.4-5, *kataischuno* refers to the poor being humiliated in the Corinthians church (1 Cor 11.22). In 1 Corinthians 1.26-31 shame is the result of confidence in human wisdom for God shamed the wisdom of philosophers through the wisdom of Christ, which is our salvation, in order for people to boast only in the Lord and not in themselves (1 Cor 2.6-8). When all the contexts are viewed, it appears that the usual meaning of the word is one's feeling of shame which is the result of one's confidence in false wisdom or placing one's confidence in a false hope. On the other hand, one does not need to be ashamed if one has spoken truthfully or placed one's hope and faith in God. Therefore it is unlikely that 1 Cor 11.4-5 has the meaning shaming one's source (i.e., Christ and the man). This is further confirmed by verse 6 – "But if it is shameful for a woman to be shorn or shaved" – for Paul used the word *aischron*, which is the neuter of *aischros*, derived from *aischos* (disfigurement, disgrace); *aischunomai*, used in verses 4-5, is also derived from *aischos*. The text signifies therefore that a woman brings shame upon herself if she disfigures or disgraces herself by cutting her hair short to resemble a man, for long hair was considered an ornament of the woman's person.[55]

The angels in 1 Corinthians 11.10 have puzzled theologians as much as "the law "in 1 Corinthians 14.34-35. Barnes, who made the woman a complete contradiction in his theology, regarded it "as one of the very few passages in the Bible whose meaning as yet it wholly inexplicable." He nevertheless concluded that the women ought to wear a veil because the angels of God witness the public worship "and because they know and appreciate the propriety of subordination and order in public assemblies." Also the Living Bible suggests that the angles rejoice over the fact that women are under the man's authority, but it is a false translation, as has already been noted. In 1 Timothy 5.21, Paul charged Timothy before God and *the elect angels* to observe everything without prejudice, doing nothing with partiality. The elect angels are eager to observe the teaching of the Gospel (1 Pet 1.12) and God has chosen to make His wisdom known to the apostate angels through the church (Eph 3.8-13). Therefore the meaning may be that women should have the right to pray and prophesy *as women*, as a testimony that the Gospel has ended the dominion of

---

55. *The Instructor*, Book II, VIII.

sin in the church, which the elect angels are observing and which teaches the Fallen angels the wisdom of God.

The source of the woman's authority over herself is her origin from the man, for being created in the image of God, she has free will. Obedience removes one's free will for one cannot obey and simultaneously act according to one's own conscience, as was later observed by Thomas Aquinas. The purpose of the woman's creation was for her to be the man's partner in God's work, wherefore Paul argued that the woman ought to have the power of free will to act according to her own conscience in her relationship to God. But although the first woman was created as an individual with free will, as seen in the event of the Fall, in which the woman took the fruit, a woman is not independent of the man, for she was created from the man.

It is important to note that the stress in 1 Corinthians 11.1-16 is not the proper hair length for men and women but the goodness of the woman's creation from the man as his equal. In the Old Testament, a Nazirite allowed his or her hair grow during the time of his separation and after fulfilling the vow, he or she shaved the consecrated head and burnt the hair as an offering to God (Num 6). We find this practice still in the New Testament: in Acts 21.20-25 Paul is asked to pay the expenses of four Jewish Christians who had taken a vow and needed to complete their separation by shaving their heads and by offering three animal sacrifices, alongside grain and drink offerings. It was not shameful for the Nazirite man to have long hair or for the Nazirite woman to shave her head, and therefore it was not the hair itself that was the problem in Corinth, but the reason why women were cutting their hair short – to resemble men in order to pray and prophesy in the church. Paul praised the Corinthians for following tradition of equality between men and women but wanted them to correct their misguided effort to make all equal by transforming women into men.

CHAPTER 10

1 Tim 2.11-15

My friend, who is pale and positive, said to me yesterday, as the tired sun was nodding: "You are too sensitive."

I admit, I am – sensitive. I am artificial. I cringe or am bumptious or immobile. I am intellectually dishonest, art-blind, and I lack humor.

"Why don't you stop all this?" She resorts triumphantly.

You will not let us.

"There you go again. You know that I –" Wait! I answer. Wait!

I arise at seven. The milkman has neglected me. He pays little attention to colored districts. My white neighbor glares elaborately. I walk softly, lest I disturb him. The children jeer as I pass to work. The women in the streetcar withdraw their skirts or prefer to stand. The policemen are truculent. The elevator man hates to serve Negroes. My job is insecure because the white union wants it and does not want me. I try to lunch, but no place near will serve me. I go forty blocks to Marshall's, but the Committee of Fourteen closes Marshall's; they say that white women frequent it.

"Do all eating places discriminate?" No, but how shall I know which do not – except –

I hurry home through crowds. They mutter or get angry. I go to a mass-meeting. They stare. I go to church. "We don't admit niggers!" Or perhaps I leave the beaten track. I seek new work. "Our employees would not work with you; our customers would object." I ask to help in social uplift. "Why – er – we will write you." I enter the free field of science. Every laboratory door is closed and no endowments are available. I seek the universal mistress, Art; the studio door is locked. I write literature. "We cannot publish stories of colored folks of that type." It's the only type I know. This is my life. It makes me idiotic. It gives me artificial problems. I hesitate, I rush, I waver. In fine – I am sensitive!

– W.E.B. Du Bois[1]

---

1. W.E.B. Du Bois, "On Being Black," W.E.B. Du Bois, *A Reader*, ed. Meyer Weinberg (New York: Harper & Row, 1970), 3-4.

~

Douglas Moo recognizes the presence of false teaching in Ephesus in his essay *What Does It Mean Not to Teach or Have Authority Over Men?*

> Many interpretations of 1 Timothy 2.11-15 rely heavily on the nature of this false teaching at Ephesus in explaining what Paul means in these verses. There is nothing wrong with this in principle; good exegesis always takes into consideration the larger context in which a text appears. However, Paul tells us remarkably little about the specifics of this false teaching, presumably because he knows that Timothy is well acquainted with the problem. This means that we cannot be at all sure about the precise nature of this false teaching and particularly, about is impact on the women in the church – witness the many, often contradictory, scholarly reconstructions of this false teaching. But this means that we must be very careful about allowing any specific reconstruction – tentative and uncertain as it must be – to play too large a role in our exegesis. [2]

Yet, despite his caution, Moo believes the false teacher's were "encouraging women to discard what we might call traditional female roles in favor of a more egalitarian approach," and that by encouraging abstinence from marriage they were tearing down traditional female roles. The emphasis on "the traditional female role" found in complementarism is a product of Protestant theology with its rejection of monasticism and emphasis on domesticity, wherefore it is unlikely that the false teachers were attempting to subvert a role which did not exist until the sixteenth century. In addition, Paul encouraged celibacy in his letter to the Corinthians,[3] although he by no means rejected marriage, for he encouraged the younger widows to marry (1 Tim 5.11-15) in accordance with 1 Corinthians 7.9.

We know more about the false teachers than Moo allows for. In Revelations

---

2. Piper and Grudem, 180-1.

3. "But I say to the unmarried and to the widows: It is good for them if they remain even as I am" (1 Cor 7.8).

2.1-8, in the letter directed to the Ephesians, Christ commended the believers for having tested "those who say they are apostles and are not," and for hating "the deeds of the Nicolaitans,"[4] a Christian Gnostic group of the first century. Irenaeus mentioned the group in his work *Against Heresies*.

> John, the disciple of the Lord, preaches this faith, and seeks, by the proclamation of the Gospel, to remove that error which by Cerinthus had been disseminated among men, and *a long time previously by those termed Nicolaitans,* who are an offset of that "knowledge" falsely so called, that he might confound them, and persuade them that there is but one God, who made all things by His Word.[5]

According to Irenaeus, the Nicolaitans had existed for a long time before John wrote his gospel, which would place them in Ephesus in the middle of the first century – the decades of Paul's missionary activities.

Paul called Gnosticism "knowledge falsely called" (*pseudonumos gnosis*) in 1 Timothy 6.20. The ones who professed the "knowledge falsely called" had strayed from the faith (1 Tim 6.21) and having strayed, had turned to idle talk, desiring to be teachers of the law, not understanding the things they were saying and constantly affirming (1 Tim 1.6-7). Paul warned Timothy, whom he had left in Ephesus, to avoid their profane and opposing arguments and to guard the Gospel which had been entrusted to him.

By the time John wrote Revelation, the Ephesians had exposed the false apostles and were commended by the apostle for hating their deeds. But the Nicolaitans were not found only in Ephesus. Ignatius, the disciple of John the Apostle, exhorted the Christians in Tralles, a city nearby Ephesus, to flee from "the impure Nicolaitans, falsely so called, who are lovers of pleasure and

---

4. According to tradition John resided in Ephesus, wherefore he would have known the Gnostic sect Nicolatians: "And there are those that heard from him that John, the disciple of the Lord, going to bathe in Ephesus and seeing Cerinthus within, ran out of the bath-house without bathing, crying, 'Let us flee, lest even the bath Fall, because Cerinthus, the enemy of the truth, is within' (Eusibius, Pamphilius, *The Church History of Eusibius*, Book IV, XI). John's Gospel and letters emphasize the reality of the incarnation, denied by the Gnostics. E.g., "By this you know the Spirit of God: Every spirit that confesses that Jesus Christ has come in the flesh is of God, and every spirit that does not confess that Jesus Christ has come in the flesh is not of God. And this is the spirit of the Antichrist, which you have heard was coming, and is now already in the world" (John 4.2-3).

5. *Against Heresies*, Book III, Ch. XI.

given to calumnious speeches."[6] He warned also the Philadelphians about the Nicolaitans who considered unlawful unions to be "a good thing" and placed the "highest happiness in pleasure."[7] Ignatius did not believe Nicolaus, one of the first deacons (Acts 6.3-5), was the originator of the group, but Hippolytus wrote that Nicolaus "departed from correct doctrine and was in the habit of inculcating indifferency [sic] of both life and food," and that he was the "cause of the wide-spread combination" of the numerous Gnostic sects.[8] Also pseudo-Tertullian thought Nicolaus was a "brother heretic."[9] Clement of Alexandria agreed with Ignatius for he wrote that a group of heretics had named themselves Nicolaitans because of his phrase "to abuse the flesh," which they interpreted to permit fornication, though Nicolaus had meant they should control its impulses.[10]

Tertullian believed the false prophetess in Thyatira had learned from the Nicolaitans, for she taught the believers to commit fornication and eating meats sacrificed to idols.[11] He may have made the connection because of the letter to the church in Pergamum, in which the Nicolaitans were compared to the teachings of Balam, "who taught Balak to put a stumbling block before the children of Israel, to eat things sacrificed to idols, and to commit sexual immorality" (Rev 2.14-5). According to Tertullian, the Nicolaitans were known for their "maintenance of lust and luxury,"[12] and Fabius Marius Victorinus (Died A.D. 370) added they believed "what had been offered to idols might be exorcised and eaten, and that whoever should have committed fornication might receive peace on the eighth day."[13]

In Gnosticism, the inner and spiritual man was redeemed by means of knowledge, for the material world, including the body, was believed to have been created through ignorance.[14] The "illuminated" Gnostics believed they were saved regardless of their conduct, because they were spiritual by nature

---

6. Ignatius, *Epistle to the Trallians*, Ch. XI.

7. Ignatius, *Epistle to the Philadelphians*, Ch. VI.

8. Hippolytus, *Refutation of All Heresies*, Book VII. XXIV.

9. *Against the Heresies*, Ch. I.

10. *Stromata*, Book III. Ch 4.

11. Tertullian, *On Modesty*, Chapter XIX.

12. *Five Books Against Marcion*, Book I, Ch. XXIX.

13. Victorinus, *Commentary on the Apocalypse of the Blessed John*, From the Second Chapter, 6.

14. Against Heresies, Book I, XXI.4.

and that which is spiritual cannot be destroyed. Hence, they ate meats offered to idols, and committed fornication – both considered major offenses by the church [15] – for good works and pure living was only necessary for the Christians, who possessed an "animal" nature.[16]

Tertullian provided his readers with a comprehensive list of the Gnostic groups and their beliefs.

> Besides all this, I add a review of the doctrines themselves, which, existing as they did in the days of the apostles, were both exposed and denounced by the said apostles. For by this method they will be more easily reprobated, when they are detected to have been even then in existence, or at any rate to have been seedlings of the (tares) which then were. Paul, in his first epistle to the Corinthians, sets his mark on certain who denied and doubted the resurrection. This opinion was the especial property of the Sadducees. A part of it, however, is maintained by Marcion and Apelles and Valentinus, and all other impugners of the resurrection. Writing also to the Galatians, he inveighs against such men as observed and defend circumcision and the (Mosaic) law. Thus runs Hebion's heresy. Such also as "forbid to marry" he reproaches in his instructions to Timothy. Now, this is the teaching of Marcion and his follower Apelles. (The apostle) directs a similar blow against those who said that "the resurrection was past already." Such an opinion did the Valentinians assert of themselves. When again he mentions "endless genealogies," one also recognizes Valentinus, in whose system a certain Aeon, whosoever he be, of a new name, and that not one only, generates of his own grace Sense and Truth; and these in like manner produce of themselves Word and Life, while these again afterwards beget Man and the Church. From these primary eight ten other Aeons after them spring, and then the twelve others arise with their wonderful names, to complete the mere story of the thirty Aeons. The same apostle, when disapproving of those who are "in bondage to elements," points us to some dogma of Hermogenes, who introduces matter as having no beginning, and then compares it with God, who has no beginning. By thus making

---

15. Ibid., Ch. VI.
16. *The Instructor,* Book I, Ch. VI.

the mother of the elements a goddess, he has it in his power "to be in bondage" to a being which he puts on a par with God. John, however, in the Apocalypse is charged to chastise those "who eat things sacrificed to idols," and "who commit fornication." There are even now another sort of Nicolaitans. Theirs is called the Gaian heresy. But in his epistle he especially designates those as "Antichrists" who "denied that Christ was come in the flesh," and who refused to think that Jesus was the Son of God. The one dogma Marcion maintained; the other, Hebion. The doctrine, however, of Simon's sorcery, which inculcated the worship of angels, was itself actually reckoned amongst idolatries and condemned by the Apostle Peter in Simon's.[17]

Christian Gnosticism developed early and Simon Magus, whom Luke mentions in Acts 8, has been accredited for its creation.[18] Simon was a native of Gitta in Samaria and known for his sorcery and magic.[19] He denied the God of the Old Testament and the prophets, and that God had created the heavens and Earth.[20] He claimed that "he himself was God over all, and that the world was formed by his angels."[21] Menander, who succeed Simon Magus, claimed to be the Savior who would help mankind gain mastery over the world-creating angels through magic and by being baptized by him, and thus gain perpetual immorality on earth, for he did not believe in the immortality of the soul and the resurrection.[22]

The Gnostics believed that salvation was attained through right knowledge, attainable only for a small elite and therefore a mediator was not needed between humanity and God. Paul reminded Timothy that he was not lying, that God desired *all* men to be saved and come to the knowledge of the truth, for there is one God and one Mediator between God and men, the Man Christ Jesus (1 Tim 2.3). Since the heresy in Ephesus involved sexual immorality, and good works were not considered applicable to the Gnostic, Paul exhorted the women in Ephesus to adorn themselves with good works instead of jewelry and expensive clothing (1 Tim 2.1-10). He warned also Timothy

---

17. *The Prescription Against Heresies*, XXXIII.
18. *Against Heresies*, Book III, Preface,1.
19. *Refutation of All Heresies,* Book IV, II.
20. *Letter to the Philadelphians,* Ch VI
21. *Against Heresies,* Book II, Ch, IX.
22. Pamphilus, *The Church History of Eusebius*, Book III, Ch. XXVI.

to avoid youthful lusts. Instead, Paul wanted him to "pursue righteousness, faith, love, peace with those who call on the Lord out of a pure heart" (2 Tim 2.22-26), for every Christian ought to depart from iniquity (2 Tim 2.19). In 2 Timothy 3.1-9 Paul mentions women whom the Gnostics had captivated and who were "loaded down with sins, led away by various lusts." They were always learning and never able to come to the knowledge of truth, for the Gnostic teaching, which Paul called fables and old wives' tales (1 Tim 1.4; 4.7) – a term used later by Irenaeus[23] – did not lead to the truth. Paul wanted Timothy to reject the profane old wives' tales and instruct the believers in the "good doctrine," which he had carefully followed (4.6-7). Paul wanted him to also be an example to the believers "in word, in conduct, in love, in spirit, in faith, in purity" (4.12) which the Gnostics had rejected and consequently had "suffered shipwreck"; Paul mentions Hymenaeus and Alexander as examples of such a fate (1.19-20). Tertullian listed also Hymenaeus and Philetus (2 Tim 2.17) as false teachers who had deserted Apostle Paul.[24]

Because the Gnostics believed in salvation through knowledge and because the Nicolaitans were lascivious, Paul wrote, "But shall be saved through childbearing, if they continue in faith, love and holiness with sobriety." In other words, Paul affirmed the gospel: salvation is made available through the birth of Christ, but the believers must also live holy lives (compare with Philippians 2.1). We find the same theme in 1 Timothy 2.15, "Now the purpose of the commandment [to abstain from false teaching] is love from a pure heart, from a good conscience, and from sincere faith, from which some, having strayed, have turned aside to idle talk."

In 1 Timothy 4.1-5 Paul warned Timothy that in later times some would forbid marriage and command abstinence from foods and these are found in the writings of Marcion, whose Gnosticism Tertullian refuted in his work, *Five Books Against Marcion*. Tertullian connected Gnosticism also to the "fables and endless genealogies," which Paul warned believers should not pay attention to.

> Let, however, any man approach the subject from a knowledge of the faith which he has otherwise learned, as soon as he finds so many names of Aeons, so many marriages, so many offsprings, so many

---

23. *Against Heresies*, Book I, Ch. XIII, XVI.
24. *The Prescription against Heretics*, Ch. III.

exits, so many issues, felicities *and* infelicities of a dispersed and mutilated Deity, will that man hesitate at once to pronounce that these are "the fables and endless genealogies" which the inspired apostle by anticipation condemned, *whilst these seeds of heresy were even then shooting forth?* [25]

The most revealing aspect in determining the nature of the false teaching in Ephesus is the Gnostics' own refusal to accept 1 and 2 Timothy. According to Tertullian, "their vain presumptions must needs refuse to acknowledge the (writings) whereby they are refuted."[26] Also Clement wrote that, "convicted by this utterance, [1 Tim 6.20] the heretics reject the Epistles to Timothy."[27]

In the fourth century, when Gnosticism no longer posed a threat for the church, the "fables and genealogies" became Jewish, perhaps because of Titus 1.14.[28] Matthew Henry, Adam Clarke, and Barnes continued the tradition of affirming the Jewish origin of the "fables and genealogies," but *Jamieson, Fausset, and Brown's Commentary* points out that Paul would never call the Jewish genealogies "fables."[29] Also the twentieth-century *Wycliffe Commentary* recognized these as Gnostic in origin.

The myths and genealogies were probably Gnostic or proto-Gnostic teachings. Gnosticism had two extremes: asceticism, as in 1 Tim 4.3, and antinomian license, as the context intimates here. Erroneous discourses on law, and Gnostic speculations left plain matters of immorality uncorrected. The dispensation of God (ASV; AV, godly edifying) is the proper issue of sound teaching, and therefore parallels the "love" of verse 5, and the "good warfare" of verse 18. Love is Paul's summary of religious and ethical duty (Rom 13.10; Gal 5.6). The sound teaching brings God's ordering or God's superintendence of the life[30]

---

25. Tertullian, *Against the Valentinians,* Ch. III.

26. *The Prescription Against Heretics,* Ch. XVII.

27. *Stromata,* Book II, Ch. XI.

28. Rufinus, *The Apology of Rufinus,* Addressed to Apronianus, in Reply to Jerome's Letter to Pammachius, Written at Aquileia A.D. 400.

29. Robert Jamieson, A.R. Fausset, and David Brown, "1 Timothy 1.4, " Jamieson, Fausset and Brown's Commentary on the Whole Bible, Electronic Database, 1997.

30. "1 Timothy 1.4," *Wycliffe Bible Commentary.*

~

Grudem and Piper do not view 1 Timothy 2.12 as "an absolute prohibition of all teaching by women" for "teaching and learning are such broad terms that it is impossible that women not teach men and men not learn from women in some sense."[31] Schreiner agrees with Grudem and Piper.

> And I think women can proclaim the gospel to men in those [secular] cultures, for 1 Timothy 2.11-15 prohibits only authoritative teaching to a group of Christians within the church, not evangelism to those outside the church. Such proclamation of the gospel is not limited to men. She should clearly explain, however (as man missionary women have done in history), that men should assume leadership roles in the governance and teaching ministry of the church as soon as it is established.... There are also some way in which women can instruct both men and women, in my opinion, if the function of authoritative teaching to men is not involved. Thus, it is appropriate for women who travel as speakers to address a mixed audience as articulate and thoughtful representatives of a feminine perspective of life.[32]

One wonders if Schreiner does not consider unbelieving men to be truly men since women are allowed to teach them regardless of the creation principle. And the question remains also why Luther allowed women to preach in the absence of a qualified man, a principle Weinrich approves of, if the prohibition for women to teach is based on Creation. Not surprisingly, Knight disagrees with Schreiner for he sees the prohibition as an unqualified one which "extends to every situation in the life of the Christian community where these is actual, recognized teaching of the Scriptures and the Christian faith to a group that includes men, e.g., a Sunday School class, a small group meeting, a couples group, etc."[33] Moo himself adds that in 1 Timothy 2.12-18, the principle cannot be separated from the form of behavior for "a woman to teach a man or to have authority over a man is, by definition, to void the principle for which Paul quotes the creation account."[34]

---

31. Piper and Grudem, 69-70.
32. Ibid., 223.
33. Ibid., 354.
34. Ibid., 191.

Prior to the twofold subjection, Adam's prior creation did not restrict public teaching only to men. For example, Chrysostom believed that Paul denied women the right to teach *because of the Fall.*

> If it be asked, what has this to do with women of the present day? it shows that the male sex enjoyed the higher honor. Man was first formed; and elsewhere he shows their superiority. "Neither was the man created for the woman, but the woman for the man." (1 Cor xi. 9) Why then does he say this? He wishes the man to have the preeminence in every way; both for the reason given above, he means, let him have precedence, and on account of what occurred afterwards. For the woman taught the man once, and made him guilty of disobedience, and wrought our ruin. Therefore because she made a bad use of her power over the man, or rather her equality with him, God made her subject to her husband. "Thy desire shall be to thy husband?" (Gen iii. 16) This had not been said to her before... *The woman taught once, and ruined all. On this account therefore he saith, let her not teach.* But what is it to other women, that she suffered this? It certainly concerns them; for the sex is weak and fickle, and he is speaking of the sex collectively. For he says not Eve, but "the woman," which is the common name of the whole sex, not her proper name. Was then the whole sex included in the transgression for her fault? As he said of Adam, "After the similitude of Adam's transgression, who is the figure of Him that was to come" (Rom v. 14); *so here the female sex transgressed, and not the male.* Shall not women then be saved? Yes, by means of children. For it is not of Eve that he says, "If they continue in faith and charity and holiness with sobriety." What faith? what charity? what holiness with sobriety? It is as if he had said, "Ye women, be not cast down, because your sex has incurred blame. God has granted you another opportunity of salvation, by the bringing up of children, so that you are saved, not only by yourselves, but by others."[35]

Because it seemed irrational that women should earn their salvation through works, and because virginity was so highly valued in the fifth century church,

---

35. Chrysostom, *Homilies on First Timothy*, Homily IX. "The weakness and light-mindedness of the female sex (*infirmitas sexus* and *levitas animi*) were the underlying principles of Roman legal theory that mandated all women to be under the custody of males" (Pomeroy, 150).

Chrysostom felt compelled to explain the inconsistency, but he could only conclude that "this is the amount of what [Paul] says."

After Gnosticism was vanquished 1 Timothy 2 was re-interpreted according to the principle of the sole guilt of Eve, which was believed to be the cause of the woman's subjection and exclusion from teaching. In 412, Jerome sent a letter to Principia in which he praised the great learning of Marcella.

> Consequently after my departure from Rome, in case of a dispute arising as to the testimony of scripture on any subject, recourse was had to her to settle it. And so wise was she and so well did she understand what philosophers call το πρεπον, that is, the becoming, in what she did, that when she answered questions she gave her own opinion not as her own but as from me or some one else, thus admitting that what she taught she had herself learned from others. For she knew that the apostle had said: "I suffer not a woman to teach," and she would not seem to inflict a wrong upon the male sex many of whom (including sometimes priests) questioned her concerning obscure and doubtful points.[36]

The first-century Christian bishop Clement of Rome wrote that the apostles "preaching through countries and cities... appointed the first-fruits [of theirs labors], having first proved them by the Spirit, to be bishops and deacons of those who should afterwards believe."[37] Since "first-fruits" signify the first ones to come to faith, and because women were among the first ones to believe, the apostles appointed also women as bishops and deacons.

∼

In 1 Timothy 2, the text changes from plural to singular at verse 11, indicating that the subject changes. Paul is writing about a woman, whom he does not permit to teach or *authentein andros*. Perseus Online Dictionary gives *authenteo* the meanings "to have full power over" and "to murder."[38] Hence Paul wrote that he did not permit the absolute rule of the woman in question,

---

36. Jerome, "Letter CXXVII," *The Letters of St. Jerome*, 7.

37. *The First Epistle of Clement to the Corinthians*, Chapter XLII.

38. Perseus Digital Library, www.perseus.tufts.edu (accessed June 29, 2009), s.v. "authenteo." Euripides wrote, "Power absolute, I say, robs men of life" (Justin on the Sole Government of God, Ch. V).

for men and women were to work together as equals. It is also not certain that we should connect *didasko* and *authentein andros*. It is possible Paul wrote, "The woman in silence let learn with all subjection, and I do not permit [the] woman to teach [in general] *nor* to rule over the man with absolute power, but to be in silence."

If the exclusion of women from teaching men is based on the order of creation and is absolute in nature, why did Paul use the word *epitrepo* ("permit") which expresses the granting or withholding of a request and is never used of a commandment based on creation?[39] For example, Moses permitted (*epitrepo*) men to divorce their wives, due to the hardness of their hearts, but Jesus revoked the permission, basing his commandment on the original creation of man and woman (Mark 10.1-12). Also Paul wrote, "Now to the married *I command* [*paraggello*], *yet not I but the Lord*: A wife is not to depart from her husband." (1 Cor 7.10) As seen in 1 Corinthians 7, Paul distinguished between that which the Lord had commanded and that which he himself judged as a faithful steward (1 Cor 7.12, 25).

We find *epitrepo* also in 1 Corinthians 14.34-35. The verse connects the withholding of permission to a law, which shows *epitrepo* needs a corresponding commandment. First Corinthians 14 and 1 Timothy 2 are the only contexts where permission is withheld in the New Testament. 1 Corinthians 14.34-35 withholds permission for women to speak in the church, but a commandment which forbids female speech in a religious setting is not found in the Old Testament or the Gospels, which strengthens the likelihood of an interpolation.[40] In 1 Timothy 2, 1) either Paul is withholding permission as a response to a request, or 2) he is forbidding teaching temporarily, in the same sense as Moses permitted divorce. In the latter case, Paul would go against a commandment which allowed women to teach due to a temporary situation; in the former he would be affirming a commandment based on the creation.

Complementarists believe Paul is withholding permission for a woman

---

39. See Matthew 8.21, 31; 19.8; Mark 10.4; 5.13; Luke 8.32; 9.59, 61; Acts 21.39, 40; 26.1, 27.3, 28.16; 1 Corinthians 14.34; 16.7; 1 Timothy 2.12; Hebrews 6.3.

40. Even if we would affirm that women were created subject to the man, it could not be used to impose silence, for even though believers are subject to God, they are not forbidden from speech in His presence; in fact most churches actively encourage people to pray more. It is because speech, not the sword, gives people power in the church that women are silenced, just as the peasants and serfs were before the Reformation.

to teach a man based on the man's prior creation and the woman's assumed subjection to the man. The immediate problem with the view is that the man's prior creation is not used as a foundation to exclude women from teaching men in the Mosaic Law or the Gospels. For example, teachings concerning marriage are found abundantly in both the Old and the New Testament and the woman's creation from the man is always the foundation for the existence of marriage (Gen 2.23-25; Mal 2.14-15; Mark 10.5-12; Eph 5.30-31). In fact, teaching is *not* restricted to men in the gospels or the epistles.

> Whoever therefore breaks one of the least of these commandments, and teaches men (*anthropos*) so, shall be called least in the kingdom of heaven; but whoever does and teaches them, he shall be called great in the kingdom of heaven. (Matt 5.19-20)

> And Jesus came and spoke to them, saying, "All authority has been given to Me in heaven and on earth. Go therefore and make disciples of all the nations, baptizing them in the name of the Father and of the Son and of the Holy Spirit, teaching them to observe all things that I have commanded you; and lo, I am with you always, even to the end of the age." Amen. (Matt 28.18-20)

> Having then gifts differing according to the grace that is given to us, let us use them: if prophecy, let us prophesy in proportion to our faith; or ministry, let us use it in our ministering; he who teaches, in teaching; he who exhorts, in exhortation; he who gives, with liberality; he who leads, with diligence; he who shows mercy, with cheerfulness. (Rom 12.6-8)

> And the things that you have heard from me among many witnesses, commit these to faithful men (*anthropos*) who will be able to teach others also. (2 Tim 2.2)

> For though by this time you ought to be teachers, you need someone to teach you again the first principles of the oracles of God; and you have come to need milk and not solid food. (Heb 5.12)

Paul wrote to Timothy, "As I urged you when I went into Macedonia – remain in Ephesus that you may charge (*paraggello*) some (*tis*) that they teach no other doctrine" (1 Tim 1.3). Timothy was to charge also women to teach no other doctrine, for the word *tis* (some) is gender neutral.[41] Hence we find that 1 Timothy mirrors the problem found in 1 Corinthians: the teaching found in 1 Timothy 1.3 is gender neutral but 2.12 appears to restrict the activity to men, and in both chapters reference is made to both the creation and fall of mankind.

It is not without significance that Grudem must base the man's authority on an inference due to the conspicuous absence of a corresponding commandment.

> The fact that God first created Adam, then after a period of time created Eve (Gen 2.7, 18-23), *suggests* that God saw Adam as having a leadership role in his family.... The creation of Adam first is consistent with the Old Testament pattern of "primogeniture," the idea that the firstborn in any generation in a human family has leadership in the family for that generation. The right of primogeniture is assumed throughout the Old Testament text.[42]

The secular custom of primogeniture is applied only to boys, wherefore Grudem makes the inference that because Adam was male, he had the privileges of the firstborn. But this inference would make only Adam – not every man – the firstborn of the human family, for not every man is a firstborn. In fact, if it is argued that *every* firstborn is a leader, women cannot be excluded from leadership, since also females are among the firstborns, as is seen in England where, as a consequence, Queens have ruled the nation. But most importantly, it is *Jesus* who is the firstborn of the creation, of the dead, and the church (Col 1.15, 18; Heb 12.23). It is He who is the heir (Heb 1.2) with whom we will inherit the kingdom (Gal 4.7) for every believer becomes a co-heir with Christ and becomes part of the household of God, wherefore also Peter reminded the husbands to give honor to their wives as co-heirs (1 Pet 3.7). All believers have God as their Father, and as is true in the natural family, the younger siblings all share the same privileges and responsibilities. Thus primogeniture as an analogy is invalid.

---

41. In Revelation 2.20 John rebukes the Christians of Thyatira for they allowed a woman to teach and seduce the people to commit sexual immorality and eat things sacrificed to idols. The stress is not on the fact that she is a woman, but that she is leading people away from the truth.

42. *Systematic Theology*, 461.

~

Although we cannot say with absolute certainty what Paul referred to in 1 Tim 2.11-15, it is most likely connected to the Gnostic heresy which was being taught in Ephesus, and therefore his withholding of permission was directed to a woman who held absolute power over men and taught a Gnostic heresy which involved the Creation and Fall accounts. We do know that the Gnostics delighted in giving the creation and Fall accounts novel meanings in an effort to explain the existence of evil in the world. The God of the Old Testament was viewed as an angry and jealous God who wanted to keep humanity in perpetual slavery to Himself.

> The Testimony of Truth, for example, tells us the story of the Garden of Eden from the viewpoint of the serpent! Here the Serpent, long known to appear in gnostic literature as the principle of divine wisdom, convinces Adam and Eve to partake of knowledge while "the Lord" threatens them with death, trying jealously to prevent them from attaining knowledge, and expelling them from Paradise when they achieve it.[43]

The Serpent becomes the hero and humanity conquers God who can only expel them from the garden in his fury. The theme found in 1 Tim 2.11-15, the man's prior creation, is often reversed in Gnostic literature as seen in *The Reality of the Rulers* (third century A.D.).

> The rulers took counsel with one another and said, "Come, let us cause a deep sleep to Fall on Adam." And he slept. Now, the deep sleep that they caused to Fall on him, and he slept, is ignorance. They opened his side, which was like a living woman. And they built up his side with some flesh in place of her, and Adam came to be only with soul. The woman of spirit came to him and spoke with him, saying, "Rise, Adam." And when he saw her, he said, "It is you who have given me life. You will be called 'mother of the living.' For she is my mother. She is the physician, and the woman, and she was given birth.... Then the female spiritual presence came in the form of a snake, the instructor, and it taught them, saying, "What did he say

---

43. Elaine Pagels, The *Gnostic Gospels*, (New York: Vintage publishers, 1989), 17.

to you? Was it, 'From every tree in the garden you shall eat, but from the tree of recognizing evil and good do not eat?'... And the woman of flesh took from the tree and ate, and she gave to her husband as well as herself, and those beings, who possessed only a soul, ate. And their imperfection became apparent in their lack of knowledge.... They turned to their Adam and took him and expelled him from the garden along with his wife, for they have no blessing, since they too are under the curse.[44]

God is not viewed as the source of salvation; instead humanity must save itself through Gnostic knowledge, wherefore Paul wrote, "For this is good and acceptable in the sight of God our Savior, who desires all men to be saved and to come to the knowledge of the truth" (1 Tim 2.3-4).

Also the woman's deception is reversed in Gnostic literature for the tree of knowledge of good and evil represents salvation through knowledge.

They [the rulers] were troubled because Adam had sobered up from all ignorance. They gathered together and took counsel and said, "Look, Adam has become like one of us, so that he understands the difference between light and darkness. Now perhaps he will be deceived as with the tree of knowledge and will come to the tree of life and eat from it and become immortal and rule and condemn us and the world. Come, let's cast him out of paradise down to the earth, the place from where he was taken, so that he will no longer be able to know anything better than we can." And so they cast Adam and his wife out of Paradise.[45]

Although it has been suggested that women are easily deceived because of 1 Tim 2.14, Paul admitted to have been deceived by sin (Rom 7.11), and he was fearful that the Corinthians would be deceived by false teachers (2 Cor 11.3). Thankfully the image of the gullible woman is being rejected by the modern church, but historically the deception of Eve has barred women from teaching in the church. Thomas Aquinas considered the woman's punishment to be more grievous than the man's and therefore her sin was also more grievous.

---

44. Willis Barnston and Marvin Meyer, ed, "The Reality of the Rulers," *The Gnostic Bible* (Boston, MA: New Seeds, 2003), 170-172.

45. Barnston and Mayer, "*On the Origin of the World*," *The Gnostic Bible*, 433

He considered her to more puffed up than the man in as much as she believed through deception that she was able to attain God's likeness by eating of the forbidden fruit while the man wished to attain to God's likeness by his own power and because he had not yet experienced God's severity. Moreover, the woman suggested sin to the man and therefore sinned against God and her neighbor, but the man consented to the sin out of good-will.[46]

~

According to Knight, the masculine language in 1 Timothy 3 is the reason for the exclusion of women from leadership in the church.[47] Yet, the only phrase which is masculine is *mias guinakos andra* ("one woman man") found in verses 2 and 12. Knight writes that *aner* ("man") is used to distinguish men from women, which is correct, but because Greek is an androcentric language, *aner* functions also as a generic term and includes women, as seen in Romans 4.6-8.

> Just as David also describes the blessedness of the man [*anthropos*] to whom God imputes righteousness apart from works: "Blessed are those whose [*hos*, neut.] lawless deeds are forgiven, and whose [*hos*, neut.] sins are covered; Blessed is the man [*aner*] to whom the LORD shall not impute sin." (Rom 4.6-8)

In Psalm 32, which Paul quotes in Romans 4.6-8, the Hebrew word for "man" is *'adam*, which means "a human being." Similarly, in Matthew 19.5 the word for "man" is *anthropos*, although Genesis 2.24 uses *'yish*, the Hebrew

---

46. Summa Theologica, Second part of second part, Q 163, Article 4. Thomas quotes Augustine's *The City of God*, "[A]nd as it is not credible that Solomon was so blind as to suppose that idols should be worshipped, but was drawn over to such sacrilege by the blandishments of women; so we cannot believe that Adam was deceived, and supposed the devil's word to be truth, and therefore transgressed God's law, but that he by the drawings of kindred yielded to the woman, the husband to the wife, the one human being to the only other human being. For not without significance did the apostle say, "And Adam was not deceived, but the woman being deceived was in the transgression;" but he speaks thus, because the woman accepted as true what the serpent told her, but the man could not bear to be severed from his only companion, even though this involved a partnership in sin. He was not on this account less culpable, but sinned with his eyes open" (City of God, Book XIV, Ch. 11).

47. Piper and Grudem, 353.

equivalent of *aner*. D.A. Carson, one of the contributors to *Recovering Biblical Manhood and Womanhood,* acknowledges that "people considered generically are regularly found in the masculine gender in Greek."[48] James, for example, used *aner* often as a generic term when writing to all believers.[49]

The overwhelmingly masculine language of the Bible has caused unexpected problems in traditional theology, one of them being the denial of the resurrection of the female body.[50] Because the body of Christ is called a man (*aner*) in Ephesians 4.13, and because the saints are being conformed into the image of the Son of God (Rom 8.29), some early church theologians concluded that women will rise as men. Augustine denied this because the female is a nature, not a vice, and therefore part of the original Creation.[51] He corrected also those who believed *adelphos* ("brother") excluded women.[52]

In the Tenth Commandment, all of Israel was told not to covet their neighbor's wife (Exod 20.17); in 1 Corinthians 7.1-2 Paul writes that it is not good for a human (*anthropos*) to touch a woman and in 1 Corinthians 7.25-28 he again writes that is it good for a human (*anthropos*) to remain as he is: the one bound the a wife should not seek to be freed, and the one who is unmarried should not seek a wife. In all cases women are included, although the language is masculine. Because Greek is an androcentric language, it is not possible to exclude women from masculine language; it is only possible to exclude

---

48. Piper and Grudem, 148.

49. See James 1.7-8, 12; 19-20, 23-24; 2.1-2,; 3.1-2.

50. When a group is considered inferior, the only option for them is to be transformed into their superiors. We find this very clearly in racism, "If I were God, what would I do to improve the lot of the Negro? If I were God, I'd make everybody white." (Peggy Streit quotes a parent from Queens, New York, in "Why They Fight for the P.A.T." *New York Times Magazine*, September 20, 1964, quoted by James P. Comer, *Beyond Black and White*, 71) When the white people began their exodus from the Northern inner city as the black people moved in, it signaled to the black people "that the 'Christian' God was a white God and that he was unwilling and incapable of accepting black as equals, unless they first whiten their skins and their souls" (Salley & Behm, 47).

51. *The city of God*, Book XXII, Ch. 17.

52. "Quarrels should be unknown among you, or at least, if they arise, they should as quickly as possible be ended, lest anger grow into hatred, and convert "a mote into a beam,"and make the soul chargeable with murder. For the saying of Scripture: "He that hateth his brother is a murderer," does not concern men only, but women also are bound by this law through its being enjoined on the other sex, which was prior in the order of creation" (Augustine, Letter CCXI. 14).

men from feminine language. In 1 Timothy 5.9, the same phrase is found in the feminine (*henoos andros gunee*) because Paul is writing exclusively about women. In 1 Timothy 3.1-2, the office of bishop is open to anyone (*ei-tis*), and therefore the masculine gender is necessary, and does not exclude women.

Ei-tis is used 62 times in the New Testament and it is never used in a gender exclusive manner.[53] It has been suggested that *mias guinakos andra* is equivalent of monogamy, but it is a false assumption, for *monogamos* is a Greek term (*monos* "single" and *gamos* "marriage") and both Greece and Rome were monogamous societies wherefore Paul did not have to forbid polygamy. But he did have to exhort both men and women to remain faithful to their spouses, wherefore the one who wished to become an overseer had to have a disposition of faithfulness. Considering that, at least, Paul and John were unmarried, and because Paul wished all to be as he was, i.e., celibate (1 Cor 7.7), it is unlikely that marriage was a requirement. Therefore it is better to understand *mias guinakos andra* as "faithful."

---

53. In 1 Cor 7.12-13 *ei-tis* is connected to *adelphos* ("brother"), and in the context the gender distinction is clear for the next sentence speaks of women. But also *adelphos* is used as a generic term for all believers, in the same manner as *aner* is used as a generic term of all humans, (See 1 Cor 10.1; Gal 1.11; 1 Thess 1.4; etc.). In James 5.19, James uses the modified form *ean tis*, when he writes, "Brethren (*adelphos*), if *anyone* among you wanders from the truth." Also women are included in *adelphos* and therefore neither *adelphos* or *ean tis* creates a gender distinction.

CHAPTER 11

1 Cor 12.26-31

When, however, they are confuted from the Scriptures, they turn round and accuse these same Scriptures, as if they were not correct, nor of authority, and [assert] that they are ambiguous, and that the truth cannot be extracted from them by those who are ignorant of tradition. For [they allege] that the truth was not delivered by means of written documents, but *vivâ voce:* wherefore also Paul declared, "But we speak wisdom among those that are perfect, but not the wisdom of this world." . . . But, again, when we refer them to that tradition which originates from the apostles, [and] which is preserved by means of the succession of presbyters in the Churches, they object to tradition, saying that they themselves are wiser not merely than the presbyters, but even than the apostles, because they have discovered the unadulterated truth. . . . It comes to this, therefore, that these men do now consent neither to Scripture nor to tradition.

– Irenaeus[1]

WEINRICH CLAIMS IN his essay *Women in the History of the Church* that the "utter paucity of instances adduced where women were given or took the function of public preaching and teaching confirms" that only men ought to be leaders in the church.[2] But if women were excluded from leadership in the patristic era, how much evidence of their previous existence in the clergy would be left for posterity to read?[3]

---

1. *Against Heresies*, Book III, Ch. II, 1-2.
2. Piper and Grudem, 279.
3. In 1988 the Soviet Union cancelled all history examinations due to the honest admission that their national heritage had been engulfed by the official lies and secrets of the

Until the Nag Hammadi library was found in upper Egypt in 1945,[4] the only source of information about Gnosticism were the scanty remarks found in the writings in the early Christian writers. Tobias Churton describes why the condemned material had to be hid in the middle of the fourth century.

> Athanasius we know was in hiding among the monks of Upper Egypt in AD 356 during a temporary 'turn-about' in his episcopal career. It was perhaps his observation while hiding there that furnished him with a view that 'some few of the simple should be beguiled from their simplicity and purity, but the subtlety of certain men, and should afterwards read other books – those called apocryphal.' Now, if these texts were buried in response to a heresy 'clearout' at the time of broadcasting of the letter, then it was almost certainly the work of monks, in particular those monks who had most to lose from being associated with the condemned literature. If condemned heretics, such people would suffer excommunication and the accompanying divorce from Christ's interests. Furthermore, the books would, according to practice be burned. We are observing a stiffening in the regime governing the Coptic (that is, Egyptian) Church.... As we shall see, the books buried in the middle of the fourth century would not fit in with the Creed. They had to go.[5]

Although the extant literary evidence of women in leadership is scanty, we do not need to rely solely on written testimonies, for some of the extant evidence of female leadership in the church is found in tombstones and buildings, which are not as easily destroyed as burnable books.

Ute E. Eisen describes two inscriptions within the mosaics of the chapel of St. Zeno which mention *episcopa* Theodora, the mother of Pope Paschal I (817-824). Her husband, Bonosus, did not possess a sacerdotal title and therefore *episcopa* does not refer to a bishop's wife. Theodora is depicted with a rectangular halo, which was used for persons of high rank, such as bishops; saints were depicted with round halos. Over the halo, the word *episcopa* is inscribed.

---

past (Taylor Branch, *Parting the Waters* [New York: Simon and Schuster Paperbacks, 1988, Preface).

4. The Gnosis Archive, www.gnosis.org (accessed June 29, 2009).

5. Tobias Churton, *The Gnostics* (New York: Barnes and Nobles Books, 1987), 8.

The attempts to interpret the mosaic have created an array of suggestions. Some have made it an honorary title for the mother of the pope, who was seen as taking the position of a wife by her son's side. Others have made her into an abbess, although an abbess was never called *episcopa,* the title 'abbess' being well known. And yet others have tried to claim an interpolation, which is farfetched since the inscription is found twice, in different locations. No one has suggested that Theodora could have been a bishop, for women just are not supposed to be bishops in the church; instead the title *episcopa* is frequently omitted in the verbal reproductions of the inscription.[6]

Kevin Madigan and Carolyn Osiek describe an inscription in mosaic in the Basilica of St. Augustine in Hippo, North-Africa, after the era of Vandal occupation which began in 431. The inscription reads, "Guilia Runa the prebyteress (*presbiterissa*), rest in peace, lived for fifty years."[7] And John Wijngaards describes a tombstone from Delphi, Greece, of a woman deacon which states, "The most devout deaconess Athanasia, established deaconess by his holiness Bishop Pantamianos after she lived a blameless life. He erected this tomb on the place where her honored [body?] lies."[8]

Yet, the most undeniable evidence of women in ecclesiastical leadership is found in the Bible. Because the women leaders found in the Bible challenge the dogma of the woman's subordination, the women in question have either been ignored – or transformed into men. Junia, for example, has become a controversial biblical figure because Paul calls her an apostle (Rom 16.7). A footnote by the editors of the Early Church Writer's collection provides us a vivid picture of how scholars have dealt with Junia's identity.

> The more probable view is that Andronicus and Junias [not Junia as Chrys., certainly not if his interpretation is correct; *that a woman should have been an apostle is out of the question*] are designated as distinguished, honorably known among (by) the apostles. (So De Wette, Philippi, Holmann, Meyer).[9]

---

6. Eisen, 200-204.

7. Kevin Madigan and Carolyn Osiek, *Ordained Women in the Early Church* (Baltimore, MD: The Johns Hopkins University Press, 2005), 197.

8. Wijngaards, 133.

9. Chrysostom, *Homilies on Romans*, Homily XXXI, Verse 7, Footnote 13.

Schreiner is candid in his essay *The Ministries of Women in the Context of Male Leadership* about the problem Junia's identity poses for complementarist theology.

> Of course, if Junias was a woman apostle (Romans 16.7), then a tension is created between the apostleship of Junias (If Junias was a woman) and the other arguments adduced in the chapter, for apostles were certainly the most authoritative messengers of God in the New Testament.[10]

He concludes that the passage is unclear and therefore no decisive decision can be made based on the information given in the Bible. Schreiner is not alone in his indecision for also Grudem writes that we cannot know if Junia was a woman because "the evidence is indecisive," and therefore we cannot be dogmatic about the name.[11] Although both Grudem and Schreiner wish to ignore Romans 16.7,[12] Grudem does not consider it sound hermeneutic, "If someone says, 'I am not going to base my decision on these verses because nobody can figure out what they mean anyway,' then he has essentially said that those passages cannot play a role in his decision about this question."[13] Grudem must remain indecisive, despite his own advice, for if he claims that the name is 'Junias,' he must provide proof, which he cannot, for according to Eldon Jay Epp, "After all, the masculine Junias was asserted (I would say invented) when no evidence for such a masculine name could be found, a circumstance still unchanged."[14] On the other hand, if he admits Junia was

---

10. Piper and Grudem, 221.

11. Ibid., 79.

12. Knight writes that according to a hermeneutical principle, the section which deals with the technical terms must be resolved first, after which a historical statement, the actual lives of real people, can be evaluated. This is a true principle, but if the lives of real people continuously conflict with the resolution, one must examine the resolution itself, for it is not possible that the real lives of the people found in the Bible are entirely out of harmony with biblical truths, unless used as a negative example. The Bible mentions women in various leadership roles: Miriam (leader), Deborah (judge), Huldah (prophet), Phoebe (deacon), Priscilla (co-worker) and Junia (apostle). These women have either been ignored or the legitimacy of the leadership has been questioned by complementarists due to their commitment to the twofold subjection of Thomas Aquinas (Piper and Grudem, 354).

13. Wayne Grudem, *Evangelical Feminism* (Wheaton, IL: Crossway, 2006), 89.

14. Eldon Jay Epp, *Junia, The First Woman Apostle* (Minneapolis, MN: Fortress Press, 2005), 27.

a woman, he must explain how she could have been a bishop for he quotes Epiphanius, "Iounias, of whom [hou] Paul makes mention, became bishop of Apameia of Syria."[15] Epiphanius used the masculine relative pronoun (*hou*), but in the endnotes Grudem admits that he is perplexed that Epiphanius designates also Priscilla as a man.[16]

Grudem quotes also Rufinus's Latin translation of Origen's commentary on Romans which has "Andronicus et Junias," a Latin masculine, singular nominative. However, Epp cites Caroline Hammond Bammel's critical edition on Origen which explains that *Iunias* ("Junias") is a variant reading from a twelfth-century manuscript subgroup E, which also includes *Iulia* ("Julia") as a variant.[17] Earlier manuscripts from the ninth century all have *Iunia* ("Junia"). In addition, Hraban of Fulda (780-856) cited Rufinus's translation of Origen literally and the name we find in his text is Junia.

Both the King James Version and New King James Version have Junia, as does Erasmus's New Testament (1516).[18] The Greek manuscripts all have Junia, except for five that have the variant Julia. In addition, some manuscripts have Junia in Romans 16.15 (where the name Julia appears), a variant which can be explained only if both of the names were feminine. Because of these variants, even Julia has become a male name in the hands of translators and commentators. Aegidius (1243/47-1316) is usually considered the first one to call Junia – and Julia – a man.[19] However, by far the greatest influence over the identity of Junia has been Luther who brought the male Junias to the masses through his German translation of the New Testament (1522) and his *Lectures on Romans*.[20]

That Junia was a woman is thus established, but was she was an apostle? Grudem attempts to make Andronicus and Junia "messengers" in the broad sense and he provides two examples: 1 Corinthians 8.23 and Philippians 2.25-6. But his case is weakened by the fact that the "brother" mentioned in 2 Corinthians 8.23 was chosen by the churches to join Titus as he traveled

---

15. Piper and Grudem, 79.
16. Ibid., Footnote 19, 479.
17. Epp, 33-34.
18. Ibid., 28.
19. Ibid., 35.
20. Ibid., 38.

to Corinth to prepare the offering gathered by the Corinthians. Andronicus and Junia were in Rome and no mention is made of them traveling as representatives of the Roman church, or any other church, to distribute offerings gathered. Similarly, Epaphroditus was sent to Paul by the Philippian church to bring him their gift and to care for him in prison (Phil. 2.25-26). Paul mentions that Andronicus and Junia were "in Christ" before him, making it very possible that they had seen the risen Christ, which was one of the qualifications for apostleship.

Epiphanius writes that Junia whom Paul mentions became a bishop of Apameia, which further strengthens the case that Junia was an apostle, for the offices of an apostle and bishop were identical in the Early Church (1 Pet 5.1; 2 John 1): "But deacons ought to remember that the Lord chose apostles, that is, bishops and overseers; while apostles appointed for themselves deacons after the ascent of the Lord into heaven, as ministers of their episcopacy and of the Church."[21]

An early witness to Junia's identity is Chrysostom who did not only call Junia a woman –he also thought she was an apostle *par excellence*.

> "Salute Andronicus and Junia my kinsmen."... Then another praise besides. "Who are of note among the Apostles." And indeed to be apostles at all is a great thing. But to be even amongst these of note, just consider what a great encomium this is! But they were of note owing to their works, to their achievements. Oh! how great is the devotion (φιλοσοφια) of this woman, that she should be even counted worthy of the appellation of apostle! But even here he does not stop, but adds another encomium besides, and says, "Who were also in Christ before me."[22]

Yet, for some Junia cannot be an apostle and a woman at the same, regardless of the evidence for "if the phrase means 'distinguished apostles,' 'Iouninan is a man... On the other hand, if the name is female, the phrase means 'of note in the eyes of the apostles.'"[23] Grudem does not dare to call Junia a man for the lack of evidence, but neither is he willing to call her a woman and give

---

21. Cyprian, "Epistle LXIV," *Epistles of Cyprian*, 3.
22. *Homilies on Romans,* Homily XXXI.
23. Piper and Grudem, *72.*

legitimacy to the existence of a female apostle and bishop. In a last effort to support his indecision, he writes that Junia was not a common woman's name in the Greek-speaking world,[24] which is true since it was a Latin name.[25]

~

Thomas R. Schreiner recognizes in his essay *The Valuable Ministries of Women in the context of Male Leadership* that female prophets existed both in Israel and the church, but in order to avoid the logical conclusion that also women were leaders, he writes, "It is instructive to note in the Old Testament that some women were prophets, but never priests." He adds that the priests had the "more settled and established positions of leadership in Israel," for they were the teachers of the Law.

The Levitical priesthood was based on Israel's Exodus from Egypt.

> "In days to come, when your son asks you, 'What does this mean?' say to him, 'With a mighty hand the LORD brought us out of Egypt, out of the land of slavery. When Pharaoh stubbornly refused to let us go, the LORD killed every firstborn in Egypt, both man and animal. This is why I sacrifice to the LORD the first male offspring of every womb and redeem each of my firstborn sons.' And it will be like a sign on your hand and a symbol on your forehead that the LORD brought us out of Egypt with his mighty hand." (Exod 13.14-16)

The Pharaoh had planned to kill all the firstborn male Israelites (Exod 1.16), but instead God destroyed the firstborn male Egyptians to free Israel from Egypt, wherefore every firstborn in Israel belonged to God. Instead of sacrificing their firstborn sons, the pagan practice which the prophets fought for centuries to eradicate, the Israelites were to redeem them with a male Levite (Num 3.5-16). God chose Aaron and his sons to serve as His priests from the Levites who functioned as a perpetual reminder of God's redeeming power as they worked in the Sanctuary.

---

24. Ibid., 80.

25. Roman women were given their father's name in the feminine form, thus Julius became Julia, Junius became Junia, Claudius became Claudia, Dianus became Diana etc. (*Pomeroy*, 165).

> They are the Israelites who are to be given wholly to me. I have taken them as my own in place of the firstborn, the first male offspring from every Israelite woman. Every firstborn male in Israel, whether man or animal, is mine. When I struck down all the firstborn in Egypt, I set them apart for myself. And I have taken the Levites in place of all the firstborn sons in Israel. Of all the Israelites, I have given the Levites as gifts to Aaron and his sons to do the work at the Tent of Meeting on behalf of the Israelites and to make atonement for them so that no plague will strike the Israelites when they go near the sanctuary." (Num 8.16-19)

The New Covenant episcopacy cannot be compared to the Levitical priesthood for the Old Covenant priesthood was based on ancestry, while the New Covenant one is based on the "power of endless life" (Heb 7.16). With Christ, a new priesthood was instituted; one that is in the order of Melchizedek and in which the High Priest will never die (Heb 7.11-25). In the Levitical Priesthood, the High Priest offered a sacrifice once a year in the holy of holies and interceded for himself and the people, but in the new priesthood the High Priest sacrificed Himself once and took away sin and thus provided eternal redemption (Heb 9.25-26). There is no longer a need for further sacrifice, but our High Priest continues to intercede on our behalf, for having been tempted himself, he is able to help us (Heb 2.17-18; 7.25). All Christians are priests in the New Covenant (1 Pet 2.5) wherefore the Levitical priesthood cannot be used to exclude women from ecclesiastical leadership in the church.

Because Schreiner must acknowledge that the prophets were the ones who spoke the word of the Lord and "what they said was absolutely authoritative – no part of it could be questioned or challenged,"[26] he has to make the women prophets "different" and therefore without authority.

> I am not suggesting that the Lord did not raise her [Deborah] up, for He did bring evident blessing to Israel through her, but it may indicate that the nature of her role as a prophet and a judge was different from that of the other judges in that she did not exercise leadership over men as the other judges did.[27]

---

26. Piper and Grudem, 217.
27. Ibid., 216.

Deborah is not to only judge who is not explicitly said to have been raised by God (e.g., Judg 3.31; 10.1-2; 12.8-15). "To raise up" (*quwm*) appears to have been a term used when decisive action was needed, such as when an enemy had to be confronted (e.g. Ps 3.7; 1 Kings 14.14). The judges God raised created peace and maintained it throughout their lives.

> Then the LORD raised [quwm] up judges, who saved them out of the hands of these raiders. Yet they would not listen to their judges but prostituted themselves to other gods and worshiped them. Unlike their fathers, they quickly turned from the way in which their fathers had walked, the way of obedience to the LORD's commands. Whenever the LORD raised up a judge for them, he was with the judge and saved them out of the hands of their enemies as long as the judge lived; for the LORD had compassion on them as they groaned under those who oppressed and afflicted them. (Judg 2.16-18)

Deborah was not an exception, "On that day God subdued Jabin, the Canaanite king, before the Israelites. And the hand of the Israelites grew stronger and stronger against Jabin, the Canaanite king, until they destroyed him... Then the land had peace forty years" (Judg 4.23-24; 5.31, NIV). Although the Bible does not mention that Deborah was specifically raised by God, she rose up when Israel needed a judge, just as other judges had before her, which naturally indicates that God "raised" her, "Village life in Israel ceased, ceased until I, Deborah, arose [*quwm*], arose a mother in Israel" (Judg 5.7).

On the Council for Biblical Manhood and Womanhood's Web site, Barbara K. Mouser writes:

> She was the wife of Lappidoth. No details are given about Deborah's husband or marriage. However, the fact that she is identified as a wife (4.4) and later identifies herself as a mother (5.7) who ministers from a particular place (4.5) warrants the understanding that Deborah's ministry did not negate her responsibilities at home.[28]

---

28. Barbara K. Mouser, "The Womanliness of Deborah: Complementarian Principles from Judges 4-5," Council of Biblical Manhood and Womanhood, www.cbmw.com (accessed June 29, 2009).

Mouser adds that Deborah could be describing herself as a mother of the entire nation, but that it would describe her "motivation, not as a judge or even as a prophetess, but rather as a mother, one concerned for the life and well-being of God's children." Also Schreiner attempts to transform Deborah into a modern homemaker, for he denies she prophesied in public. According to Schreiner, her role was limited to private and individual instruction for she sat under a palm tree.[29] The writers of the *Jamieson, Fausset, and Brown Commentary* disagree.

> She dwelt under the palm tree-or, collectively, a palm grove. Stanley ('Sinai and Palestine,' p. 145) takes it to have been 'a well-known and solitary landmark,' and from the distinct specification of the locality, 'probably the same spot as that called Baal-tamar' (Judg 20.33), the 'sanctuary of the palm.' *It is common in the present day in the East to administer justice in the open air, or under the canopy of an umbrageous tree.* The traditionary [sic] spot which Deborah frequented is still pointed out; and it is remarkable that a great meeting or fair is statedly [sic] held at the place, as it has been uninterruptedly since her time, at which, among other matters of business, disputes are settled and quarrels adjusted between rival tribes.[30]

All of Israel came to Deborah (Judg 4.5), for it was a common practice that people gathered under a tree, which afforded shade in an era in which large houses were practically nonexistent (Judg 9.6).

Rabbi Joseph Telushkin explains in *Biblical Literacy* that Deborah was "far more than a local magistrate,"[31] for as she summons Barak, "the foremost Israelite soldier of the age, he comes immediately," and acts according to her words. Mouser sees Deborah's summoning of Barak as proof that "war is the work of men" for it is not "normative, desirable, or glorious for women to go to battle with men." Accordingly she concludes that Deborah could not have been a judge due to her mistaken belief that all judges were warriors.

---

29. Piper and Grudem, 216.
30. "Judges 4.5," *Jamieson, Fausset, and Brown Commentary*.
31. Rabbi Joseph Telushkin, *Biblical Literacy* (New York: Morrow, 1997), 167.

Also Schreiner attempts to dismiss Deborah as an example of a woman in leadership in the Bible by pointing out that she was not a warrior-judge.

> The only passage that creates any difficulty… is Judges 4, where Deborah commands Barak what to do and is a judge in Israel. But there are several reasons why this is in harmony with the notion of male headship explained in 1 Corinthians 11.2-16: Deborah is a special case because she seems to the only judge in Judges who has no military function. The other judges also lead Israel into victory in battle, but Deborah receives a word from the Lord that Barak is to do this (Judges 4.6-7). Deborah is not asserting leadership for herself; she gives priority to a man. [32]

However, similarly to Moses, Deborah was a prophet-judge (Exod 18.14-15) and as Deborah sent Barak, Moses sent Joshua to fight the battle (Exod 17.9). Neither did Samuel, who was the last prophet-judge to rule over Israel, fight himself; he sent the men of Israel to the war. Whereas Mouser tries to make Deborah's ministry "home-based," and therefore feminine, Samuel is the true "home-based" judge, for although Samuel traveled in a circuit between Bethel, Gilgal and Mizpah, he always returned to Ramah, "for his home was there," and "there he judged Israel." (1 Sam 7.2-17)

In the footnotes, Schreiner makes a final attempt to assert that Deborah could not have ruled over men for in Isaiah 3.12 women ruling over men is a sign of God's judgment. [33] But what does Isaiah 3 actually say? Isaiah is predicting the destruction of Jerusalem and Judah by Babylon. Verse 12 speaks of the time *after* the judgment; it is not the *reason* for the judgment. As a result of the persistent sinning of the people, God was about to remove the warriors, the judges, prophets, and elders from Jerusalem, and the only ones left would be a few men, the women, and children. The young people would oppress the elderly; there would be such a lack of men that they would attempt to make anyone left a leader. Adam Clarke provides an alternative interpretation of Isaiah 3.12, which is a distinct possibility since ancient Hebrew did not have vowels, "This verse might be read, "The collectors of grapes shall be

---

32. Piper and Grudem, 216.
33. Ibid., Footnote 5, 504.

their oppressors; and usurers (*noshim*, instead of *nashim*, women) shall rule over them."

Mouser perpetuates also the argument that Israel did what was right in their own eyes during the era of the judges wherefore Deborah cannot be used as an example of women in leadership.

> Those who seek to extrapolate doctrine or practice from Deborah need to remember that Judges 4-5 is the historical report of a very rare circumstance in a far-from-ideal setting. These chapters are given for our edification, but should not be seen as precedents or used to overturn clear commands of Scripture.

Once again we find that if we use the same criterion to evaluate the legitimacy of Moses' role as judge, we would have to dismiss his role as a judge as an illegitimate example.

> You shall not at all do as we are doing here today – *every man doing whatever is right in his own eyes* – for as yet you have not come to the rest and the inheritance which the LORD your God is giving you. (Deut 12.8)

The judges were raised *because* people did what was right in their own eyes. The cycle found in the book of Judges is that of sin – oppression – deliverance, but it was not exclusively a post-Exodus problem; rather it has been the cycle of human life since the entrance of sin, experienced on the personal level, as well as on a larger scale. The judges were also an inherent part of the theocracy of Israel, an office instituted by Moses in the wilderness to settle disputes in accordance with the Law (Exod 18.13-27). An Israelite who did not listen to a judge was executed (Deut 17.12-13), wherefore it is not possible that a judge could function without divine authority.

Mouser believes also that Hebrews 11.32-34 is "the clearest statements that Barak, not Deborah, is the judge." If this is the case we should also conclude that Rahab was the hero in conquering of Jericho since she, not Joshua, is mentioned in Hebrews 11.30-31. On the contrary, the Bible explicitly states that Deborah was a judge, for why do we find her in the book of Judges if she was not one? In addition she was a prophet and God's spokesperson. The Law clearly states that when a prophet is false and does not speak for God, the event will not come to pass (Deut 18.21-22). Is it believable that a prophet could set herself up as a judge without God's approval, settle disputes and teach the law without the proper authority, and still function as a prophet?

Finally, Mouser perpetuates the myth that egalitarian women want to replace men for had Deborah been egalitarian, "her goal would have been to take Barak's job, not exhort him to do it." Mouser's view is based on the erroneous belief that women are continuously attempting to conquer men and become their rulers. The belief that a woman rejects God's will if she does not hand over all power to men is an ingenious way to keep women from challenging male rule in the home and church. But it is not unbiblical to challenge an illegitimate rule and Gregory of Nyssa offers a compelling reason why it occurs.

> That were like a usurpation, viz. not to assign the command to a superiority of Being, but to divide a creation that retains by right of nature equal privileges into slaves and a ruling power, one part in command, the other in subjection; as if, as the result of an arbitrary distribution, these same privileges had been piled at random on one who after that distribution got preferred to his equals. Even man did not share his honour with the brutes, before he received his dominion over them; his prerogative of reason gave him the title to command; he was set over them, because of a variance of his nature in the direction of superiority. And human governments experience such quickly-repeated revolutions for this very reason, that it is impracticable that those to whom nature has given equal rights should be excluded from power, but her impulse is instinct in all to make themselves equal with the dominant party, when all are of the same blood.[34]

The similarity between Islam's exclusion of women from leadership and the complementarist denial of Deborah's legitimate role as a judge is striking. Just as one verse (1 Tim 2.12) seemingly denies authority from women in Christianity, one *Hadith* ("tradition") excludes women from leadership in Islam, "Those who entrust their affairs to women will never know prosperity."[35] Fatima Mernissi explains how "this *Hadith* is the sledgehammer argument used by

---

34. *Against Eunomius,* Book I, Ch. 35.
35. Mernissi, 1

those who want to exclude women from politics."[36] She quotes Muhammad 'Arafa's *The Rights of Women in Islam* in which he claims that women have never participated alongside men in public affairs. Because 'A'isha, the Prophet's wife, led military battles in the early decades of the faith, 'Arafa dismisses her by stating, "[T]his individual act of a woman companion cannot be claimed [to legitimate the participation of women in political affairs], given that the voice of Allah and his prophet is clear on this point."[37] Thomas Aquinas quoted 1 Timothy 2.11 in order to deny women spiritual jurisdiction, and he added Aristotle's opinion "that it is a corruption of public life when the government comes into the hands of a woman."[38] Could Islam, Christianity and Greek philosophy truly be in such agreement on the subject unless the exclusion of women from leadership was based on an external system of belief?

Another similarity is found in Al-Afghani's conviction that had 'A'isha not spearheaded the military activities the Muslim world would have been one of peace and prosperity, instead of being divided into the *Sunnis* and *Shi'ites*. Mernissi writes that according to Al-Afghani, "Allah wanted to use the experience of 'A'isha to teach Muslims a lesson" – that women were created for procreation and homemaking, not public affairs.[39] 'A'isha is a Muslim Eve, Deborah and Sarah all in one for had Eve not taken the fruit there would never have been sin; had Sarah not given Hagar to Abraham the Jews and Arabs would never have hated each other, and Deborah should have had enough sense to stay home instead of judging Israel under a palm tree.

~

James A. Borland, in his essay *Women in the Life and teachings of Jesus*, uses Jesus' choice of apostles as a foundation for his exclusion of women from leadership.

> Christ promised that the apostles would sit on twelve thrones ruling the twelve tribes of Israel (Matthew 19.28; Luke 22.30). Christ promised the apostles reception of special revelation (John 16.13-15)

---

36. Ibid., 4.
37. Ibid., 5.
38. *Summa Theologica*, Supplement, Question 19, Article 3, Rep 4.
39. Mernissi, 7.

and a special teaching ministry of the Holy Spirit (John 14.26). As a testimony of the fact that male leadership in the church has been permanently established by Christ, the names of the twelve apostles are forever inscribed on the very foundations of heaven itself. "Now the wall of the city had twelve foundations, and on them were the names of the twelve apostles of the Lamb" (Revelation 21.14, NKJV)... No woman in Christ's ministry was called, commissioned, or named an apostle, or even performed in the role of an apostle. These roles and functions Christ reserved for men.[40]

But as with Schreiner, his entire argument falls apart if even one woman is found to have been an apostle, wherefore there has been such an effort to transform Junia into a man.

Jesus did not establish an all male leadership because his closest disciples were men. The Twelve were all male because they were the New Covenant counterpart to the twelve tribes of the Old Covenant, just as the seventy disciples Jesus sent were the counterpart to the seventy Moses chose (Luke 10.1-4; Num 11.16-25). Barnabas (A.D. 100) wrote, "To these He gave authority to preach the Gospel, being twelve in number, corresponding to the twelve tribes of Israel."[41] Also Irenaeus (A.D. 180) wrote, "In a foreign country were the twelve tribes born, the race of Israel, inasmuch as Christ was also, in a strange country, to generate the twelve-pillared foundation of the Church."[42]

There is no indication in the theology of the first three centuries that the Twelve Apostles held any other significance than that of corresponding to the twelve tribes of Israel. A text which comes close to Borland's theology is found in the fourth century work *Constitutions of the Holy Apostles*.

> We do not permit our "women to teach in the Church," but only to pray and hear those that teach; for our Master and Lord, Jesus

---

40. Piper and Grudem, 121.

41. *The Epistle of Barnabas*, Chapter VIII.

42. *Against Heresies*, Book IV, XXI. The same is also found in Revelation, "Also she had a great and high wall with twelve gates, and twelve angels at the gates, and names written on them, which are the names of the twelve tribes of the children of Israel: three gates on the east, three gates on the north, three gates on the south, and three gates on the west. Now the wall of the city had twelve foundations, and on them were the names of the twelve apostles of the Lamb" (Rev 21.12-14).

Himself, when He sent us the twelve to make disciples of the people and of the nations, did nowhere send out women to preach, although He did not want such. For there were with us the mother of our Lord and His sisters; also Mary Magdalene, and Mary the mother of James, and Martha and Mary the sisters of Lazarus; Salome, and certain others. For, had it been necessary for women to teach, He Himself had first commanded these also to instruct the people with us. For "if the head of the wife be the man," it is not reasonable that the rest of the body should govern the head.[43]

The work claims to have been written by the apostles themselves to create the illusion of having apostolic authority, but it was written in an era of theological controversy and increased intolerance within the church. Women were already being actively excluded from leadership by the councils and the novel use of the Twelve as a justification for excluding women became a permanent part of traditional theology.

The tribes may have received their beginning and names from the sons of Jacob, but it did not exclude women from being in the leadership in Israel, as shown by the examples of Miriam, Deborah and Huldah, for Israel as a nation included both men and women. Similarly, although the Twelve were the foundation of the church, the church includes both men and women, and as in Israel, women are also found in the leadership of the church. Tribal identity, which was important in the pre-Christ Israel, has become superfluous in Christianity;[44] clergy is no longer hereditary, nor is the inheritance divided, for it is God who places each member in the Body according to the His good pleasure and the gifting of the Holy Spirit determines one's role in the church – not one's gender, race or class.[45]

A belief related to the conclusion that only men should be in leadership

---

43. *Constitutions of the Holy Apostles,* Book III. VI.

44. The twelve tribes had to remain distinct until the time of Christ, for had the tribes dissolved, the identity of the Messiah would have been impossible to determine. Tribal identity was preserved through inheritance; women could freely exchange tribes as they married, unless they had inherited their father's property (Num 27.8-11).

45. Evangelism is not restricted to women because Mary was the first one to bring the message of the resurrected Savior; instead Borland writes, "The important point is that God did use women along with men at this strategic juncture in human history." He adds that "the duty and high privilege of witnessing for Christ is still open to every believer, without distinction as to gender" (Piper and Grudem, 120). Why is the proclaiming of the Gospel

because the Twelve were all men, is that God is male and therefore only men can represent God on Earth. In Catholicism the priesthood is reserved for men because it is traced back to the Last Supper during which Jesus is believed to have entrusted the Eucharist, and the priesthood, to the twelve disciples, Peter being the chief of the Twelve. Only the priest can confer eternal life through the sacraments of the church. Protestantism does not fall far behind in allowing only men to baptize and confirm the new birth which has occurred within.

The representation of God is not reserved only to men, for as Gregory of Nazianzen pointed out, the designation "Father" does not make God male, for gender belongs to our world, not the eternal Godhead.

> For it does not follow that because the Son is the Son in some higher relation (inasmuch as we could not in any other way than this point out that He is of God and Consubstantial), it would also be necessary to think that all the names of this lower world and of our kindred should be transferred to the Godhead. Or maybe you would consider our God to be a male, according to the same arguments, because he is called God and Father, and that Deity is feminine, from the gender of the word, and Spirit neuter, because It has nothing to do with generation.[46]

Also Arnobius affirmed that although God's name is masculine, He does not have a gender, for He is a Spirit.

> And yet, that no thoughtless person may raise a false accusation against us, as though we believed God whom we worship to be male, – for this reason, that is, that when we speak of Him we use a masculine word, – *let him understand that it is not sex which is expressed, but His name, and its meaning according to custom, and the way in which we are in the habit of using words.* For the Deity is not male, but His name is of the masculine gender: but in your ceremonies you cannot say the same; for in your prayers you have been wont to say *whether*

gender neutral although a woman was the first evangelist, but the teaching of the Gospel is restricted to the male portion of the church because the first apostles were all men?

46. Gregory of Nazianzen, "*Oration XXXII, The Fifth Theological Oration, On the Holy Spirit,*" *Orations.*

thou art god or goddess, and this uncertain description shows, even by their opposition, that you attribute sex to the gods. We cannot, then, be prevailed on to believe that the divine is embodied; for bodies must needs be distinguished by difference of sex, if they are male and female. For who, however mean his capacity, does not know that the sexes of different gender have been ordained and formed by the Creator of the creatures of earth, only that, by intercourse and union of bodies, that which is fleeting and transient may endure being ever renewed and maintained?[47]

The Christian God has been depicted as a white male for centuries, for Christian theologians have traditionally been white European males who have defined God in their own image – a persistent human habit as described by Jennifer Michael Hecht in her book *Doubt, a History*.

In the light of knowledge of other cultures, Xenophanes began to feel that the idea of these gods was sort of silly, not just because they acted childishly, but also because they were so very Greek, so much created in the image of Hellenistic society. With this critique, Xenophanes began the great tradition of trying to imagine where the idea of gods came from, famously claiming that if oxen and horses and lions could paint, they would depict the gods as black and flat-nosed, while the Tharicans picture them with blue eyes and red hair.[48]

∽

Schreiner, who did not believe Deborah was a legitimate judge, does not believe that the term "laborers" signifies that women were leaders in the early church.

The terms fellow-worker and laborer are vague. There are many ways that women could have been fellow-workers and laborers without holding leadership positions over men. The clear teaching of Paul elsewhere (1 Cor 11.2-16; 14.33b-36, 1 Timothy 2.11-15) must be the

---

47. Arnobius, *Adversus Gentes*, Book III, 8.
48. Jennifer Michael Hecht, *Doubt, a History, The great Doubters and Their Legacy of Innovation from Socrates and Jesus to Thomas Jefferson and Emily Dickison* (San Francisco, CA: Harper, 2003), 7.

guide for understanding the role rather than the appeal to terms that are too vague to support the idea of women sharing full leadership with men.[49]

Exactly how vague are these terms? Paul called the following persons his fellow-workers (*synergos*): Timothy (Rom 16.21), Titus (2 Cor 8.23), Priscilla and Aquila (Rom 16.3), Urbanus (Rom 16.9), Apollos (1 Cor 3.6-9) Epaphroditus (Phil 2.25), Euodia, Syntyche, and Clement (Phil 4.1-3), Aristarchus, Marcus, and Jesus, which is called Justus (Col 4.10-11), Philemon (Philem 1), Mark, Aristarchus, Demas, and Luke (Philem 24).

Paul used laborer (*kopiao*) to describe his own ministry (1 Cor 15.10), and the ministry of Mary (Rom 16.6), Tryphena, Tryphosa, and Persis (Rom 16.12). Both *synergos* and *kopiao* are connected to preaching (1 Cor 15.9-11; Gal 4.11-13), teaching (1 Tim 5.17; Col 1.28-29; Phil 2.16), and leadership (1 Cor 16.16, 1 Thess 5.12-13; 1 Tim 5.17).

Because Paul exhorted the Corinthians to submit to the household of Stephanas who had devoted themselves to the ministry of the saints, and to all who work and labor (1 Cor 16.16), it has been inferred that also women were leaders. Schreiner objects to the argument that women were part of the household and therefore leaders, for according to him it proves too much, i.e., even children should be included.[50] But Paul wrote he baptized the household of Stephanas (1 Cor 1.16); did he baptize only the men?

Chrysostom, who delighted in writing about the actual persons found in the Bible, wrote about Euodia and Syntyche, whom Paul called his coworkers.

> "Labored with me." What sayest thou? Did women labor with thee? Yes, he answereth, they too contributed no small portion. Although many were they who wrought together with him, yet these women also acted with him amongst the many. The Churches then were no little edified, for many good ends are gained where they who are approved, *be they men, or be they women*, enjoy from the rest such honor.[51]

---

49. Piper and Grudem, 218.
50. Ibid., 219.
51. *Homilies on Philippians*, Homily XIII.

Regarding women deacons, Schreiner writes that we do not need to come to a firm decision, for deacons did not teach or govern the church,[52] yet Schreiner favors the existence of women deacons in his comment found in the footnotes.

> Another argument in favor of woman deacons is that Paul says nothing about the wives of elders in 1 Timothy 3.1-7. Such an omission is hard to explain if he is speaking of the wives of deacons in 1 Timothy 3.11. One would expect that higher qualifications would be demanded of wives of elders than of wives of deacons. But if Paul is referring to women who were deacons, then the omission of women among elders is because women could not be elders, although they could be deacons. Of course, those who argue for full inclusion of women do not use this particular argument because it would exclude women from being elders, even though they could be deacons.[53]

Schreiner ignores the word *ei-tis* ("anyone") in 1 Timothy 3.1 which qualifies both men and women to seek the position as overseers. He neglects also the fact that the phrase found in 1 Timothy 3.2 – *mias guinakos andra* – is found also in 1 Timothy 3.12, wherefore it is absolutely essential that we must come to a firm decision about women deacons. For it is proven that 1 Timothy 3.11 speaks of women deacons, the phrase cannot exclude women from being overseers.

Incidentally, Knight disagrees with Schreiner for he sees the role of the deacons as one of leadership, which is also the Catholic position.

> Most Christians and churches who have made the application to "elders" have done so also for "deacons," noting that they, too, are designated in masculine terms (1 Timothy 3.12; also Acts 6.3, where the Greek word used for "men" [aner] is the word used to distinguish men from women rather than one used for men as mankind whether male or female [anthropos].) They have noted furthermore that the role of deacons is still one of leadership, even if the leadership is in the area of service. At the same time it should be noted that women (or wives) are referred to in this section of deacons (1 Timothy 3.11). This

---

52. Piper and Grudem, 220.
53. Ibid., 504.

has led to two understandings. The first is that the text distinguishes them from the deacons (who are males), does not designate them as deacons, but mentions them because they serve with and alongside the deacons in diaconal service. It is my judgment that this view understands the passage correctly and furthermore that it is the wives of deacons who are in view.[54]

As with Junia, if deacons are part of leadership, the women in 1 Timothy 3.11 are wives; if deacons are not part of leadership, the women are deacons.

The same grammatical construction used of deacons in 1 Timothy 3.8-13 is found in 1 Corinthians 7.12-14.

> But to the rest I, not the Lord, say: If any *brother* has a wife who does not believe, and she is willing to live with him, let him not divorce her. And *a woman* who has a husband who does not believe, if he is willing to live with her, let her not divorce him. For the unbelieving husband is sanctified by the wife, and the unbelieving wife is sanctified by the husband; otherwise your children would be unclean, but now they are holy.

The woman in verse 13 is not married to the "brother" in verse 12. Instead, both the "brother" and "woman" belong to the same "category," (i.e., Christians married to unbelievers). It is therefore unlikely that the women in 1 Timothy 3.11 are married to the deacons mention in 1 Timothy 3.8, but are deacons themselves.

Polycarp, the disciple of John the Apostle, applied all of the qualifications found in 1 Timothy 3.8-12 to deacons in general.

> Knowing, then, that "God is not mocked," we ought to walk worthy of His commandment and glory. In like manner should the deacons be blameless before the face of His righteousness, as being the servants of God and Christ, and not of men. They must not be slanderers (F), double-tongued (M), or lovers of money (M), but temperate (F) in all things, compassionate, industrious, walking according to the truth of the Lord, who was the servant of all.[55]

---

54. Ibid., 353.
55. *The Epistle of Polycarp to the Philippians*, Ch. V.

Also Clement of Alexandria included women as deacons, although he erreneously placed the text in the second letter to Timothy.

> Scimus enim quae cunque de feminis diaconis in altera ad Timotheum praestantissimus docet Paulus

> We also know about the directions about women deacons which are given by the noble Paul in his second letter to Timothy.[56]

Chrysostom stated without ambiguity that the phrase *mias guinakos andra* referred also to women deacons, not wives of deacons.

> Some have thought that this is said of women generally, but it is not so, for why should he introduce anything about women to interfere with his subject? He is speaking of those who hold the rank of Deaconesses. *"Let the Deacons be husbands of one wife." This must be understood therefore to relate to Deaconesses.* For that order is necessary and useful and honorable in the Church. Observe how he requires the same virtue from the Deacons, as from the Bishops, for though they were not of equal rank, they must equally be blameless; equally pure.[57]

Since the women in 1 Timothy 3.11 were not wives, but deacons, and the phrase *mias guinakos andra* was applicable to them, the phrase cannot be used to exclude women from leadership in the church.

Phoebe is a controversial figure in the Bible for she is called *diakonos* ("deacon'). Knight considers the term *diakonos* found in Romans 16.1-2 to be used in a nontechnical and nonofficial sense.[58] Schreiner is once again doubtful about the identity of a woman with an official title, for he writes that "one cannot be sure" whether Phoebe was a deacon. [59]

But Chrysostom recognized Phoebe as an office-holding deaconess.

---

56. *Stromata*, Book III, Ch. VI.
57. *Homilies on 1 Timothy*, Homily XI.
58. Piper and Grudem, 353.
59. Ibid., 219.

Wishing then that they should feel on easy terms, and be in honor, he addressed each of them, setting forth their praise to the best advantage he might. For one he calls beloved another kinsman, another both, another fellow-prisoner, another fellow-worker, another approved, another elect. And of the women one he addresses by her title, *for he does not call her servant of the Church in an undefined way* (because if this were so he would have given Tryphena and Persis this name too), *but this one as having the office of deaconess*, and another as helper and assistant, another as mother, another from the labors she underwent, and some he addresses from the house they belonged to, some by the name of Brethren, some by the appellation of Saints. And some he honors by the mere fact of addressing them, and some by addressing them by name, and some by calling them first-fruits, and some by their precedence in time, but more than all, Priscilla and Aquila.[60]

Chrystostom was an Eastern bishop, and Weinrich recognizes the existence of women deacons in the East and their disappearance by the twelveth century. He does not believe the Western church had a developed female diaconate,[61] but Madigan and Osiek disagree.

There is no evidence for female deacons in the West until the fifth century, about the same time, curiously, that the inscriptions about female presbyters appear.... The Western epigraphical evidence for female deacons is slim, probably because of the vagaries of inscriptional survival, in view of the efforts of councils of the fifth and sixth centuries to eliminate them. The canons and episcopal letters below, on access of women to the altar, should also be compared. That so much effort was given to suppression has to indicate more of a custom than the few inscriptions and literary references reveal.[62]

It is also important to remember the destrucion of Christian literature during the last persecution by Emperor Diocletian, which was ended in A.D. 311 by Galerius.[63] How much was lost is unknown, but to assume that the lack of literary evidence prior to the fifth century proves the non-existence

---

60. *Homilies on Romans*, XXXI.
61. Piper and Grudem, 265.
62. Madigan and Osiek, 139, 143.
63. *A World History of Christianity*, 34-35.

of a western female diaconate is as if a future historian would assume that Jews did not exist in large numbers in Europe prior to 1940s because of the small number of Holocaust survivors. Madigan and Osiek suggest that the diaconate was imported from the east where it flourished, a view they share with Weinrich.[64] But the end of the fourth century was the beginning of the divide between the western and eastern churches, which would become permanent after the Latin crusaders sacked Constantinople in 1204. In the 380s Pope Damasus of Rome ordered the use of Latin in the western liturgy, which further enforced the linguistic divide between the western and eastern churches, which was already felt in the western theologicans inability to read the literature written in Greek, as seen in a letter from Augustine in which he asks for more translations.[65] It is unlikely that the West would adopt a pratice from the East at this critical junction of church history when the two traditions were drifting apart and the bishops of Rome and Constantinople were caught in a struggle for eminence. But most importantly, the suggestion does not answer the question where the eastern churches received its tradition from.[66]

Madigan and Osiek cite three councils, the Council of Orange (441), Council of Epaon (517) and Council of Orleans (533), in which the ordination of female deacons was forbidden. If women deacons did not exist in the West, why forbid the practice?[67] But by far the most remarkable evidence of the existence of deaconnesses in the West is a letter by Pope Benedict VIII (A.D. 1017) to the Bishop of Porto in Portugal.

---

64. Piper and Grudem,, 276.

65. Charles Freeman, *Egypt, Greece and Rome* (New York: Oxford University Press, 2004), 600.

66. The order of women deacons is said to have been created due to the inability of men to visit women in their homes, but Jerome was indignant about the habit of some men to purposefully seek the diaconate to gain access to women, "There are others – I speak of those of my own order – who seek the presbyterate and the diaconate simply that they may be able to see women with less restraint.... Certain persons have devoted the whole of their energies and life to the single object of knowing the names, houses, and characters of married ladies" ("Letter XXII. *To Eustochium,*" The Letters of St. Jerome, 28).

67. The complementarist effort to forbid the ordination of women which is occurring in the modern church is a good comparison.

In the same way, we concede and confirm to you and to your successors in perpetuity every episcopal ordination (ordinationem episcopalem), not only of presbyters but also of deacons or deaconnesses (diaconissis) or subdeacons.[68]

John Wijngaards recognizes that "since the Middle Ages, it has been commonly assumed in the [Catholic] Church, without any solid ground, that women had been excluded by God from holy orders."[69] Paul K. Jewett noted that the exclusion of women, both in the Catholic and Protestant theology, has been based on the woman's subjection to the man as a created order.

We see then that so far as the nature fo the ministerial office bears on the question of woman's ordination, the ultimate issue proves to be her relationship of subordiantion to the man. This is true regardless of one's specific theological view of ordination werein the essential element is the sacramental comminssioning of a priest to pronounce absolution and celebrate the sacrifice of the Mass, or whether one has a Protestant and evangelical view wherein the essential element is the setting apart of a minister to preach the gospel and shephers the flock of God. In both traditions it is the woman's relationship to the man that disqualifies her for ordination.[70]

In the *Summa* we find the objection that the female sex is not an impediment to receiving orders for the office of a prophet is greater than the office of a priest. In addition women became martyrs and devoted themselves to the religious life, and since the power of orders is founded in the soul, but sex is not in the soul, also women should receive Orders. To this Thomas Aquinas answered:

On the contrary, It is said (1 Timothy 2.12): "I suffer not a woman to teach (in the Church), nor to use authority over the man." Further, the crown is required previous to receiving Orders, albeit not for the validity of the sacrament. But the crown or tonsure is not befitting

---

68. Madigan and Osiek, 147.

69. Wijngaards, 133.

70. Jewett, 163.

to women according to 1 Corinthians 11. Neither therefore is the receiving of Orders.[71]

Thomas believed that the male sex is required for receiving Orders, for it is not possible for a woman to signify eminence of degree for she is in the state of subjection to the man. In addition, the male sex is necessary for the lawfulness of the sacraments, but not for the validity because deaconesses and priestesses [presbytera] are mentioned in the *Decretals*. Thomas reconciled his exclusion of women and the existence of women within the orders with the explanation that the deaconess reads homilies in church and the *presbytera* is a widow because "presbyter" means "elder."[72]

Ute E. Eisen explains how, "In his argument Epiphanius attempts to show that women who held different titles (deaconesses, widows, presbytides) really exercised the same office, namely that of deaconess – an effort that is not surprising in light of the premise already formulated, that women could not be anything but deaconesses."[73] Against Epiphanius's fourth-century theology, we may note that in the first-century church deacons were ambassadors between the churches,[74] ministers of the mysteries of Christ, servants of the church,[75] and entrusted with bringing the Eucharist to those who were absent from the weekly service.[76] That the deacons were called "servants of the church" is important, for only deacons are called servants of the church in the Bible.

---

71. *Summa Theologica*, Supplement, Question 39, Article 1.

72. Thomas believed the woman was subject to the man because of his Aristoetlian belief that the wiser should rule. The modern church is no longer able to use the argument since it has been proven that the woman is equally intelligent, wherefore the current argument is based on the Divine Command Theory: a dogma must be obeyed because God has commanded it, not because it is logical, necessary or reasonable. Hence Ortlund writes, "Under God, a wife may not compete for that primary responsibility [to lead their partnership in a God-glorifying direction]. It is her husband's *just because he is the husband*, by the wise decree of God" (Piper and Grudem, 105). We find the same reasoning in Islam. According to Peter N. Stearns the Koran says, "Men have authority over women because of what God has conferred on the other in preference to the other" (Peter N. Stearns, *Gender in World History*, [Routledge, 2000], 39).

73. Eisen, 119-120.

74. *The Epistle of Ignatius to the Philadelphians*, Chapter X.

75. *The Epistle of Ignatius to the Trallians*, Chapter II.

76. *The First Apology of Justin*, Chapter LXVII.

The civil authorities are called servants of God (Rom 13.4), the apostles were ministers of the New Testament (2 Cor 3.6), servants of God and of Christ (2 Cor 6.4; 11.23), and co-workers (*synergos*) were called ministers of God and Christ (1 Thess 3.2; Col 1.7). Since Phoebe is called a servant of the church in Cenchrea, and she was a messenger to the Church of Rome, she was an official deacon who ministered in the mysteries of Christ.

～

Ute E. Eisen quotes Epiphanius' *Panarion Against Eighty Heresies* (ca. 374-377) in which he writes about Christians who ordained women as bishops and presbyters.

> They have women bishops, women presbyters, and everything else, all of which they say is in accord with 'in Christ Jesus there is neither male or female.' They ordain women among bishops and presbyters because of Eve [not hearing] the word of the Lord: 'your desire shall be for your husband, and he shall rule over you' (Gen 3.16). But the apostolic word remains hidden from them: 'I permit no woman to speak or to have authority over a man' (1 Tim 2.12) and again: 'man is not from woman, but woman from man (1 Cor 11.8) and 'Adam was not deceived but Eve was first deceived and became a transgressor.'[77]

Eisen explains how Epiphanius tries to convince his reader that only heretics ordained women, but the Canon XI of the Synod of Laodicea (written between 341-381) orders that *presbytides* or women presiders should not be ordained in the Church. As with deaconesses, why deny a practice that does not exist? Epiphanius defines *presbytides* as the oldest of the deaconesses, an order which he claims is identical with the order of widows, but the Canon XI uses *prokathesthai* ("preside, stand before, lead') which is also found in Ignatius's letter to the Magnesians, "I exhort you to study to do all things with a divine harmony, while your *bishop presides* in the place of God, and your presbyters in the place of the assembly of the apostles, along with your deacons."[78] Eisen further quotes Jean Galot whose comment is highly enlightening.

---

77. Eisen, 118.
78. *Epistle to the Magnesians*, Ch 6.

If one should trust the title of the Canon, *It is not allowed to appoint women-priests in the church,* one could understand the *presbitidi* in the sense of "priestess." But such a definition seems unthinkable in the Catholic Church, and there has been an attempt to identify these *presbitidi* either with higher deaconesses, or as deaconesses, or as elderly women responsible for the overseeing of the women of the church.[79]

Also Madigan and Osiek write that, "While synods and councils, both East and West, repeatedly condemned the practice of women prebyters, the epigraphical evidence suggest their ongoing existence, even if in small numbers."[80] Since their disappearance, there has been a great effort to equate woman elders with widows, the widows with deaconesses and the deaconesses with lay-women without an official function to deny the existence of women officeholders in the church.

Schreiner, for example, does not believe *presbytides* refers to female elders in Titus 2.3 for according to him, the usual word for "elders" is *presbyteros* which "could easily have been made feminine (*presbytera*) if Paul wanted to refer to women elders.[81] If Schreiner is correct, "older women" should be translated "woman elder" in 1 Timothy 5.1-2.

> Do not rebuke an older man (*presbuteros*) harshly, but exhort him as if he were your father. Treat younger men (*neoterous*) as brothers, older women (*presbytera*) as mothers and younger women (*neoteras*) as sisters, with absolute purity. (NIV)

The usual translation, and interpretation, of the above text is that Paul is talking about elderly people. But if the words *presbytas* and *presbytidas* were used of the elderly and *presbyteros* and *presbyteras* of officeholders, how can 1 Timothy 5.1-2 refer to the elderly?

The combination of *presbytero* and *neos* found in 1 Timothy 5.1-2 appears also in 1 Peter 5.5.

> Young men (*neoteroi*), in the same way be submissive to those who are older (*presbuteros*). All of you, clothe yourselves with humility toward

---

79. Piper and Grudem, 119.
80. Ibid., 163.
81. Ibid., 220.

one another, because, "God opposes the proud but gives grace to the humble."

The context of 1 Peter 5 speaks of elders and laity (younger in faith, not age). Similarly, in Titus 2, the word for the younger men and women is *neos*. Clement of Alexandria called laity "the young," and also Matthew Henry recognized that Paul was writing about office-holding elders. Incidentally, Madigan and Osiek write that *presbytis* and *presbytera* are two forms which have more or less the same meaning.[82]

Clement of Alexandria called laity "the young."[83] Also Matthew Henry recognized that Paul was writing about office holding elders."[84]

In the Constitutions of the Holy Apostles (fourth century) we find a group of women who are defined as "elder women." They cannot be part of laity, for they are named after the virgins and widows.

> When thou callest an assembly of the Church as one that is the commander of a great ship, appoint the assemblies to be made with all possible skill, charging the deacons as mariners to prepare places for the brethren as for passengers, with all due care and decency. And first, let the building be long, with its head to the east, with its vestries on both sides at the east end, and so it will be like a ship. In the middle let the bishop's throne be placed, and on each side of him let the presbytery sit down; and let the deacons stand near at hand, in close and small girt garments, for they are like the mariners and managers of the ship: with regard to these, let the laity sit on the other side, with all quietness and good order. And let the women sit by themselves, they also keeping silence.... In the next place, let the presbyters one by one, not all together, exhort the people, and the bishop in the last

---

82. Madigan and Osiek, 171. Epiphanius attempted to deny the existence of women elders by differentiating between *presbytidas* ("elderess") and *presbyeridas* ("presbyteress"), and by claiming the latter had never existed in the church. Yet, Canon 11 of the Synod of Laodicea used the word *presbytides* for women presiders who had an official function (Eisen, 119, 121).

83. "Let us therefore respect those who are over us, and reverence the elders; let us honour the young, and let us teach the discipline of God (Stromata, Book IV, XVII).

84. "To be very tender in rebuking elders-elders in age, elders by office" (1 Tim 5.1," *Matthew Henry's Commentary on the Whole Bible: New Modern Edition*).

place, as being the commander. Let the porters stand at the entries of the men, and observe them. *Let the deaconesses also stand at those of the women, like shipmen.* For the same description and pattern was both in the tabernacle of the testimony and in the temple of God.... Let the young persons sit by themselves, if there be a place for them; if not, let them stand upright. *But let those that are already stricken in years sit in order.* For the children which stand, let their fathers and mothers take them to them. Let the younger women also sit by themselves, if there be a place for them; but if there be not, let them stand behind the women. Let those women which are married, and have children, be placed by themselves; but let *the virgins, and the widows, and the elder women, stand or sit before all the rest;* and let the deacon be the disposer of the places, that every one of those that comes in may go to his proper place, and may not sit at the entrance.[85]

By the time the constitution was written, women were segregated from men in the church, but they had not yet been excluded from serving as deacons and elders. However, they were no longer allowed near the altar, for by the fourth century the leadership model of the Church had changed from the domestic overseer in the private home to the monarchial bishop who presided in God's stead over a public assembly. The bishop was seated on a raised dais from which he governed the Church[86] and it was from this seat that Chrysostom wanted to exclude women.

In what sense then does he say, "I suffer not a woman to teach?" He means to hinder her from publicly coming forward, and from the seat on the bema, not from the word of teaching. Since if this were the case, how would he have said to the woman that had an unbelieving husband, "How knowest thou, O woman, if thou shalt save thy husband?" Or how came he to suffer her to admonish children, when he says, but "she shall be saved by child-bearing if they continue in faith, and charity, and holiness, with sobriety?" How came Priscilla to instruct even Apollos? It was not then to cut in sunder private conversing for advantage that he said this, but that before all, and which it was the teacher's duty to give in the public assembly; or again,

---

85. *Constitutions of the Holy Apostles*, Book II, Sec. VII. On Assembling in the Church.
86. Torjesen, 157.

in case the husband be believing and thoroughly furnished, able also to instruct her. When she is the wiser, then he does not forbid her teaching and improving him.[87]

Weinrich cites Tertullian's *Prescription Against Heretics* in which he "complains that among them no distinctions are made between catechumens and believers, women and men, neophyte and experienced faithful, layman and priest."[88] He makes the inference that Tertullian was writing about a practice that didn't exist in the Church, for it would make his writing pointless. But since Tertullian envisioned a Church which resembled Rome, his complaint was that these groups were not hierarchical enough. Weinrich believes Tertullian rejected Gnostic egalitarianism when he called the women "wanton" (*procaces*), but in fact, Roman women were called *procaces* when they attempted to function outside their proper sphere, the household.[89] Since the church had grown and moved from the household to the public assembly, a dilemma had been created: how to deal with the social mores which restricted women's activities to the home? Tertullian solved the problem by excluding women from the laity and by veiling their faces so they would remain in the private - even when they were in public.[90]

In his essay *The Church as Family,* Vern Sheridan Poythress describes the analogy which he believes exists between the church and the family:

> The leadership within the family is vested in the husband and father (Eph 5.22-6.4).... Women, by contrast, are not to be placed in authority in the church, because such a role would not harmonize with the general relations between men and women in marriage, as established at creation (1 Timothy 2.11-14). Thus, the differences between men and women within the context of marriage and family

---

87. *Homilies on Romans,* Homily XXXI.

88. Piper and Grudem, 274.

89. Torjesen, 165.

90. Tertullian recognized that even a (male) layperson could perform the functions of the priesthood in the absence of the bishop and therefore his complaint was about the woman performing functions which he reserved to men alone by excluding women also from the laity.

carry over into differences in roles that men and women may assume within the church.[91]

Poythress creates his analogy due to the assumption that the husband and the overseer have the same authority over those entrusted in their care. But if the overseers are the "fathers" of the church, and women can become "mothers" of the church, the laity must necessarily be regarded as "children." Poythress recognizes the logical conclusion of his argument, but he does not notice the inherent fallacy embedded in it.

> Ephesians 5.22-6.4 and other passages about the family clearly leave open a great many possibilities for the exact form of managerial arrangements. In these matters, a wise leader attempts to work out arrangements that best use and enhance the gifts of each family member. But Ephesians 5.22-6.4 does nevertheless draw some clear boundary lines. Children should submit to their parents, and conversely parents have responsibility for managing their children.... The analogy between the natural family and God's household therefore suggests the same procedures for God's household. Responsibilities for management may, in broad sense, be delegated and distributed throughout God's household. But the overseers, as fathers in the household, possess more ultimate authority.[92]

If the laity is regarded as the children, they must submit to both the "fathers" and the "mothers," as children do in the natural family. This causes a problem with 1 Timothy 2.12 ("I do not permit a woman to teach or to have authority over a man; she must be silent") for Poythress's reasoning allows women to teach men who are part of the laity and have authority over them as mothers do with their children. In fact, his argument is a powerful testimony of the validity and necessity of women elders in the church.

Yet, although Poythress regards the laity as children, he refers to 1 Timothy 5.1-2 when describing the proper treatment of the members of the church.

> Conduct toward any other member of the household must take into account not merely sweepingly general obligations to love but the

91. Piper and Grudem, 238.
92. Ibid., 245.

concrete distinctions introduced by differences in status within the household: treating some like fathers, others like brothers, others like mothers, others like sisters. Hence, 1 Timothy 5.1-2 presupposes the structure of an argument. The church is like a family. Therefore you must treat fellow church members like fellow family members.[93]

How can the overseer be a "father" if older men are to be treated as fathers and the younger men as brothers? To solve the contradiction, Poythress makes the overseer take God's place in the church, "God's Fatherhood is expressed in His rule over us and that rule is exercised in part through mature, father-like overseers."[94]

Poythress's analogy would be valid if he believed *male elders* should be treated as fathers, *female elders* as mothers, younger men (in faith) as brothers and younger women as sisters (1 Tim 5.1-2). If this was Poythress's argument, the church would truly be like a family, but in his analogy, the overseer takes God's place, and his relationship to the church becomes that of Christ-church instead of father-child. The relationship between the laity and an overseer is not the one flesh unity which exists between the man and the woman, and Christ and the church, wherefore Poythress's analogy fails.

---

93. Ibid., 236.
94. Ibid., 246.

CHAPTER 12

Gal 3.28

Now Pythagoras made an epitome of the statements on righteousness in
Moses, when he said,
"Do not step over the balance," that is, do not transgress equality in distribu-
tion, honouring justice so.
"Which friends to friends for ever, binds, to cities, cities – to allies, allies,
For equality is what is right for men; but less to greater ever hostile grows,
And days of hate begin," as is said with poetic grace.
Wherefore the Lord says, "Take My yoke, for it is gentle and light."
And on the disciples, striving for the pre-eminence, He enjoins equality with
simplicity,
Saying "that they must become as little children." Likewise also the apostle
writes, that
"No one in Christ is bond or free, or Greek or Jew.
For the creation in Christ Jesus is new, is equality, free of strife – not grasping
– just."
For envy, and jealousy, and bitterness, stand without the divine choir.

                                                    – CLEMENT OF ALEXANDRIA[1]

~

THE NATURAL INFERIORITY of women, slaves and Barbarians (non-Greeks)
taught by Aristotle and imported into the church by Clement in the second
century, was a radical departure from the natural equality of all believers
espoused by Paul (Gal 3.28; Col 3.11). The change did not take place over-

---

1. *The Stromata*, Book V, Ch.

night for in A.D. 369, Gregory of Nazianzen wrote a laudatory oration for his brother Caesarius in which he affirmed the abolishing of earthly distinctions.

> This is the purpose of the great mystery for us. This is the purpose for us of God, Who for us was made man and became poor, to raise our flesh, and recover His image, and remodel man, that we might all be made one in Christ, who was perfectly made in all of us all that He Himself is, that we might no longer be male and female, barbarian, Scythian, bond or free (which are badges of the flesh), but might bear in ourselves only the stamp of God, by Whom and for Whom we were made, and have so far received our form and model from Him, that we are recognized by it alone.

One of the consequences of the synthesis of Aristotle's philosophy with theology was the gradual removing of both women and slaves from leadership as the rule of inferiors was considered hurtful. In the Arabic Canons, attributed falsely to the council of Nicea (325), Canon II prohibits the ordination of slaves. In the thirteenth century, Thomas Aquinas forbade the ordination of slaves because a slave could not serve his carnal master and exercise his spiritual ministry at the same time, for he could not give what was not his, although Thomas did acquiesce that a slave could in principle be ordained for freedom was not required for the validity of the sacrament, only for its lawfulness. But because "the reception of spiritual power involves also an obligation to certain bodily actions, and consequently it is hindered by bodily subjection," it was not advisable.[2] If a slave was ordained with the owner's knowledge, the slave became a freedman. But in case a slave was ordained without the owner's consent, the bishop and those who presented him were to pay the owner double of the slave's value, if the knew him to be slave, or if the slave had possessions of his own, he was obligated to buy his freedom or return to slavery, regardless of his ordination.[3]

Through the European Renaissance, Reformation and Enlightenment, the biblical concept of equality became eventually an inseparable part of western ideology, for where Christian ethics are infused into the customs and beliefs of a society universal brotherhood becomes a reality – even when the church

---

2. *Summa Theologica,* Supplement, Question 39, Article 1, Reply to objection 1
3. Ibid, Article 3, Reply to objection 5

resists it. The great irony of church history is that whereas the modern secular society affirms the natural equality of all humans based on biblical principles, the church still clings to its dogmas which are based on secular philosophy. With the rise of modern science, a byproduct of the European Renaissance, Aristotle was set aside, for as Marjorie Grene points out, "in some important respects biology, like all modern science, really is, and must be, un-Aristotelian."[4] The direct result of the replacing of Aristotle's philosophy with biology, psychology, and sociology was the inclusion of women in both civic and ecclesiastical leadership in the twentieth century as the natural inferiority of women was rejected.

The Industrial Revolution eroded the old class system in which one's birth determined one's place in the social fabric. Education became imperative in the new social order and women soon realized they had to gain admittance to higher education if they were to succeed in the new society.[5] Rosalind Rosenberg describes in *Beyond Separate Spheres* the forces at work to prevent women from gaining admittance to higher education in the nineteenth century America – and their failure.

The Protestant dogma of the all-encompassing vocation of marriage and motherhood for all women permeated the nineteenth-century society. As women begun to enter colleges, in separate facilities at first, the medical profession set out to oppose their inroad.

> Clarke was not the first doctor to assert that women's unique physiology limited her social role. The conviction that women's subordinate position was biologically ordained had roots in antiquity, and it was a commonplace in nineteenth-century medical discussion to note that the womb exerted a supremely powerful force from which men were free. As one physician explained, it was as though the "Almighty, in creating the female sex, had taken the uterus and built a woman around it." The womb the doctors emphasized, dominated a woman's mental as well as physical life, producing a weak, submissive, uncreative, emotional, intuitive, and generally inferior personality.[6]

---

4. Marjorie Grene, "Aristotle and Modern Biology," *Journal of the History of Ideas* (July-Sept, 1972) www. culturaleconomics.atfreeweb.com (accessed June 29, 2009).

5. Rosenberg, 4.

6. Ibid., 5-6.

The strong appeal to the inevitableness of biology had not existed before the middle of the nineteenth century, and its introduction was largely due to the greater availability of (separate) college education for women and an increase in opportunities that was created by the Industrial Revolution, which threatened the sexual segregation of the Victorian era.[7] Philosophy was no longer providing adequate answers due to increase in knowledge, and evolutionary biology became the new source for answers for those wishing to preserve gender segregation – but also for those who sought its demise.[8]

In evolutionary biology, the womb dominated the whole woman, making her a less intelligent person. In addition, women's brain, being lighter, was not believed to be suited for intellectual exertion; instead "her affinity for lower forms of life" became the perfect example for the evolutionary belief that "there is no fundamental difference between men and the higher mammals in their mental faculties."[9] To this Antoinette Brown Blackwell objected, "How incredibly singular, blind and perverse, then is the dogmatism which has insisted that man's larger brain, measured by inches in the cranium, must necessarily prove his mental superiority to Woman."[10]

John Hopkins anatomist Dr. Franklin Mall concluded that the only method to link brain weight, sex and intelligence was for the researchers to know the sex and to look for specific characteristics. Mall suggested that the scientists begin by not knowing the sex to ascertain that the differences they claimed existed were truly there. None did, for as soon as it was found that girls did generally better in school, the sexless intelligence became the norm. To this, Dr. Helen Thompson Woolley commented with heavy irony:

> So far as I know, no one has drawn the conclusion that girls have greater native ability than boys. One is tempted to indulge in idle speculation as to whether this admirable restraint from hasty generalization would have been equally marked had sex findings been reversed.[11]

---

7. Ibid., 6.
8. Ibid., 14.
9. Ibid., 8-9.
10. Ibid., 106.
11. Ibid., 106.

The inferior woman disappeared as soon as it was discovered that the beliefs that had so long supported the inferiority of women, and her restricted role, were in fact caused by the lack of education and equal opportunity.

~

S. Lewis Johnson Jr. recognizes that Galatians 3.28 nullifies the distinctions of race, social rank and sex in the church, but he believes it has to do with our equality as sons and daughters of God, not our social roles.[12] But the only social role Johnson believes is still valid is female subjection, for he maintains that although Paul was not about to abolish slavery, he provided the justification for the future abolishing of the institution.[13]

As a parallel, we can note William MacDonald, who is convinced that all distinctions between Jews and Gentiles have been removed, but that distinctions based on social rank and sex are still valid today because Paul gave separate instructions to wives and slaves. MacDonald circumvents the existence of slavery in the New Testament by applying the instructions for the slaves to modern day employees.[14] But ignoring the fundamental questions about personal freedom and human dignity does not explain how Paul could have approved of slavery, while Christians have successfully used the Bible to argue for its abolishing. Thus we must further examine Johnson's claim, that female subjection was rightly preserved while slavery was abolished *after* the Bible was written.

Wayne Grudem argues in his essay *An Overview of Central Concerns*, co-authored by John Piper, that Paul did not approve of slavery.

> Paul's regulation for how slaves and masters related to each other do not assume the goodness of the institution of slavery. Rather, seeds for slavery's dissolution were sown in Philemon 16 ("no longer a slave, but better than a slave, as a dear brother."), Ephesians 6.9 (Masters... do not threaten [your slaves]"), Colossians 4.1 ("Masters, provide your slaves with what is right and fair"), and 1 Timothy 6.1-2 (masters are

---

12. Piper and Grudem, 158.
13. Ibid., 159.
14. MacDonald, "Ephesians 6.5."

"brothers"). Where these seeds of equality came to full flower, the very institution of slavery would no longer be slavery.[15]

Yet, although believing women are called sisters (1 Tim 5.2), and although husbands should not treat their wives harshly (Col 3.19) but love them as they love themselves (Eph 5.25), Grudem does not see a parallel between women and slaves, for he refutes "the trajectory position" when applied to gender, although he explicitly approves of it in the case of slavery.

> [W]e do see the apostles in a process of coming to understand the inclusion of the Gentiles in the church (Acts 15; Gal 2.1-14; 3.28). But the process was completed within the New Testament, and the commands given to Christians in the New Testament say nothing about excluding Gentiles from the church. We do not have to progress on a "trajectory" beyond the New Testament to discover that. Christians living in the time of Paul's epistles were living under the new covenant. And we Christians living today are also living under the new covenant.... That means that *we are living in the same period in God's plan for "the history of redemption" as the first-century Christians.* And that is why we can read and apply the New Testament directly to ourselves today. To attempt to go beyond the New Testament documents and derive our authority from "where the New Testament was heading" is to reject the very documents God gave us to govern our life under the new covenant until Christ returns.... Most evangelical interpreters say that the Bible does not command or encourage or endorse slavery, but rather tells Christians who were slaves how they should conduct themselves, and also gives principles *that would modify and ultimately lead to the abolition of slavery.*[16]

Grudem recognizes that "Scripture sometimes regulates undesirable relationships without condoning them as permanent ideals," and his criterion for an "undesirable relationship" is that it is not based on the creation order. Since, "the existence of slavery is not rooted in any creation ordinance," it was rightly abolished, but because creation gives "an unshakable foundation for marriage

---

15. Piper and Grudem, 65.
16. *Evangelical Feminism,* 57, 77.

and its complementary roles for husband and wife,"[17] male headship should be preserved. However, not all human relationships that should be preserved are based on the creation order; civil governments, for example, were instituted because of sin, to punish lawbreakers.[18] Thus, the criterion is not whether the relationship was instituted at creation, but whether it was instituted by God for the benefit of humanity.

Despite his arguments in favor of abolition, slavery continues to cause problems for Grudem, for the proslavery arguments used in the nineteenth-century sound very much like the ones used by complementarists of the twentieth-century. Grudem attempts to solve the problem by making a distinction between first- and nineteenth-century slavery.

> [Slavery] was the most common employment situation on the Roman Empire in the time of the New Testament. A bondservant could not quit his job or seek another employment until he obtained his freedom. But there were extensive laws that regulated the treatment of such bondservants and gave them considerable protection. Bond-servants could own their own property and often purchased their freedom by about age 30, and often held positions of significant responsibility such as teachers, physicians, nurses, managers of estates, retail merchants, and business executives.... The first-century institution of "bondservants" is far different from the picture that comes to mind when modern readers hear the word "slavery." This helps us understand why the New Testament did not immediately prohibit the institution of "bondservants," while at the same time giving principles that led to its eventual abolition. And it helps to understand why the Christians in England and the United States who campaigned for the abolition of slavery based on the moral teachings of the Bible saw it as a far worse institution, one that was not at all supported by the

---

17. Piper and Grudem, 65-66.

18. "For since man, by departing from God, reached such a pitch of fury as even to look upon his brother as his enemy, and engaged without fear in every kind of restless conduct, and murder, and avarice; God imposed upon mankind the fear of man, as they did not acknowledge the fear of God, in order that, being subjected to the authority of men, and kept under restraint by their laws, they might attain to some degree of justice, and exercise mutual forbearance through dread of the sword suspended full in their view" (Against Heresies, Book V, XXIV, 2).

Bible but was so cruel and dehumanizing that it had to be abolished completely and forever.[19]

According to Sarah B. Pomeroy, although the minimum age for manumission was thirty (Lex Aelia Sentia, A.D. 4), many slaves obtained their freedom earlier. That a slave could obtain his or her freedom through marriage or by saving enough through the original tipping system to pay back the purchase price did not mean that that a majority of slaves became freedmen. As an example we may note that over half of the wives of imperial slaves and freedmen were dead before thirty, most dying between twenty and twenty-five, and the mortality rate of the slaves of poorer classes was most likely even higher.[20]

Revealingly, while Grudem portrays the first-century slavery as benign, Rachel Pendergraft, a spokesperson for the Knights of the Ku Klux Klan, uses the same argument in her article *The Shocking Story of Real Slavery in America,* in defense of the nineteenth-century American black slavery.

> Shocking it is then, to learn that Negro slaves didn't really have it that bad. No, it wasn't within their power to travel abroad if they wished, but then again they weren't at the mercy of an African witch doctor or head hunter either. But aside from being removed from the savagery of Africa did they benefit at all from their new home? Robert Fogel a 1993 Nobel Prize winner says yes.... he is best known for his book Time on the Cross: The Economics of American Negro Slavery. The book that Fogel co-authored with Stanley Engerman, has startled historians and has caused an outcry among many for its radical conclusion that slaves were commonly better off than northern free laborers. Among the examples in the book that establish their assertion: Black women slaves were allowed maternal leave, were taken well care of and received attentive care during the pregnancy. They had one-year maternity leave after the birth of their child. Slaves were now allowed to work while they were sick, even if there were suspicions that the slaves were faking it, it was usually considered best

---

19. *Evangelical Feminism* 78-9. The difference between Roman and American slavery was used in the seventies to highlight the fact that Roman slavery was not limited to skin color, which was believed to have been the case in Rome. Salley and Behm carefully pointed out that their comparison did not justify slavery in any form (Salley and Behm, 88-89).

20. Pomeroy, 194-195.

to allow the slaves a few days rest rather than take a chance. Slaves were allowed to conduct a home business if they wished to do so and were even allowed to make and sell their wares and crafts in town at the market place. Slaves were also given generous incentive programs and rewarded for their production, such rewards were usually cash bonuses. There was an average retirement age after which the slave was well cared for by the plantation owner and would usually spend time on business or helping with the slave children. Slaves usually lived their whole lives in a close knit "slave community" where they ran their own affairs. Families were rarely split apart and slaves were encouraged to marry as the owners felt that breaking up families was simply poor business – it created unhappy slaves, which would affect production. They even had family garden plots where they were able to raise food for their family, Negroes in the south had guaranteed housing, food, clothing, medical care, business opportunities, support after retirement and a bonus program.[21]

Pendergraft ignores the cruelty of black slavery in order to support her racist theology, which maintains that white people are called by God to lead the rest of the world, and have done so in the past with compassion. Similarly, Grudem omits the starvation, physical abuse, the sexual exploitation – which included children – and the threat of crucifixion, "the slave's penalty,"[22] to explain why the nineteenth-century slave owners were not able to use the Bible to support their view. Both Pendergraft and Grudem treat the singularly most devastating part of slavery – being considered someone's property – as casually as a person rising from the dinner table treats world hunger, which mirrors the indifference of Horace, the Roman writer (65-68 B.C.), as described by Edith Hamilton.

> It goes without saying that he never took note of slaves, but it is worthy of remark that a man sensitive and quick of feeling as he was would write of their terrible punishments with complete unconcern. He does say mildly that a man who has a slave crucified because he stole a bit of food must be out of his mind, but he speaks of slaves being beaten

---

21. Rachel Pendergraft, "The Shocking Story of Real Slavery in America," The Knights of the Ku Klux Klan, www.kkk.com.

22. Hamilton, 37.

as a matter of course, of "the horrible scourge," with pieces of metal attached to the lashes, and of others of the methods of torture devised to keep in order a class grown dangerous because of its enormous size. A man of position, says Horace, is mean if he walks out with only five slaves attending him; on the other hand, one can be seen with two hundred has passed the limit of good sense. And yet in spite of their great numbers they were so completely without human significance, so casually mistreated and murdered in that city accustomed by all the favorite forms of amusement to mortal agony and violent death, that their condition never drew a passing thought from even the very best, a man like Horace, a thinker, gentle, kindly, dutiful. His bewilderment, if he could be recalled to life and confronted with out point of view, would be pitiful. He was wise and good, yet he lived with a monstrous evil and never caught a glimpse of it. So does custom keep men blind.[23]

Custom does indeed blind people. Grudem denounces racism, which was the foundation of black slavery, but upholds female subjection, which Pendergraft in turn refutes with indignation as an importation from Judaism. Similar blindness to injustice is found in the nineteenth-century suffrage movement and the mid-twentieth century civil rights movement. An exasperated Elizabeth Cady Stanton fought against black men gaining the suffrage before white women,[24] and the Baptist pastor Martin Luther King Jr. did not consider women fit for leadership in the civil rights movement.[25]

Finally, Grudem tries to evade the charge by the somewhat defensive statement, "We must remember the real possibility that it is not we but the evangelical feminists today who resemble nineteenth century defenders of slavery in the most significant way: using arguments from the Bible to justify conformity to some very strong pressures in contemporary society (in favor of slavery then, and feminism now)."[26] But if the pressure from the contemporary society caused the Southern slave owners to pick up their Bibles to defend slavery, why did Kentucky wait until 1976, and Mississippi until 1995, to

---

23. Ibid., 125.
24. Geoffrey C. Ward and Ken Burns, *Not For Ourselves Alone, The Story of Elizabeth Cady Stanton and Susan B. Anthony* (New York: Alfred A. Knopp, 1999), 111.
25. Branch, 258.
26. Piper and Grudem, 66.

ratify the Thirteenth Amendment which ended slavery in 1865? It is far more believable that the slave owners picked up their Bibles because of the universal sin of greed, fortified by racism. Slavery was extremely profitable for the plantation owners and the ending of slavery would have meant drastically reduced profits. The greed of the plantation owners can be seen clearly in that black people were coerced to work for low wages on the same plantations they had been freed from, and that Jim Crow (segregation) continued to severely limit the freedom and rights of the black people for another century. As a parallel we can note that Roman slavery was not ended because it was considered immoral, but because it became unprofitable.[27]

> Slavery in the Roman Empire did not suddenly end, but it was slowly replaced when new economic forces introduced other forms of cheap labor. During the late empire, Roman farmers and traders were reluctant to pay large amounts of money for slaves because they did not wish to invest in a declining economy. The legal status of "slave" continued for centuries, but slaves were gradually replaced by wage laborers in the towns and by land-bound peasants (later called serfs) in the countryside. These types of workers provided cheap labor without the initial cost that slave owners had to pay for slaves. Slavery did not disappear in Rome because of human reform or religious principle, but because Romans found another, perhaps even harsher, system of labor.[28]

Grudem's attempt to evade the charge makes it clear that he is anxious to distance himself from the nineteenth-century slave owners, but he cannot deny that the central belief of complementarism is female obedience to male authority as a religious duty. And it is this belief which ties complementarism to American black slavery.

> Although many slaveowners shared the motivations of the clergy, their concerns tended to be more pragmatic. They wanted to cultivate

---

27. Fatima Mernissi notes a similar development within Islam, "The paradoxical result is that, despite Islam's opposition to slavery in principle, it only disappeared from the Muslim countries under pressure from and intervention by the colonial powers" (Mernissi, 129).

28. "Slavery in Ancient Rome" www.crystalinks.com/romeslavery.html (accessed June 29, 2009).

docility and efficiency in their slaves and combat the attacks of the abolitionists by demonstrating the stability of their conservative, yet humane, social order. If slaves could be taught to believe that obedience to their masters was a religious duty, then the authority of the planters would be established upon a solid foundation.[29]

Columbus Salley and Ronald Behm observe that the form of Christianity taught to the slaves was designed to support slavery "almost to the exclusion of the historic dogmas of the Christian faith."[30] The justification for slavery was that it was natural, ordained by God, and benefitted the slave, because it was approved by both the Old and New Testament and because the black people were cursed due to Noah's son Ham.[31] The slaves were taught that "slavery had divine sanction, that insolence was as much an offense against God as against the temporal master."[32] Grudem admits that "some slave owners tried to use the Bible to support slavery in nineteenth-century America, but opponents of slavery used the Bible too, and they were far more persuasive, and they won the argument."[33] But he cannot avoid the similarity between his own arguments and those of the slave owners for complementarism tells women their subjection is ordained by God, is beneficial, is approved by both the Old and the New Testament, and that insolence is an offense against God as much as it is towards the husband.

It is not enough to destroy an institution for the underlying philosophy will create another mutated form of the previous institution: the belief in white superiority, which created black slavery, created segregation after the end of slavery, and later transformed itself into ghettoization.[34] Similarly, the

---

29. George A. Rogers, R. Frank Saunders, *Swamp Waters and Wiregrass: Historical Sketches of Coastal Georgia* (Macon, GA: Mercer University Press, 1984), 44.

30. Salley and Behm, 20.

31. Ibid. 23. That someone is believed to be cursed by God has been a method of assigning subjection and inferiority to a group. Women were considered inferior because of the assumed curse of Eve; Jewish people were considered cursed by God because of deicide (murder of God) and black people have been considered inferior because of the curse of Ham. None were based on logic, for God did not curse Eve or Adam, nor Ham (Noah cursed Canaan whose descendants, the Canaanites, became the servants of Israel (Joshua 17.13), nor the Jewish people for we are all responsible for the death of Christ.

32. Ibid., 21.

33. *Evangelical Feminism*, 79.

34. Salley and Behm, 44.

subjection of women was based on their assumed inferiority which became institutionalized in the many laws and customs which segregated women from men and excluded women from the political, educational, and social institutions. Although the legal standing of women was changed, the underlying philosophy of male superiority created "equal but different," which continued to exclude women from leadership and full participation in society.

Slavery exists in the Bible for a reason and should not be explained away, for as long as sin exists, people will enslave others. In the church, however, slavery as an impossibility for how can own one's brother or sister?

Women of the Victorian era were accountable before the law, which they had gained as a result of the witchcraze as husbands refused to be punished – hanged or burned on the stake – for the crimes of their wives, the old system which had ensured the man's control in the home. Prior to the sixteenth-century "the European legal system lumped women, children, serfs, and slaves into the category of dependent property and therefore largely ignored them, except when they got too far out of line."[35] In the nineteenth century Anglo-Saxon world, a woman was by law required to obey her husband who was her lord and master, and without positive political rights, women had little hope to change their condition for the better.[36] Frederick Douglass (1818-1895), the great abolitionist, wrote in his newspaper, the North Star, in favor of female suffrage.

> All that distinguishes man as an intelligent and accountable being is equally true of woman; and if that government only is just which governs by the free consent of the governed, there can be no reason in the world for denying to woman the exercise of the elective franchise, or a hand in making and administering the laws of the land. Our doctrine is that "right is of no sex."[37]

---

35. *Witchcraze*, 41.

36. A group cannot defend itself from exploitation without political rights, as observed by John Stuart Mill, "And we know that legal protection the slaves have, where the laws are made by the masters" (Mill, 97).

37. Ward and Burns, 41.

Douglass was a half a century ahead of his time in his affirmation of the woman's equal intelligence, perhaps because he had felt the injustice of discrimination personally as a black man. Similarly to the slave owners, men refused to grant women, whom they considered inferior and lacking in reason, equal rights without a prolonged fight; seventy-two years after the initial effort to secure the ballot, President Wilson ended the legal minority of women – and the man's lordship – in 1920. Yet, the church would continue to argue that the woman was obligated to obey the man, although it lacked the legal means to enforce the obedience and could only appeal to the woman's sense of religious duty and the newly formulated concept of "equal but different," which was created to maintain the *status quo*, endangered as it was by the new legal standing of the woman.[38]

A similar attempt to avoid full equality is found in "equal but separate," the concept created to enforce segregation after slavery was officially abolished in 1865.[39] Dr. Martin Luther King Jr. exposed the inherent hypocrisy of the concept by pointing out that eleven o'clock every Sunday was the most segregated hour in the United States.[40] Neither "equal and separate" nor "equal but different" can be defended using logic for equality and inequality cannot co-exist, as was recognized already in the third century by Arnobius.

> In our opinion, however, that which is good naturally, does not require
> to be either corrected or reproved; nay more, it should not know what

---

38. "Equal but separate" would prevent also black men from becoming leaders in the mainstream Protestant churches, "Yet another evidence of white racism in the white church is the refusal of white Christians to accept a black leadership which will not compromise with racism in any form and which challenges the *status quo*" (Salley and Behm, 113).

39. "The [white] Protestant church, a major southern social institution, was among the first groups to segregate after the Civil War and to accept racism as the basis of race relations. Protestantism helped pave way for the capitulation to racism at the turn of the century." "Baptist and Methodist churches were by far the most popular among former slaves. The independent African Methodist Episcopalian Church and the African Methodist Episcopal Zion Church which had been organized by freedmen in the North during the slavery period experienced phenomenal growth. They were formed largely because the white society would not tolerate the presence of blacks as equals in common public worship" (Salley and Behm, 32-33).

40. James P. Comer recollects the astonishment he felt when he realized that also many white people were Christians, "I did not know that so many white people ever went to church. I could not understand how they could go to church and treat blacks the way they did" (Comer, 22).

evil is, if the nature of each kind would abide in its own integrity, for neither can two contraries be implanted in each other, nor can equality be contained in inequality, nor sweetness in bitterness.[41]

Although the nineteenth century is considered pristine by many due to its heavy emphasis on female submission, nostalgia and selective memory distorts the picture. Sarah Grimke, who was active in the abolition movement, advocated also for women's rights. In her *Letters on the Equality of the Sexes and the Condition of Woman* (1837), Grimke described the reality of life in the Victorian Era.

She merges her rights and her duties in her husband, and thus virtually chooses him for a savior and a king, and rejects Christ as her Ruler and Redeemer. I know some women are very glad of so convenient a pretext to shield themselves from the performance of duty; but there are others, who, under a mistaken view of their obligations as wives, submit conscientiously to this species of oppression, and go mourning on their way, for want of that holy fortitude, which would enable them to fulfill their duties as moral and responsible beings, without reference to poor fallen man. O that woman may arise in her dignity as an immortal creature, and speak, think and act as unto God, and not unto man! There is, perhaps, less bondage of mind among the poorer classes, because their sphere of duty is more concentrated, and they are deprived of the means of intellectual culture, and of the opportunity of exercising their judgment, on many moral subjects of deep interest and of vital importance. Authority is called into exercise by resistance, and hence there will be mental bondage only in proportion as the faculties of mind are evolved, and woman feels herself as a rational and intelligent being, on a footing with man. But women, among the lowest classes of society, so far as my observation has extended, suffer intensely from the brutality of their husbands. Duty as well as inclination has led me, for many years, into the abodes of poverty and sorrow, and I have been amazed at the treatment which women receive at the hands of those, who arrogate to themselves the epithet of protectors. Brute force, the law of violence, rules to a great extent in the poor man's domicile; and woman is little more than his drudge. They are

---

41. Adversus Gentes, Book II. 50.

less under the supervision of public opinion, less under the restraints of education, and unaided or unbiased by the refinements of polished society. Religion, wherever it exists, supplies the place of all these; but the real cause of woman's degradation and suffering in married life is to be found in the erroneous notion of her inferiority to man; and never will she be rightly regarded by herself, or others, until the opinion, so derogatory to the wisdom and mercy of God, is exploded, and woman arises in all the majesty of her womanhood, to claim those rights which are inseparable from her existence as an immortal, intelligent and responsible being.... If man is constituted the governor of woman, he must be her God; and the sentiment expressed to me lately, by a married man, is perfectly correct: 'In my opinion,' said he, 'the greatest excellence to which married woman can attain, is to worship her husband.' He was *a professor of religion* – his wife a lovely and intelligent woman. He spoke out what thousands think and act. Women are indebted to Milton for giving to this false notion, 'confirmation strong as proof of holy writ.' His Eve is embellished with every personal grace, to gratify the eye of her admiring husband; but he seems to have furnished the mother of mankind with just enough intelligence enough to comprehend *her supposed inferiority to Adam, and to yield unresisting submission to her lord and master.* Milton puts into Eve's mouth the following address to Adam: "My author and disposer, what thou bidst, unargued I obey; so God ordains – God is thy law; thou mine: to know no more, is woman's happiest knowledge and her praise." This much admired sentimental nonsense is fraught with absurdity and wickedness. If it were true, the commandment of Jehovah should have run thus: Mans hall have no other gods before ME, and woman shall have no other gods before MAN." [42]

A telling example of the attitude of the church towards women who spoke in public was the treatment of Grimke, who was openly criticized for her speeches in favor of abolition in the 1830s. A "Pastoral Letter of the General Association of Congregational Ministers of Massachusetts" was issued in response of her speeches in front of a mixed audience, called "promiscuous" in those days. The ministers did not only disapprove that women had left their

---

42. Sarah Grimke, "Letter XIII, Relation of Husband and Wife," *Letters on the Equality of the Sexes and the Condition of Woman,* " 1837.

"private sphere," but seemed also to have been annoyed that the laity was bold enough to request a discussion without their initiation and concluded that there must be something "wrong in that zeal or in the principle which excite it."[43]

Frederick Douglass noted that "the cause of the slave has been peculiarly woman's cause."[44] The struggle for civil rights is intrinsically connected to women's rights, for both are concerned with basic human rights, not only in the Anglo-Saxon world, but also around the world; in the late sixties, anthropologist Susan C. Seymour noticed how the struggle for civil rights movement also helped stimulate a women's rights movement in India.[45]

~

A parallel text to Galatians 3.28 is 1 Corinthians 7 in which Paul describes the practical implications of our oneness in Christ: husbands and wives do not have authority over their own bodies (v. 4), neither is the man favored in the dissolution of the union, which is permitted only in case the unbeliever wishes to depart (vv. 10-16); although marriage was mandatory in Judaism, Paul was of the opinion that it is good to be married, but it is better to abstain whether one was a man or a woman, for the married have many troubles from which the celibate is spared (vv. 25-40); neither circumcision (Jew) nor uncircumcision (Gentile) matters, only keeping the commandments of God (v. 19); a slave is a freedman in Christ, as the free is Christ's slave, and thus the earthly distinctions are obliterated (vv. 21-24).[46] Galatians 3.28 cannot refer only to faith and God's acceptance of us as his children, for God spoke equally with Abraham (freeborn Jewish male) and Hagar (female Gentile slave) before the time of Christ. Even in the Mosaic Covenant, a stranger could become "as

43. Pastoral Letter of the General Association of Massachusetts, June 28, 1837, from Margaret Zulich, Wake Forest University, 4.1; 4.3; 11.1 http://www.assumption.edu/ahc/abolition/PastoralLetter (accessed June 29, 2009).

44. Ward and Burns, 33.

45. Susan C. Seymour, *Women, Family, and Child Care in India, A World in Transition* (Cambridge University Press, 1999), 11.

46. "The thought of the apostle, then, must be that in Christ the basic divisions which have threatened human fellowship, are done away. Not distinctions which enrich fellowship, but divisions which destroy fellowship by leading to hostility and exploitation – these have no more place in Christ" (Jewett, 143).

the native" through the circumcision of all the males in the household (Exod 12.48-49). It was not God who restricted access to Himself to a few chosen; it was His people who created a hierarchy of human worth.

The key to the correct understanding of Galatians 3.28 is not the phrase "you are all sons of God through faith" but the phrase "for as many of you as were baptized into Christ have put on Christ" (v. 27). For that one has "put on Christ" has practical implications, not only abstract ones.

> But now you yourselves are to put off all these: anger, wrath, malice, blasphemy, filthy language out of your mouth. Do not lie to one another, since you have put off the old man with his deeds, and have put on the new man who is renewed in knowledge according to the image of Him who created him, where there is neither Greek nor Jew, circumcised nor uncircumcised, barbarian, Scythian, slave nor free, but Christ is all and in all. (Col 3.7-11)

Paul continued by exhorting the believers to "put on tender mercies, kindness, humility, meekness, longsuffering; bearing with one another, and forgiving one another, if anyone has a complaint against another; even as Christ forgave you, so you also must do" (3.12-13). They were also to "put on love, which is the bond of perfection" (v. 14). It is in this context that we find Colossians 3.18-4.1, a contracted form of Ephesians 5.21-33, which also follows a similar exhortation. In Colossians 3.25 Paul reminded the slaves that "he who does wrong will be repaid for what he has done, and there is no partiality." He warned also the masters in Ephesians 6.9 that their heavenly Master did not show partiality, wherefore they were to cease from threatening their slaves. James wrote to the believers that God had chosen the poor to be heirs of the kingdom and that they dishonored the poor when they showed partiality towards the rich and did not love their neighbor as themselves (James 2.1-9). Treating one's neighbor as one wants to be treated in return is loving one's neighbor and we find this principle in Ephesians 5.28, "So husbands ought to love their own wives as their own bodies; he who loves his wife loves himself." The demanding of preferential treatment because of one's sex, class or race is against the principle of natural equality of all humans as described in Galatians 3.28.

CHAPTER 13

1 Tim 5.14-15

The dream of diversity is like the dream of equality.
Both are based on ideals we celebrate even as we undermine them daily...
The segmentation of society means that often we don't have arguments across
the political divide.
Within their little validating communities, liberals and conservatives
Circulate half-truths about the supposed awfulness of the other side.
These distortions are believed because it feels good to believe them.

— David Brooks[1]

~

Because the dividing difference between men and women is believed to be ruling and childbearing, the only role available for women in patriarchy is that of a wife and mother. Complementarism continues Luther's tradition of assigning motherhood as the only vocation available for women, as seen in Knight's essay *The Family and the Church.*

> God relates the effect of the curse respectively to that portion of His creation mandate (as already established in Genesis 1 and 2) that most particularly applies to the woman on the one hand and to the man on the other hand. God has said to them: "Be fruitful and multiply, and fill the earth, and subdue it; and rule over... every living thing that moves on the earth (Genesis 1.28). Now he relates the curse to that aspect of the creation mandate that is the particular responsibility of

---

1. *David Brooks,* "People Like Us," The Atlantic (Sept, 2003), http://www.theatlantic .com/doc/200309/brooks (accessed June 29, 2009).

234

the woman and of the man and in so doing indicates the particular role that He has determined each is to fulfill.... In short, God speaks about what is unique to her as a woman, namely, being a mother and a wife... Then he delineates what is the main calling for man, namely, the responsibility of breadwinner and provider for his wife and family.[2]

Knight finds the roles by dividing Genesis 1.28 into two categories and assigning "being fruitful" to the woman and "ruling" to the man, which puts the woman on par with the animals for they were told to be fruitful, but not to rule due to their lack of reason (Gen 1.21-22).[3] Knight's arbitrary division makes the woman's entire existence revolve around her sexual function, and her entitlement to financial support from the breadwinning husband is due to her performances as a wife.

The division of the mind and the body is the traditional method of assigning women into the domestic sphere, found already in antiquity, the woman being considered suited only for procreation, not intellectual exertion. However, the Roman *matron*, whom we meet in the Bible, would not recognize herself in the modern homemaker.

> The wealthy Roman woman played a different role as wife and mother than her counterpart in Classical Athens. The fortunes of Romans were far greater, and they had not only more but more competent slaves. The tasks enumerated by Xenophon for the well-to-do Athenians wife were, even among the traditional-minded Romans, relegated to a slave, the chief steward's wife (*vilica*). Nevertheless, the Roman matron bore sole responsibility for the management of her town house, and although her work was mainly the supervision of slaves, she was expected to be able to perform such chores as spinning and weaving. Household duties did not hold a prominent place in a woman's public image: the Roman matron could never be considered

---

2. Piper and Grudem, 347.

3. Ortlund disagrees with Knight, "Further, Moses doubtless intends to imply the equality of the sexes, for both the male and female display the glory of God's image with equal brilliance: "... in the image of God he created him; male and female he created them." This is consistent with God's intention, stated in verse 26, that both sexes should rule. "... and let *them* rule..." (Piper and Grudem, 97).

a housewife as could the Athenian.... Freed from household routines, virtuous women could visit, go shopping, attend festivals and recitals, and supervise their children's education.[4]

Neither could the Proverbs 31 woman be considered a modern homemaker who is only concerned with the processing but not the producing of materials, for she bought fields, planted vineyards, produced clothing and food items, and considered her merchandise good. The twentieth-century homemaker was essentially a product of the nineteenth century which changed the attitude towards work performed by women. As a result of the Industrial Revolution, the work done traditionally by women, such as the making of cloth, medicine and, foods, was taken over by factories, and the wealth extracted from the underpaid working class began to accumulate into the hands of upper class men who displayed their wealth by having an "ornamental" wife who did not work as her ancestors had; instead she supervised the work done by others.[5] The middle class housewife of the early twentieth century, no longer needed servants, for she had electricity and machines which greatly reduced the labor involved, but what was she supposed to do with her time?[6] The "woman question" was partially answered by Helen Cambell: to keep the world clean was the one great task for women.[7] With little else to do, women set out to eradicate the dreaded germs with a passion and by the 1950s women spent nearly

---

4. Pomeroy, 169-170.

5. Barbara Ehrenreich and Deirdre English, *For Her Own Good* (Anchor, 1989) 117-118; Gail Collins writes, "All this discussion about women's role [before the woman's rights movement] was directed at a minority of all American households – most wives and daughters were still on the farm, doing the same rough chores their grandmothers had performed. As late as 1840, only one in nine Americans lived in a town with 2,500 or more people, and many urban women were too poor to contemplate their appropriate role in society. Still, thanks to the publishing industry, housewives in raw settlements and isolate farms devoured magazines that lectured them about their rights and duties as True Women, along with hints on how to decorate and elegant parlor and raise a decorous child." (Gail Collins, *America's Women, 400 Years of Dolls, Drudges, Helpmates and Heriones* [New York: Perennial, 2003], 93).

6. The working-class women followed the work traditionally performed by women to the factories, (Ehrenreich and English, 158) but the middleclass housewife was left with the Domestic Void. "As the Ladies' Home Journal [1911] editorialized, social stability required that the void be filled: "As a matter of fact, what a certain type of woman needs today more than anything else is some task that "would tie her down." Our whole social fabric would be better for it. Too many women are dangerously idle" (Ibid., 165).

7. Ibid, 174.

eighty hours a week cleaning their homes. (Women who worked outside the home, did the same housework in half the time.)[8] Although home economics had attempted to make homemaking a career in which the housewife was the manager by offering scientific advice how to effectively manage a home, in the end, the manager and the worker were one and the same, and the time gained by efficiency only raised the standard which created more work in an endless cycle.[9]

Cleaning one's home is not a fulfilling career, and Betty Friedan described the problem that had no name in the 1950s.

> The problem lay buried, unspoken for many years in the minds of American women. It was a strange stirring, a sense of dissatisfaction, a yearning that women suffered in the middle of the twentieth century in the United States. Each suburban wife struggled with it alone. As she made the beds, shopped for groceries, matched slipcover material, ate peanut butter sandwiches with her children, chauffeured Cub Scouts and Brownies, lay beside her husband at night – she was afraid to ask even of herself the silent question – "Is this all?" For over fifteen years there was no word of this yearning in the millions of words written about women, for women, in all the columns, book and articles by experts telling women their role was to seek fulfillment as wives and mothers.[10]

Yet, the illusion that the scientific approach to homemaking would make it a career worth pursuing has not been eradicated from the popular mind,[11] as seen in Dorothy Patterson's essay *The High Calling of Wife and Mother in Biblical Perspective.*

---

8. *The Feminine Mystique*, 241.

9. Ehrenreich and English, 178.

10. *The Feminine Mystique*, 15.

11. "The hope that education will make housework interesting dies hard. A 1974 home economics text states: " Much has been written concerning the boredom and frustration of the American homemaker. People who do things poorly are often bored and/or frustrated. The homemaker who is educated for homemaking us able to use her knowledge in a creative way for the attainment of a personally satisfying happy life and for the achievement of the social, economic, aesthetic, and scientific values in successful family life." (Ehrenreich and English, 171, Footnote, Quotes Eileen E. Quigley, Introduction to Home Economics [New York: MacMillan, 1974], 58-59).

> Homemaking, if pursued with energy, imagination, and skills, has
> as much challenge and opportunity, success and failure, growth and
> expansion, perks and incentives as any corporation... Homemaking
> – being a full-time wife and mother – is not a destructive drought of
> usefulness but an overflowing oasis of opportunity; it is not a dreary
> cell to contain one's talents and skills but a brilliant catalyst to channel
> creativity and energies into meaningful work.[12]

Sheila Wray Gregoire is more honest in her book *To Love, Honor and Vacuum*.

> Having to do less housework will probably make you happier all on its
> own, as long as you maintain a reasonable level of order in your home.
> Why? Because studies show that housework can be one of the most
> depressing jobs, whether you're doing a whole day of it or just fifteen
> minutes of dishes. There are reasons for this: you usually do it alone,
> nobody thanks you when you finish something, and besides that, it's
> never really done! [13]

Domestic science failed to provide an answer to the "woman question" because of the inherent boredom of housekeeping, which was not a fulfilling vocation for the average well-educated woman, who had nearly equal opportunities outside the home. Most societies relegate domestic work to uneducated slaves or servants, but the disappearance of slaves and domestic servants, and the increased standard of cleanliness, made it necessary for the well-educated woman to do the work; an arrangement necessary lest every man would find himself in front of the dish sink.

~

No one argued in the fifties whether women were inferior or superior to men, for they were "simply different." The "woman question" had vanished, having been replaced with the happy housewife – or so it was thought. In

---

12. Piper and Grudem, 377
13. Sheila Wray Gregoire, *To Honor, Love and Vacuum* (Grand Rapids, MI: Kregel Publications, 2003), 53-54.

1960 the bubble burst.[14] Newspapers and television reported about the unhappiness of the American housewife, and education was blamed for making them dissatisfied with the domestic life. It was even suggested that women should no longer be admitted to the four-year colleges and universities, or be allowed to vote.[15] The educators and newspaper columnists had accurately identified the source of the problem – education and political rights – for it was no longer possible to squeeze the educated and legally equal woman into the old mold of the uneducated legal minor.

A solution was sought high and low, but they consisted mostly of age-old panaceas such as handing one's self to God. A decade later, Christenson echoed the earlier suggestions but he conceded that being solely a homemaker would not make a woman happy.

> A wife is more than a mother, housekeeper, cook, counselor, and chauffeur. She will not find the deep places of her heart satisfied with bowling, bridge, PTA meetings, or even church work. On the other hand, if her sole source of happiness lies in her husband or her children, she is also doomed to disappointment. God did not intend us to find satisfaction apart from Himself. A wife who puts Jesus first will be a joy to her 'lord' and to her Lord (see 1 Pet 3.6). A radiant wife who once sought escape in intellectual pursuits, recently disclosed her secret for finding fulfillment in life: "It 's doing what Jesus wants me to do!" She went on to say that Jesus can change our attitudes: He can even change the routine tasks that were once a drudgery into a joy. "Be rooted in Christ, not in your husband; then you are free to be a worthwhile person, a good wife."[16]

But what if Jesus wants the wife to become a doctor, a teacher – or a pastor? Christenson's Jesus would never suggest such a thing; instead he changes the wife's attitude so the housework becomes a joy instead of a drudgery. Christenson was more concerned that wives stop nagging at their husbands than trying to find a solution for the desperate housewives, for he continued, "Jesus gives you the invitation to take your anxieties to the cross, and to leave the

---

14. *The Feminine Mystique*, 18-19.

15. Ibid., 23.

16. Larry Christenson, *The Christian Family* (New York: Bethany House Publishers, 1970), 48.

reforming of your husband in God's hands. The wife who is trusting in God is not nagging her husband." The wives certainly thought something was wrong with their husbands for, "if a woman had a problem in the 1950's and 1960's, she knew that something must be wrong with her marriage, or with herself."[17] That she thought something was wrong with herself was not a problem, for she had to only become more feminine, more submissive, and less anxious for the life she could not have to realize how lucky she was to be a woman.

Yet, another decade later, in 1980, Dr. Dobson advised women to "get into exercise classes, group hobbies, church activities, Bible studies, bicycle clubs," instead of remaining at home and considering their husbands their only source of conversation and comfort, for he believed the source of the problem was the lack of female companionship. [18] Although his advice was sound, he missed the point, for it was not the companionship of the other women that was important, but the fact that *they used to work together*. Dobson could only suggest the same tired, worn out solution, for he, like others before him, did not perceive the root of the problem: the belief that a woman's life should be limited to homemaking.

Back in the sixties, when it appeared that a simple solution was not forth-coming, the final answer was, "This is what being a woman means, and what is wrong with American women that they can't accept their role gracefully?"[19] No one suggested that women should work for the dreaded career woman had been drowned under the many commercials which were geared towards creating the myth of the happy housewife who had money to buy all the newest detergents and appliances and nothing else to do than to use them.[20]

The woman living in the colonial era had the work, but not the education or political rights; the 1950s woman had the education and political rights, but not the work. Women had achievement near equality with men by the 1940's, and a career woman was not considered an anomaly, but then came the fruitless carnage of WW II and the atom bomb, and the American people decided to go home.

---

17. *The Feminine Mystique*, 19.
18. Dr. James C. Dobson, *Straight Talk to Men and Their Wives* (Word Books, 1980), 110.
19. *The Feminine Mystique*, 24.
20. Ibid., 228.

We were all vulnerable, homesick, lonely, frightened. A pent-up hunger for marriage, home and children was felt simultaneously by several different generations; a hunger which, in the prosperity of postwar America, everyone could suddenly satisfy. The young GI, made older than his years by the war, could meet his lonely need for love and a mother by re-creating his childhood home. Instead of dating many girls until college and profession were achieved, he could marry on the GI bill, and give his own babies the tender mother love he was no longer baby enough to seek for himself. Then there were the slightly older men: men of twenty-five whose marriages had been postponed by the war and who now felt they must make up for lost time; men in their thirties kept first be depression and then by war from marrying, or if married, from enjoying the comforts of home.[21]

While it is true that a career woman had to often choose between love and a career before World War II, the glorification of the home which had existed in the previous century, was intensified by the war, and women were diverted from thinking about a career altogether. With the GI Bill the nation of renters was changed into a nation of homeowners,[22] and the young men who would not have entered college did so after the war and gained well-paying jobs which enabled them to support the women who chose to set up a home and raise a family. But the safety of the home, which had appeared so alluring for those who had lived in constant fear for years, lost its charm in a few years and boredom ascended over suburbia.

The boredom of the housewives caused an exhaustion which could not be cured, for housework could not be made interesting enough to make women feel useful. And although "the overwhelming majority of the women felt that a job was more satisfying than the housework," work was not considered an alternative; instead there was a surrender to the fact of life that to be tired was part of being a housewife. The husbands, who were told time after time to reward their wives with praise, obviously failed to do so for Dee Jepsen concludes with Dr. James Dobson that feminism was created because men were not "appreciating women for the important role they were playing."[23] In

---

21. Ibid., 182-3.
22. Ibid., 96.
23. Piper and Grudem, 392.

the fifties, husbands were at the end obliged to pitch in to keep the home running smoothly for their wives were too tired.[24] But Friedan identified also another reason for the domesticating of the husbands.

> Why should anyone raise an eyebrow because a latter-day Einstein's wife expects her husband to put aside that lifeless theory of relativity and help her with the work that is supposed to be the essence of life itself: diaper the baby and don't forge to rinse the soiled diaper in the toilet paper before putting it in the diaper pail, and then wax the kitchen floor.[25]

Eventually the wife dominated the home even more than the wartime generation by her expertise and "know-it-alls," which left very little room for the husband's assumed authority.[26] In addition, the attempt to make the 50's woman a subservient housewife through channeling her energy into shopping and cleaning made her the maker or breaker of American business world and through her decisions she controlled the destiny of men who gained their livelihood in these enterprises just as she controlled the home, her domain.

Elisabeth Elliot was dismayed by the effect she believed secular culture had on theology and to illustrate her point she quoted Francis Schaeffer who wrote, "Tell me what the world is saying today, and I'll tell you what the church will be saying seven years from now."[27] Schaeffer's words found their fulfillment in the book *Me? Obey Him?* written by Elliot's college friend Elizabeth Rice Handford in which she echoed the commercial advertising of the fifties.[28] Handford offered "The Balanced Housewife" as God's plan for womanhood, although

---

24. *The Feminine Mystique*, 250.

25. Ibid., 247.

26. Ibid., 257.

27. Piper and Grudem, 395.

28. Friedan describes how the marketers of the fifties realized that the Career Woman had to go because she was too critical and unwilling to buy all the latest gadgets to enhance her life, "The moral of the study was explicit: "Since the Balanced Homemaker represents the market with the greatest future potential, it would be to the advantage of the appliance manufacturer to make more and more women aware of the desirability of belonging to this group. Educate them through advertising that it is possible to have outside influences (without becoming a Career Woman). The art of good homemaking should be the goal of every normal woman" (*The Feminine Mystique*, 210).

she modified the fifties concept somewhat since by 1972, the Career Woman had returned, albeit still somewhat embarrassed of her own existence.

> Just because she is obedient does not mean she is limited only to the interests that traditionally have been feminine. It will include cooking, clothing, housekeeping and child-tending, of course, *but those are an essential part of her life.* But within the framework of her husband's authority, she may follow any inclination in her leisure time: welding sculptures, or turning up an automobile motor, or following major leagues baseball, or trout casting.... There is no one description of a woman who, honoring her husband, then finds a whole wide world outside, created by God to be explored and enjoyed. And she savors it to full.... It is a blessed fact that this [work], too, is available to the woman who honors and obeys her husband. I don't promise you can be famous trial lawyer or the doctor who discovers the cure for cancer or author of the great American novel, or prima donna of the Metropolitan Opera. (It's conceivable that a woman with talent could do these and still be an obedient wife.)[29]

Thus the greed of the market formed the woman's role in society and theology. It is naturally an ongoing process; the 1920s generation changed their former way of life and "by abandoning the natural, men and women imprisoned themselves in molds" created by advertising.[30] The fifty's experiment of making every woman into a housewife failed, but later generations would feel the ripple-effect of the intense glorification of shopping as a way to find happiness and fulfillment, which would lead to the near-destruction of the financial system in the early twenty-first century.[31]

---

29. Handford, *Me? Obey Him?*, 88-89.

30. Oscar and Lilian Handlin, *Liberty and Equality* (HarperCollins, 1994), 14.

31. The housewife lost much of her early prestige in the sixties and the single girl, who took an active part in the society, became the new norm and marketers were not slow to recognize the advantage. Instead of saving, people began to spend as the new theme became instant gratification. "A clearheaded capitalist could only rejoice at the new self-indulgent mood of young women." (Ehrenreich and English, 319) In 1977 the advertisers would still point out that the young woman did not live beyond her means, but this caution would be thrown out the window with the advent of the credit card.

Theology tends to get stuck, usually in the era of the founder of a particular movement, and roles, especially gender based ones, are frozen into the era which is later believed to be the Golden Era. One has to only glance at the halo, which hovers above the '50s, to realize the tendency to glorify a bygone era. John Stuart Mill objected against a form of Christianity which exists only to stereotype existing forms of government and society and to protect them against change,[32] and he was right in his estimation for a government can only provide a partial answer to the problems of humanity, wherefore governments are changed frequently either through election or revolution.

Capitalism is often believed to be an outgrowth of Christianity but it is the logical outcome of the evolutionary principle of the survival of the fittest. The struggle for survival in nature allows only for a few predators on the top of the food chain, and it is also true of the free market.

> As the result of the development of capitalism we witness an ever-increasing process of centralization and concentration of capital. The large enterprises grow in size continually, the smaller ones are squeezed out. The ownership of capital invested in these enterprises is more and more separated from the function of managing them.... The initiative has been shifted, for better or worse, in the fields of capital as well as in those of labor, from the individual to the bureaucracy. An increasing number of people cease to be independent, and become dependent on the managers of the great economic empires.... The human problem of modern capitalism can be formulate in this way: Modern capitalism needs men who co-operate smoothly and in large numbers; who want to consume more and more; and whose tastes are standardized and can be easily influenced and anticipated. It needs men who feel free and independent, not subject to any authority or principle or conscience – yet willing to be commanded, to do what is expected of them, to fit into the social machine without friction; who can be guided without force, led without leaders. Prompted without aim – expect the one to make good, to be on the move, to function, to go ahead. What is the outcome? Modern man is alienated from himself, from his fellowman, and from nature. [33]

---

32. Mill, 85.
33. Fromm, 71.

Capitalism in its rawest form does not allow for alturism, which is well attested by the nineteenth-century slave and child labor, and the ill-paid working class whose labor made the wealth of few possible. A strong middle class exists only when government regulations hinder the concentration of wealth in the hands of few by the redistribution of wealth. James P. Comer responded in 1972 to the argument presented by the white majority that the black people expected the get everything for free without work.

> Middle America has gained much of its security through such government-assistance programs as the GI bill, Farmers Home Administration, Social Security, public education, the Small Business Administration, Medicare, and so forth. Their trade unions have guaranteed them additional security through medical and life insurance plans, tuition programs, cost-of-living increases, paid vacations and numerous other benefits. Government and private assistance, not just "rugged individualism," has made opportunity available for large numbers of white Americans.[34]

Life in a capitalistic society does not offer many cushions from the cold reality of life and Patterson is not pleased that the only work recognized by society is that which is paid.[35] But the problem is not fixed by sending women home with poetic declarations of their worth, for if society requires financial independence from its citizens, those who are dependent will always be vulnerable. Christians are waking up to the reality of capitalism, as is seen in that James Dobson believes America's greatest need is for husbands to begin to guide their families instead of "pouring every physical and emotional resource into the mere acquisition of money."[36] The total control of communal assets by the governing body, which was also practiced by the early church, is possible only in a sinless world, wherefore Communism it is not a viable option for a secular society.[37] Because the individual needs the community as much as the

---

34. Comer, 73

35. Piper and Grudem, 368.

36. Ibid., 39.

37. "Communism will work in a sinless world, and only in a sinless world. This is perhaps the reason communism must assume as a basic postulate that sin does not exist. This accounts in part for the success of communal religious groups" (Stephen J. Tonsor, *Equality, Decadence, and Modernity* [Wilmington, DE: ISI Books, 2005], 6).

community needs the individual, the community must care for the individual as the individual cares for the community; a political system which provides an incentive for individual effort while caring for the weaker members provides a healthy society in which the individual can thrive.[38]

~

The glorification of the housewife became necessary to uphold the system which was built on quicksand.

> Toying with the question, how can one hour of housework expand to fill six hours (same house, same work, same wife), I came back again to the basic paradox of the feminine mystique: that it emerged to glorify woman's role as housewife at the very moment when the barriers to her full participation in society were lowered, at the very moment when science and education and her own ingenuity made it possible for a woman to be both wife and mother and to take an active part in the world outside the home. The glorification of "woman's role," then, seems to be in proportion to society's reluctance to treat women as complete human beings; for the less real function that role has, the more it is decorated with meaningless details to conceal its emptiness.[39]

This is also true of Christianity now that women are close to gaining full equality in the church: they are reminded that a homemaker "cannot be duplicated for any amount of money, for "she is worth far more than rubies." [40] And whereas women in the fifties discovered that they were able to do the same housework, which often was undone by dinnertime, in a fraction of the time when they studied or worked, or had other serious interests outside the home, Dorothy Patterson prescribes the same remedy as Christenson in *Christian Family*: "The best way to make homemaking a joyous task is to offer it as unto to the Lord; the only way to avoid the drudgery in such mundane tasks

---

38. The problem of sustaining the individual's effort while ensuring the care of the weak without causing widespread abuse of the system can never be fully solved, for humanity follows the pattern of harmony-sin-redemption found most clearly in Judges, wherefore the system has to be continuously adjusted and perfection can never be achieved.

39. *The Feminine Mystique*, 238-239.

40. Piper and Grudem, 367.

is to bathe the task with prayer and catch a vision of the divine challenge in making and nurturing a home." [41] But why does the task need to be bathed in prayer if it is "a brilliant catalyst to channel creativity and energies into meaningful work"? Because homemaking follows the law of myth rather than that of logic.

> Logic and reason deal with the relationship between facts. They tend, therefore, to speak in the indicative mood – as does Professor Ginzenberg when he notes the long history of working women and the economic value of their labor. Myth, however, will not be argued down by facts. It may seem to be making straightforward statements, but actually these conceal another mood, the imperative. Myth exists in a state of tension. It is not really describing a situation, but trying by means of this description to bring about what it declares to exist. One might think that the hopeful, optative mood was more appropriate to wish fulfillment, but myth is more demanding that that. It does not merely wish, it wills; and when it speaks, it commands action.[42]

The myth of homemaking demands that it *must* be joyous even though facts deny it and prayer must be used to overcome the inherent drudgery and boredom.

The women writers who prescribe homemaking to other women usually do not live such circumscribed lives themselves. Besides the obvious fact that they are published writers, they have other positions, such as a pastor's wife (with all the respect the position commands), counselor, or a missionary. This distinct group in between men and women exists partly because patriarchy lumps all women into one group and some women find ways to organize a pecking order,[43] but also because they are comfortable with their role, as explained by Janeway.

> In fact, I suspect that the weakening of the myth of female weakness is going to affect men's attitudes more dramatically then it is those of women. For one thing, a great many women are going to want to hang on to the myth. They were raised to believe that they

---

41. Ibid., 367.
42. Janeway, 37.
43. Stearns, 12.

had a special place in the world and that special characteristics fitted them for certain tasks and unfitted them for others. They want to be fulfilled by motherhood. ... Woman's role has been widening fast enough for them, its restrictions have eased enough, and though they know that inequities remain, they don't feel them directly enough to want to take action. Out of habit and custom and because they believe in the myth themselves, they are content with the rate of change.[44]

Motherhood is the last one of the exclusively female vocations, which used to define the separate male and female spheres. Men have taken over the producing of food items, clothing and medicine and it is only natural that women are reluctant to give up the one vocation, which gives them a sense of power and accomplishment without a guarantee that men will not eclipse them entirely. Men on the other hand fear that women will take over if they agree to equality and it is this distrust which ultimately keeps both men and women from embracing equality.[45]

Despite all the efforts to assure women that "anatomy was destiny," the tidal wave of women leaving the home could not be contained. Friedan had asked in 1963, "When motherhood, a fulfillment held sacred down to ages, is defined as a total way of life, must women themselves deny the world and the future open to them? Or does the denial of that world *force* them make motherhood a total way of life?" [46]And the women responded by re-defining motherhood as an essential part of their lives but not as an all-encompassing vocation.[47] But before we place all blame or credit on the women themselves,

---

44. Janeway, 281.

45. James P. Comer wrote, "I realize now that anxiety about pleasing a white authority or a white majority can prevent blacks from speaking out for black rights, and can lead black social activists into settling for watered-down compromises" (Comer, 21). Women feel often a need to please the male authorities wherefore they are willing to accept the compromise of "equal but different" instead of full equality.

46. Ibid., 58.

47. The infant needs a caregiver who is committed to his or her wellbeing, and although there is much talk about the family and the importance of the parent-child relationship during the first year of the infant's life, there is little, or no effort, to ensure that mothers and fathers can afford to remain home. This reluctance is not only due to capitalism, but also because of the doctrine of the man's headship which makes the wife's financial dependency necessary.

contrary to the fifties woman, the sixties woman did not have a GI Bill and had to therefore finance her own education, find a loan for her home and somehow finance the lifestyle which the fifties marketers and psychoanalysis had created and which was not made possible with only one income.

> It wasn't only that the life of the full-time housewife was becoming psychologically untenable. It was also turning out to be financially untenable. There was a fatal catch in the mid-century domestic ideal. The picture of the "good life" included a house (Cape, ranch or pseudo-colonial), three or four kids, and of course the full-time homemaker who held everything together. The problem was the first two items (house and kids) turned out to be so expensive that the third (full-time mother) often had to go.[48]

But if women are going to work, their children must be cared for. During World War II, daycare was widely available for women's work was considered essential for the war effort. But after the war ended, day care centers disappeared and "the very suggestion of their need brought hysterical outcries from educated housewives as well as the purveyors or the mystique."[49] In addition, the old stigma of daycare being a last resort for the poor is still very much with us.

> In the 1880s and 1890s, some associations also began the establish day nurseries in working-class neighborhoods. Typically located in rented brownstones, the nurseries provided a place where the working mother could safely leave her young children for a nominal fee, about 5 cents a day.... The nurseries insisted that the children be brought to them spotlessly clean at 6:30 every morning, a difficult task for a woman who worked a 12-hour day and whose tenement lacked hot water.... Not surprisingly, the nurseries were not popular among working mothers. If Bloomingdale Nursery enrolled a total of 1800 children, it generally had less than 50 in daily attendance. The Cleveland Nursery had 142 children listed on its books in 1891, but only 25 were present on any given day. In fact, the nurseries generally received

---

48. Ehrenreich and English, 310.
49. *The Feminine Mystique,* 185.

children from the woman who had no other option; they were, in a sense, a last resort.[50]

Poverty and moral failure were intrinsically connected in the nineteenth-century mindset and thus the woman who was morally superior was able to care for her children at home, although the ornamental housewife more often than not left the care of her children to the servants. It appears that the upper class did not see, or care to see, the link between their own wealth and the poverty of the working class, and because social services were largely left to the upper and middle-class women who did more harm than good with their patronizing attitude, the myth of the uncared for children of the working mother was created. Naturally there were also countless middle-class women who found themselves suddenly impoverished and with no resources to care for the children as many small businesses were put out of business by larger companies, but there was a great effort to hide the facts because appearance mattered more than reality.[51] The Century of the Child, which was created to address child abuse, such as the extensive use of child labor (2,250,000 American children under fifteen were fulltime laborers at the end of the nineteenth century),[52] caused standards to rise until parents were considered unfit if they were "too busy, tired, lazy, egocentric or indifferent to ride herd on their kids every minute every day," according to Dr Max Rafferty, former Superintendent of Public Instruction in California.[53] He believed also that a parent who did not know what her child did every minute of the day should loose the custody of her children. Dr. Rafferty was clearly influenced by the feminine mystique of the fifties which had convinced everyone that the "children will be tragically deprived if she [the mother] is not there every minute." [54] But although he blamed "the dropout parents" for the juvenile delinquency of the sixties,[55] it appears that delinquency was already created in the fifties when mothers where home and watched every step "junior" took.

---

50. Rothman, 89-90.
51. Rothman, 49.
52. Ehrenreich and English, 204.
53. *The Christian Family*, 81.
54. *The Feminine Mystique*, 247.
55. *The Christian Family*, 79.

Strange new problems are being reported in the growing generations of children whose mothers were always there, driving them around, helping them with their homework – an inability to endure pain or discipline or pursue any self-sustained goal of any sort, a devastating boredom with life. Educators are increasingly uneasy about the dependence, the lack of self-reliance, of the boys and girls who are entering college today. "We fight a continual battle to make our students assume manhood," said a Columbia dean.[56]

The Women's Rights Movement did not take off until 1970 when women marched down Fifth Avenue in New York and raised awareness of their existence,[57] just as women had in 1912 and 1913 to gain the vote.[58] The Church responded promptly; the same year Larry Christensen published *The Christian Family*, in which he considered the movement satanic in its origin.

How much evil has come upon home and church because women have lost the protective shield of a husband's authority! We have let Satan beguile us into believing that it is degrading for a wife to be submissive and obedient to her husband's authority. The whole teaching is dismissed as a foolish vaunting of the "male ego," a Neanderthal vestige which our enlightened age has happily outgrown. The Bible, however, has no desire to exalt any ego, male or female. The Divine Order set forth for the family serves the elemental purpose of protection, spiritual protection. A husband's authority and a wife's submissiveness to that authority, is a shield of protection against Satan's devices. Satan knows this, and that is why he uses every wile to undermine and break down God's pattern of Divine Order for the family.[59]

Women's Lib vs. Adam's Rib was published four years later, in which Bro Kirk Luehrs and Stephen C. Graham upheld the beliefs that the woman was created an assistant for the man (Gen 2.18-24), that woman's punishment was to serve the man (Gen 3.16), and that women have ruled men by their nagging

---

56. *The Feminine Mystique,* 29.

57. *It Changed My Life,* 192.

58. "Women's History," http://www.womenshistory.about.com/library/pic/bl_p_ny_suffrage_1913_c.htm (accessed June 29, 2009).

59. *The Christian Family,* 37.

and tears, although "we are all equal in the sight of God... where there is love, there is no need to rule, for all would be servants to our Lord."[60]

In 1977 Gene A. Getz wrote *The Measure of a Woman* in which he blamed the Women's Rights Movement for causing resentment in women who, according to him, had earlier been entirely happy in their role as fulltime homemakers.[61] Yet, doctors reported of symptoms and neuroses that had not been seen before the fifties and psychiatrists reported that unmarried women were happier than married women.[62] Doctors prescribed tranquilizers and many a housewife was taking them "like couch drops,"[63] just as the nineteenth-century woman had been prescribed laudanum (tincture of opium) and alcohol to cure the debilitating effects of boredom.[64]

A study conducted in the early sixties in England revealed that ninety percent of young mothers in the middle twenties were either working or planned to work as soon as the children were in school and this occurred before the Woman's Right Movement took off in the late sixties.[65] It was not feminism that created the desire to work in women; it was women's desire to work which created feminism.

Piper recognizes that most women have always worked.

> The point of saying that man should feel a responsibility to provide for woman is not that the woman should not assist in maintaining support for the family or for society in general. She has always done this historically because so much of domestic life required extraordinary labors on her part just to maintain the life of the family.... It is possible to be excessively demanding or excessively restrictive on a woman's role in sustaining the life of the family. Proverbs 31 pictures a wife with great ability in the business affairs of the family.[66]

---

60. Bro Kirk Luehrs and Stephen C. Graham, *Women's Lib vs. Adam's Rib* (Portland, OR: Telefriend. Inc., 1974) 17, 31, 37.

61. Getz, 75.

62. *The Feminine Mystique*, 25.

63. Ibid., 31.

64. Ehrenreich and English, 87.

65. Janeway, 225-226.

66. Piper and Grudem, 42.

But employers are not always willing to meet the needs of working mothers, for as Elizabeth Janeway observed astutely, "If society assumes implicitly that women shouldn't work because their place is at home, and regards women who work as flying in the face of custom or even nature, then there is no need for society to do anything to help them out."[67] Thus we do not have a social network which would allow women to work. Nor does the society provide paid maternal leave and other benefits, which would diminish the many hardships that most working women experience today; instead we make them feel guilty for wanting to "find themselves" or call them selfish for wanting to have a career while their children "suffer."[68] On the other hand a man who works less than his wife is considered neglectful, since the measure of a man is his paycheck. Thus social pressure creates rigid roles which keep men and women in their "proper" spheres with the explicit approval of the church.

---

67. Janeway, 190.

68. There is nothing wrong for a woman to stay home with her children if she wishes to and can afford it, just as any wealthy person is able to abstain from working. The inherent hypocrisy of homemaking is that class mentality makes a distinction between rich and poor, and although theologians claim that it is necessary for the wellbeing of the children, yet they do not seek means to ensure that *all* children can remain home, by placing the responsibility to support single mothers and poor working women on the government - or the church, which is a biblical practice. If it is the quality of childcare which is objectionable, why not start co-operative childcare centers in the church to ensure the proper upbringing of children and peace of mind for both parents and theologians?

Epilogue

CHRISTIANS ARE OFTEN unaware that the existing New Testament manuscripts contain as many variants as there are words in the New Testament,[1] and that scholars do not always agree as to the original meaning of a particular text. The manuscripts which contain most variants come from the first three centuries during which the manuscripts were copied by Christians whose literacy level was not always adequate to the task.

> Indeed we have solid evidence that this was the case, as it was a matter of occasional complaint by Christians reading those texts and trying to uncover the original words of their authors. The third century church father Origen, for example, once registered the following complaint about the copies of the Gospels at his disposal: "*The difference among the manuscripts have become great, either through the negligence of some copyists or through the perverse audacity of others; they either neglect to check what they have transcribed, or, in the process of checking, they made additions or deletions as they please.*"[2]

Although the fourth-century manuscripts created in the *scriptoria* exhibit more uniformity than the earlier versions, the later versions were based on the earlier error-riddled manuscripts. The natural question is: did the fourth-century scribes always choose the right word from the many existing variants?

Bart D. Ehrman explains further that although the majority of the errors in the manuscripts are easy to detect and do not alter the meaning of the text, some of the deliberate changes have had a profound effect on traditional theology, especially when the change has altered the subsequent interpreta-

---

1. Bart D. Ehrman, *Misquoting Jesus* (New York: Harper Collins, 2005), 89-90.
2. Ibid., 51-52.

tion of the Bible.[3] We have already noted that as a result of the interpolated verses in 1 Corinthians 14, Christian theologians have argued that Genesis 3.16 mandates the subjection and silencing of women in the church. In addition, the changed meaning of Genesis 3.16 became the foundation of Thomas Aquinas's twofold subjection, which in turn changed the interpretation of the New Testament.

But it was not only the changed interpretation of Genesis 3.16 which caused Thomas Aquinas to alter the meaning of Genesis 2.18-24 in A.D. 1250. The reason is found also in the second period of medieval history which comprised the twelfth and thirteenth centuries.

> By the twelfth century reform was universally conceded to be grievously needed. Then came the second stage in the attempt to Christianize society, this time not so much by permeation as by domination. The Church became not merely a temporary power but a theocracy. The movement which effected the change originated in a monastery but is named Gregorian, after Pope Gregory VII, who espoused its program to reform alike the monasteries, the Church, and the world.[4]

To prevent the secular rulers from interfering with the internal affairs of the church, the church had to dominate the society. Because the laity could not perform the sacraments, the sacramental system became the foundation for the dominion and as a result, the most insignificant priest, by virtue of his office, was greater than the most noble of the worldly rulers, who could not confer heavenly salvation, only earthly peace.[5] The problem the new theocracy encountered was whether a woman could hold an ecclesiastical office and rule men – even the emperor. Although the woman's rule was not deemed acceptable, the church lacked the theological justification for the definite exclusion of women from the orders. Thomas solved the problem by making the woman subject to the man from creation. That Thomas used Aristotle's philosophy to create the twofold subjection was not an obstacle, for few knew what the

---

3. Occasionally a scribe would detect a change as seen in the fourth-century *Codex Vaticanus* where the comment, "Fool and knave, leave the old reading, don't change it!" is found in the margin (Ehrman, 44).

4. Roland H. Bainton, *The Reformation of the Sixteenth Century* (Boston, MA: Beacon Press, 1952), 8.

5. Ibid.,10.

Bible actually said in the era of the Vulgate, and those who did approved of the change.

Dogmas do not co-exist harmoniously, for often one denies what the other affirms. Consider, for example, the decree found in The First Vatican Council, which convened for its first session on the 8th of December, 1869.

> For the doctrine of the faith which God has revealed is put forward not as some philosophical discovery capable of being perfected by human intelligence, but as a divine deposit committed to the spouse of Christ to be faithfully protected and infallibly promulgated. Hence, too, that meaning of the sacred dogmas is ever to be maintained which has once been declared by holy mother church, and there must never be any abandonment of this sense under the pretext or in the name of a more profound understanding. [6]

According to the above decree, the church should not uphold Thomas Aquinas's twofold subjection, based as it is on human intelligence, yet it is found in Catholic theology alongside with Augustine's denial of the woman's subjection as a created order. Protestant theologians bypass such a dilemma because of their commitment to the Bible as their final authority, but they must take into account the uncertainty of not knowing exactly what the Bible says, for we no longer possess the original manuscripts. The large amounts of variants and interpolations, such as the *Adulterous Woman* (John 8.3-11) and the Johannine Comma (1 John 5.7-8) makes dogmatism impossible for how can one be entirely certain that the text one uses was part of the original text?[7]

We will end our inquiry into biblical equality with one final question: is it possible for a Christian to uphold the man's authority as a divinely ordained doctrine? Only if one rejects the truth in favor of error. It is time to let the dogma of female subordination die.

---

6. The First Vatican Council, Session 3, April 24th 1870, Chapter 4.13-4.

7. A good example of a variant caused by a scribal error is Rev 1.5 which is translated, "Unto him that loved us, and washed us from our sins in his own blood," in the KJV. "Washed" is *lousanti* in the Greek, whereas "released" is *lusanti*. Modern translations opt for lusanti as seen in the NAS, "To Him who loves us, and released us from our sins by His blood" (Ehrman, 93).

Appendix A

Kephale in Early Christian Writings

THE FOLLOWING EARLY Christian Writers gave *kephale* the meaning "beginning" which creates an insoluble unity of the source and the person born or created.

Ignatius, disciple of John the Apostle (30-107)

Irenaeus (ca 180)

Tertullian (145-200)

Clement of Alexandria (153-217)

Origen (185-254)

Cyprian (200-258)

Novatian (210-280)

Arnobius (297-303)

Athanasius (298-373)

St. Basil (329-379)

Gregory of Nazianzen (329-389)

St. Ambrose (340-397)

Rufinus (344-408)

Councils of Ariminum and Seleucia (359)

Four discourses against the Arians (356-360)

Hilary of Poitiers (died 367)

John Chrysostom (347-407)

Aurelius Augustine (354-430)

Socrates Scholasticus (born 379)

Leo the Great (Ca. 390-461)

Ignatius, Apostolic Father (30-107) "Flee, therefore, those evil offshoots [of Satan], which produce death- bearing fruit, whereof if any one tastes, he instantly dies. For these men are not the planting of the Father. For if they were, they would appear as branches of the cross, and their fruit would be incorruptible. By it [Through the Cross], He calls you through His passion, as being His members. The head, therefore, cannot be born by itself, without its members; God, who is [the Saviour] Himself, having promised their union. (Ignatius to the Trallians, Chapter XI)

Irenaeus (ca 180) "As the Head rose from the dead, so also the remaining part of the body – of everyman who is found in life… Remember, therefore, my beloved friend, that thou hast been redeemed by the flesh of our Lord, re-established by His blood; and "holding the Head, from which the whole body of the Church, having been fitted together, takes increase" – that is, acknowledging the advent in the flesh of the Son of God, and [His] divinity (deum), and looking forward with constancy to His human nature (hominem)" (Against Heresies, Book III, XIX; Book V, XIV.4)

Tertullian (145-200) When, therefore, he speaks of their "following the commandments and doctrines of men," he refers to the conduct of those persons who "held not the Head," even Him in whom all things are gathered together; for they are all recalled to Christ, and concentrated in Him as their initiating principle – even the meats and drinks which were indifferent in their nature. (Five Books Against Marcion, Book V, Ch XIX)

Clement of Alexandria (153-217) And it is the name of God that is expressed; since, as the Son sees the goodness of the Father, God the Saviour works, being called the first principle of all things, which was imaged forth from the invisible God first, and before the ages, and which fashioned all things which came into being after itself. Nay more, the oracle exhibits the prophecy which by the Word cries and preaches, and the judgment that is to come; since it is the same Word which prophesies, and judges, and discriminates all things.... This discourse respecting God is most difficult to handle. For since the first principle of everything is difficult to find out, the absolutely first and oldest principle, which is the cause of all other things being and having been, is difficult to exhibit. For bow can that be expressed which is neither genus, nor difference, nor species, nor individual, nor number; nay more, is neither an event, nor that to which an event happens? No one can rightly express Him wholly. For on account of His greatness He is ranked as the All, and is the Father of the universe. Nor are any parts to be predicated of Him. For the One is indivisible; wherefore also it is infinite, not considered with reference to inscrutability, but with reference to its being without dimensions, and not having a limit. And therefore it is without form and name. And if we name it, we do not do so properly, terming it either the One, or the Good, or Mind, or Absolute Being, or Father, or God, or Creator or Lord. (Stromata, Book V, Ch VI, XII)

Origen (185-254) "Who is the head of all things, alone having as head God the Father, for it is written, "The head of Christ is God," seeing clearly also that it is written, no one knows the Father, save the Son, nor does anyone know the Son, save the Father" (for who can know what wisdom is, save He who called it into being) who can investigate with certainty the universal nature of His Word, and of God Himself, which nature proceeds from God, except God alone, with whom the Word was." (Origen de Principiis, Book II, ch IV.3, VI.1)

Cyprian (200-258) So that, while they feign things like the truth, they make void the truth by their subtlety. This happens, beloved brethren, so long as we do not return to the source of truth, as we do not seek the head nor keep the teaching of the heavenly Master... As there are many rays of the sun, but one light; and many branches of a tree, but one strength based in its tenacious root; and since from one spring flow many streams, although the multiplicity seems diffused in the liberality of an overflowing abundance, yet the unity is still preserved in the source. Separate a ray of the sun from its body of light, its unity does not allow a division of light; break a branch from a tree, – when broken, it will not be able to bud; cut off the stream from its fountain, and that which is cut off dries up. Thus also the Church, shone over with the light of the Lord, sheds forth her rays over the whole world, yet it is one light which is everywhere diffused, nor is the unity of the body separated. Her fruitful abundance spreads her branches over the whole world. She broadly expands her rivers, liberally flowing, yet her head is one, her source one; and she is one mother, plentiful in the results of fruitfulness: from he womb we are born, by her milk we are nourished, by her spirit we are animated. (Treatise I, On the Unity of the Church, 3, 4)

Novatian (210-280) But now, whatever He is, He is not of Himself, because He is not unborn; but He is of the Father, because He is begotten, whether as being the Word, whether as being the Power, or as being the Wisdom, or as being the Light, or as being the Son; and whatever of these He is, in that He is not from any other source, as we have already said before, than from the Father, owing His origin to His Father, He could not make a disagreement in the divinity by the number of two Gods, since He gathered His beginning by being born of Him who is one God. In which kind, being both as well only-begotten as first-begotten of Him who has no beginning, He is the only one, of all things both Source and Head. And therefore He declared that God is one, in that He proved Him to be from no source nor beginning, but rather the beginning and source of all things (A treatise of Novatian Concerning the Trinity, Ch XXXI)

Arnobius (297-303) But let this monstrous and impious fancy be put far *from us*, that Almighty God, the creator and framer, the author of things great and invisible, should be believed to have begotten souls so fickle, with no seriousness, firmness, and steadiness, prone to vice, inclining to all kinds of sins... then that, forgetting that they have one origin, one father and head, they should shake to their foundations and violate the rights of kinship. (Arnobius, Adversus Gentes, Book II, 45)

Athanasius (298-373) For neither is safe to say that the Son is from nothing, (since this is no where spoken of Him in divinely inspired Scripture,) nor again of any other subsistence before existing beside the Father, but from God alone do we define Him genuinely to be generated. For the divine Word teaches that the Ingenerate and Unbegun, the Father of Christ, is One.

Nor may we, adopting the hazardous position, 'There was once when He was not,' from unscriptural sources, imagine any interval of time before Him, but only the God who has generated Him apart from time; for through Him both times and ages came to be. Yet we must not consider the Son to be co-unbegun and co-ingenerate with the Father; for no one can be properly called Father or Son of one who is co-unbegun and co-ingenerate with Him. But we acknowledge that the Father who alone is Unbegun and Ingenerate, hath generated inconceivably and incomprehensibly to all: and that the Son hath been generated before ages, and in no wise to be ingenerate Himself like the Father, but to have the Father who generated Him as His beginning; for 'the Head of Christ is God.' (1 Cor. xi. 3.) (Councils of Ariminum and Seleucia, Part II, History of Arian opinions, Council of Sirmium)

Basil, Doctor of the Church (329-379) "If, say they, the Saviour is a vine, and we are branches ... He called US branches not of His Godhead, but of His flesh, as the Apostle says, we are 'the body of Christ, and members in particular, and again, know ye not that your bodies are the members of Christ?' If the head of the 'man is Christ, and the head of Christ is God, and man is not of one substance with Christ, Who is God (for man is not God), but Christ is of one substance with God (for He is God) therefore God is not the head of Christ in the same sense as Christ is the head of man. The natures of the creature and the creative Godhead do not exactly coincide. God is head of Christ as Father; Christ is head of us, as Maker. (Prolegomena Sketch of the Life and Works of Saint Basil, II. Works On John XV. I. "I Am the Vine.")

Gregory of Nazianzen, Doctor of the Church (329-389) "God begetteth not a false god, as we have said, nor did He deliberate and afterwards beget; but He begat eternally, and much more swiftly than our words or thoughts: for we speaking in time, consume time; but in the case of the Divine Power, the generation is timeless. And as I have often said, He did not bring forth the Son from non existence into being, nor take the non-existent into sonship: but the Father, being Eternal, eternally and ineffably begat One Only Son, who has no brother. Nor are there two first principles; but the Father is the head of the Son; the beginning is One. For the Father begot the Son VERY GOD, called Emmanuel; and Emmanuel being interpreted is, God with us (Lecture XI.14)

<u>Ambrose, Doctor of the Church</u> (340-397) "It is written, say they, that "the head of every man is Christ, and the head of woman is man, and the head of Christ is God." Let them, if they please, tell me what they mean by this objection—whether to join together, or to dissociate, these four terms. Suppose they mean to join them, and say that God is the Head of Christ in the same sense and manner as man is the head of woman. Mark what a conclusion they Fall into. For if this comparison proceeds on the supposed equality of the terms of it, and these four – woman, man, Christ, and God – are viewed together as in virtue of a likeness resulting from their being of one and the same nature, then woman and God will begin to come under one definition. But if this conclusion be not satisfactory, by reason of its impiety, let them divide, on what principle they will. Thus, if they will have it that Christ stands to God the Father in the same relation as woman to man, then surely they pronounce Christ and God to be of one substance, inasmuch as woman and man are of one nature in respect of the flesh, for their difference is in respect of sex. But, seeing that there is no difference of sex between Christ and His Father, they will acknowledge then that which is one, and common to the Son and the Father, in respect of nature, whereas they will deny the difference lying in sex. Does this conclusion content them? Or will they have woman, man, and Christ to be of one substance, and distinguish the Father from them? Will this, then, serve their turn? Suppose that it will, then observe what they are brought to. They must either confess themselves not merely Arians, but very Photinians, because they acknowledge only the Manhood of Christ, Whom they judge fit only to be placed on the same scale with human beings. Or else they must, however contrary to their leanings, subscribe to our belief, by which we dutifully and in godly fashion maintain that which they have come at by an impious course of thought, that Christ is indeed, after His divine generation, the power of God, whilst after His putting on of the flesh, He is of one substance with all men in regard of His flesh, excepting indeed the proper glory of His Incarnation, because He took upon Himself the reality, not a phantom

likeness, of flesh. Let God, then, be the Head of Christ, with regard to the conditions of Manhood. Observe that the Scripture says not that the Father is the Head of Christ; but that God is the Head of Christ, because the Godhead, as the creating power, is the Head of the being created. And well said [the Apostle] "the Head of Christ is God;" to bring before our thoughts both the Godhead of Christ and His flesh, implying, that is to say, the Incarnation in the mention of the name of Christ, and, in that of the name of God, oneness of Godhead and grandeur of sovereignty. But the saying, that in respect of the Incarnation God is the Head of Christ, leads on to the principle that Christ, as Incarnate, is the Head of man, as the Apostle has clearly expressed in another passage, where he says: "Since man is the head of woman, even as Christ is the Head of the Church;" whilst in the words following he has added: "Who gave Himself for her." After His Incarnation, then, is Christ the head of man, for His self- surrender issued from His Incarnation. The Head of Christ, then, is God, in so far as His form of a servant, that is, of man, not of God, is considered, But it is nothing against the Son of God, if, in accordance with the reality of His flesh, He is like unto men, whilst in regard of His Godhead He is one with the Father, for by this account of Him we do not take aught from His sovereignty, but attribute compassion to Him. But who can with a good conscience deny the one Godhead of the Father and the Son, when our Lord, to complete His teaching for His disciples, said: "That they may be one, even as we also are one." The record stands for witness to the Faith, though Arians turn it aside to suit their heresy; for, inasmuch as they cannot deny the Unity so often spoken of, they endeavour to diminish it, in order that the Unity of Godhead subsisting between the Father and the Son may seem to be such as is unity of devotion and faith amongst men, though even amongst men themselves community of nature makes unity thereof. (Exposition of the Christian Faith, Book IV, Chapter III, 28- 34)

Rufinus (344-408) "For He is born One of One, because there is one brightness of light, and there is one word of the understanding. Neither does an incorporeal generation degenerate into the plural number, or suffer division, where He Who is born is in no wise separated from Him Who begets. He is "only" (unique), as thought is to the mind, as wisdom is to the wise, as a word is to the understanding, as valour is to the brave. For as the Father is said by the Apostle to be "alone wise," so likewise the Son alone is called wisdom. He is then the "only Son." And, although in glory, everlastingness, virtue, dominion, power, He is what the Father is, yet all these He hath not unoriginately as the Father, but from the Father, as the Son, without beginning and equal; and although He is the Head of all things, yet the Father is the Head of Him. For so it is written, "The Head of Christ is God." (Rufinus, A Commentary on the Apostles' Creed, 6)

<u>Councils of Ariminum and Seleucia</u> (359) *The Creed according to the Council of the East.* "If any man says that the Son is incapable of birth and without beginning, saying as though there were two incapable of birth and unborn and without beginning, and makes two Gods: let him be anathema. For the Head, which is the beginning of all things, is the Son; but the Head or beginning of Christ is God: for so to One who is without beginning and is the beginning of all things, we refer the whole world through Christ. To declare the Son to be incapable of birth is the height of impiety. God would no longer be One: for the nature of the one Unborn God demands that we should confess that God is one. Since therefore God is one, there cannot be two incapable of birth: because God is one (although both the Father is God and the Son of God is God) for the very reason that incapability of birth is the only quality that can belong to one Person only. The Son is God for the very reason that He derives His birth from that essence which cannot be born. Therefore our holy faith rejects the idea that the Son is incapable of birth in order to predicate one God incapable of birth and consequently one God, and in order to embrace the Only-begotten nature, begotten from the unborn essence, in the one name of the Unborn God. For the Head of all things is the Son: but the Head of the Son is God. And to one God through this stepping-stone and by this confession all things are referred, since the whole world takes its beginning from Him to whom God Himself is the beginning" (Council convened at 359, On the councils, or the faith of the Easterns, XXVI, 59-60)

<u>Hilary of Poitiers, Doctor of the Church</u> (died 367) "But concerning the dispensation by which He assumed our body, he adds, and He is the head of the body, the Church: Who is the beginning, the first-born from the dead: that in all things He might have the pre-eminence. For it was the good pleasure of the Father that in Him should all the full-

ness dwell, and that through Him all things should be reconciled to Him. The Apostle has assigned to the spiritual mysteries their material effects. For He Who is the image of the invisible God is Himself the head of His body, the Church, and He Who is the first-born of every creature is at the same time the beginning, the first born from the dead: that in all things He might have the pre-eminence, being for us the Body, while He is also the image of God, since He, Who is the first-born of created things, is at the same time the first-born for eternity; so that as to Him things spiritual, being created in the First-born, owe it that they abide, even so all things human also owe it to Him that in the First-born from the dead they are born again into eternity. For He is Himself the beginning, Who as Son is therefore the image, and because the image, is of God. Further He is the first-born of every created thing, possessing in Himself the origin of the universe: and again He is the head of His body, the Church, and the first-born from the dead, so that in all things He has the pre-eminence. And because all things consist for Him, in Him the fullness of the Godhead is pleased to dwell, for in Him all things are reconciled through Him to Him, through Whom all things were created in Himself. (On the Trinity, Book VIII, 50)

<u>Chrysostom, Doctor of the Church</u> (347-407) "But the head of the woman is the man; and the head of Christ is God." Here the heretics rush upon us with a certain declaration of inferiority, which out of these words they contrive against the Son. But they stumble against themselves. For if "the man be the head of the woman," and the head be of the same substance with the body, and "the head of Christ is God," the Son is of the same substance with the Father. "Nay," say they, "it is not His being of another substance which we intend to show from hence, but that He is under subjection." What then are we to say to this? In the first place, when any thing lowly is said of him conjoined as He is with the Flesh, there is no disparagement of the Godhead in what is said, the Economy admitting the expression. However, tell me how thou intendest to prove this from the passage? "Why, as the man governs the wife, saith he, "so also the Father, Christ." Therefore also as Christ governs the man, so likewise the Father, the Son. "For the head of every man," we read, "is Christ." And who could ever admit this? For if the superiority of the Son compared with us, be the measure of the Fathers' compared with the Son, consider to what meanness thou

wilt bring Him. So that we must not try all things by like measure in respect of ourselves and of God, though the language used concerning them be similar; but we must assign to God a certain appropriate excellency, and so great as belongs to God. For should they not grant this, many absurdities will follow. As thus; "the head of Christ is God:" and, "Christ is the head of the man, and he of the woman." Therefore if we choose to take the term, "head," in the like sense in all the clauses, the Son will be as far removed from the Father as we are from Him. Nay, and the woman will be as far removed from us as we are from the Word of God. And what the Son is to the Father, this both we are to the Son and the woman again to the man. And who will endure this? But dost thou understand the term "head" differently in the case of the man and the woman, from what thou dost in the case of Christ? Therefore in the case of the Father and the Son, must we understand it differently also. "How understand it differently?" saith the objector. According to the occasion . For had Paul meant to speak of rule and subjection, as thou sayest, he would not have brought forwardthe instance of a wife, but rather of a slave and a master. For what if the wife be under subjection to us? it is as a wife, as free, as equal in honor. And the Son also, though He did become obedient to the Father, it was as the Son of God, it was as God. For as the obedience of the Son to the Father is greater than we find in men towards the authors of their being, so also His liberty is greater. Since it will not of course be said that the circumstances of the Son's relation to the Father are greater and more intimate than among men, and of the Father's to the Son, less. For if we admire the Son that He was obedient so as to come even unto death, and the death of the cross, and reckon this the great wonder concerning Him; we ought to admire the Father also, that He begat such a son, not as a slave under command, but as free, yielding obedience and giving counsel. For the counsellor is no slave. But again, when thou hearest of a counsellor, do not understand it as though the Father were in need, but that the Son hath the same honor with Him that begat Him. Do not therefore strain the example of the man and the woman to all particulars. (Homilies on First Corinthians, Homily XXIV)

Augustine, Doctor of the Church (354-430)

1. Mutually Connected Objects: "And with respect to the circumstance that, in that enumeration of mutually connected objects which

is given when it is said, "All things are yours, and ye are Christ's, and Christ is God's," as also, "The head of the woman is the man, the Head of the man is Christ, and the Head of Christ is God," there is no mention of the Holy Spirit; this they affirm to be but an application of the principle that, in general, the connection itself is not wont to be enumerated among the things which are connected with each other. Whence, also, those who read with closer attention appear to recognize the express Trinity likewise in that passage in which it is said, "For of Him, and through Him, and in Him, are all things." "Of Him," as if it meant, of that One who owes it to no one that He is: "through Him," as if the idea were, through a Mediator; "in Him," as if it were, in that One who holds together, that is, unites by connecting. (A Treatise on faith and the creed, 19)

2. Unity: "For one man He hath taken to Him, because unity He hath taken to Him.... But they that abide in the bond of Christ and are the members of Him, make in a manner one man, of whom saith the Apostle, "Until we all arrive at the acknowledging of the Son of God, unto a perfect man, unto the measure of the age of the fullness of Christ." Therefore one man is taken to Him, to which the Head is Christ; because "the Head of the man is Christ." (Commentary on Psalm LXV)

"Nor is it strange that though distant we are near, though unknown we are well known to each other; for we are members of one body, having one Head, enjoying the effusion of the same grace, living by the same bread, walking in the same way, and dwelling in the same home. In short, in all that makes up our being, – in the whole faith and hope by which we stand in the present life, or labour for that which is to come, – we are both in the spirit and in the body of Christ so united, that if we fell from this union we would cease to be. (Letters of Saint Augustine Letter XXX, 2)

3. Starting Point: If, then, the baptizer is not his origin and root and head, who is it from whom he receives faith? Where is the origin from which he springs? Where is the root of which he is a shoot? Where the head which is his starting-point? Can it be, that when he who is baptized is unaware of the faithlessness of his baptizer, it is then Christ who gives faith, it is then Christ who is the origin and root and head? Alas for human rashness and conceit! Why do you not allow that it is always Christ who gives faith, for the purpose of making a

man a Christian by giving it? Why do you not allow that Christ is always the origin of the Christian, that the Christian always plants his root in Christ, that Christ is the head of the Christian?... But unless we admit this, either the Apostle Paul was the head and origin of those whom he had planted, or Apollos the root of those whom he had watered, rather than He who had given them faith in believing; whereas the same Paul says, "I have planted, Apollos watered, but God gave the increase: so then neither is he that planteth anything, nor he that watereth, but God that giveth the increase." Nor was the apostle himself their root, but rather He who says, "I am the vine, ye are the branches." How, too, could he be their head, when he says, that "we, being many, are one body in Christ," and expressly declares in many passages that Christ Himself is the head of the whole body? (Augustine, In answer to the letters of Petilian, the Donatist, Bishop of Certa, Book I, Chapter 4.5)

4. Beginning: "Begetter, the latter the Begotten; the former not of the Son, the latter of the Father: the former the Beginning of the latter, whence also He is called the Head of Christ, although Christ likewise is the Beginning, but not of the Father; the latter, more-over, the Image of the former, although in no respect dissimilar, and although absolutely and without difference equal (omnino et indifferenter aequalis) (A Treatise on faith and the creed, Chapter 9.18.)

5. Incarnation: "But as "the Word was made flesh, and dwelt among us," the same Wisdom which was begotten of God condescended also to be created among men. There is a reference to this in the word, "The Lord created me in the beginning of His ways." For the beginning of His ways is the Head of the Church, which is Christ endued with human nature (homine indutus), by whom it was purposed that there should be given to us a pattern of living, that is, a sure way by which we might reach God. (A Treatise on faith and the creed, Chapter 4.6)

6. Servant: According to the form of God, it is said "Before all the hills He begat me," that is, before all the loftinesses of things created and, "Before the dawn I begat Thee," that is, before all times and temporal things: but according to the form of a servant, it is said, "The Lord created me in the beginning of His ways." Because, according to the form of God, He said, "I am the truth;" and according to the form of a servant, "I am the way." For, because He Himself, being the

first-begotten of the dead, made a passage to the kingdom of God to life eternal for His Church, to which He is so the Head as to make the body also immortal, therefore He was "created in the beginning of the ways" of God in His work. For, according to the form of God, He is the beginning, that also speaketh unto us, in which "beginning" God created the heaven and the earth; but according to the form of a servant, "He is a bridegroom coming out of His chamber. "According to the form of God, "He is the first-born of every creature, and He is before all things and by him all things consist;" according to the form of a servant, "He is the head of the body, the Church." According to the form of God, "He is the Lord of glory."(On the Trinity, Book I, Chapter 12)

7. <u>One Man:</u> "Christ is speaking: whether Head speak or whether Body speak; He is speaking that hath said, "Why persecutest thou Me?" He is speaking that hath said, "Inasmuch as ye have done it to one of the least of Mine, to Me ye have done it." The voice then of this Man is known to be of the whole man, of Head and of Body: *that need not often be mentioned, because it is known.* (St. Augustine on the Psalms, Psalm LXX) "...But since there were to be His members, that is, His faithful ones, who would not have that power which He, our God, had; by His being hid, by His concealing Himself as if He would not be put to death, He indicated that His members would do this, in which members He Himself in fact was. For Christ is not simply in the head and not in the body, but Christ whole is in the head and body. What, therefore, His members are, that He is; but what He is, it does not necessarily follow that His members are. For if His members were not Himself, He would not have said, "Saul, why persecutest thou me?" For Saul was not persecuting Himself on earth, but His members, namely, His believers. He would not, however, say, my saints, my servants, or, in short, my brethren, which is more honorable; but, me, that is, my members, whose head I am." (25. (h1) Tractate XXVII, John VII. 1–13.)

8. <u>Universal Body:</u> "...or this same Christ, the only-begotten Son of God, the Word of the Father, equal and co-eternal with the Father, by whom all things were made, was Himself also made man for our sakes, in order that of the whole Church, as of His whole body, He might be the Head.... so all the saints who lived upon the earth previous to the birth of our Lord Jesus Christ, although they were

born antecedently, were nevertheless united under the Head with that universal body of which He is the Head. (On the catechizing of the uninstructed, Chapter 19)

9. <u>Mediator:</u> "That they are made alive in Christ, because they belong to the body of Christ? that they belong to the body of Christ, because Christ is the head even to them? and that Christ is the head even to them, because there is but one Mediator between God and men, the man Christ Jesus? But this He could not have been to them, unless through His grace they had believed in His resurrection. (A treatise on the grace of Christ and the original sin, in two books, Book II, On Original sin, Ch 31)

12. <u>One Flesh</u>: "...Our Lord Jesus Christ speaketh in the Prophets, sometimes in His own Name, sometimes in ours, because He maketh Himself one with us; as it is said, "they twain shall be one flesh." Wherefore also the Lord saith in the Gospel, speaking of marriage, "therefore they are no more twain, but one flesh." One flesh, because of our mortality He took flesh; not one divinity, for He is the Creator, we the creature. Whatsoever then our Lord speaks in the person of the Flesh He took upon Him, belongs both to that Head which hath already ascended into heaven, and to those members which still toil in their earthly wandering. (Psalm CXXXIX)

13. <u>Cornerstone:</u> "We recognize the corner stone: the corner stone is Christ. There cannot be a corner, unless it hath united in itself two walls: they come from different sides to one corner, but they are not opposed to each other in the corn corner. The circumcision cometh from one side the uncircumcision from the other; in Christ both peoples have met together: because He hath become the stone, of which it is written, "The stone which the builders rejected, hath become the head of the corner." (Psalm XCV.6)

<u>Socrates Scholasticus</u> (born 379) "But we know that the Father alone being inoriginate and incomprehensible, has ineffably and incomprehensibly to all begotten, and that the Son was begotten before the ages, but is not unbegotten like the Father, but has a beginning, viz. the Father who begat him, for "the head of Christ is God." (The Ecclesiastical History Book II, Chapter XIX)

<u>Leo the Great, Doctor of the Church</u> (Ca. 390- 461) "There is no doubt therefore, dearly-beloved, that man's nature has been received

by the Son of God into such a union that not only in that Man Who is the first-begotten of all creatures, but also in all His saints there is one and the self-same Christ, and as the Head cannot be separated from the members, so the members cannot be separated from the Head. For although it is not in this life, but in eternity that GOD is to be "all in all ," yet even now He is the inseparable Inhabitant of His temple, which is the Church, according as He Himself promised, saying, "Lo! I am with you all the days till the end of the age." (Leo the Great, pope of Rome, 440, Sermon LXIII, ch III)

APPENDIX B

Colossians and Ephesians

THE FOLLOWING WORDS and concepts are found in Colossians and Ephesians:

Heard of your faith (C 1.4 E 1.15); Love for all the saints (C 1.4 E 1.15); Word of the truth of the gospel (C 1.15 E 1.13); Do not cease to pray for you (C 1.9 E 1.16); Wisdom and revelation/ wisdom and spiritual understanding (C 1.9 E 1.17); Inheritance in/of the saints (C 1.12 E 1.18); Head of the body, the Church (C 1.18 E 1.22); Fullness (C 1.19 E 1.23); Peace (C 1.20 E 2.14); Blood (C 1.20 E 2.13); Aliens (C 1.21 E 2.11); Sufferings/prisoner (C 1.24 E 3.1); Body (C 1.24 E 3.6); Minister (C 1.25 E 3.7); Mystery (C 1.26 E 3.9); Hidden from ages and from generations/the beginning of ages (C 1.26 E 3.9); Riches (C 1.24 E 3.8); Hearts (C 2.2 E 3.17); Rooted and built up/grounded in love (C 2.7 E 3.17); Filled with all the fullness of God/you are made full in Him (C 2.10 E 3.19); Raised from the dead/ascended (C 2.12 E 4.10); Without blame (C 2.15 E 1.4); Concept: False teachings (C 2.16 E 4.14); Not holding on to the head/grow up in all things to the head (C 2.19 E 4.15); Nourished/joined and knit together (C 2.20 E 4.16); Anger (C 3.8 Eph 4.26); Lying (C 3.9 E 4.25); Old man... have put on the new man (C 3.9-10 E 4.24); Forgiving one another as Christ forgave you (C 3.13 E 4.32); Love (C 3.14 E 5.2); Psalms and hymns and spiritual songs... In your hearts to the Lord (C 3.16 E 5.19); Giving thanks to God the Father through Him (C 3.17 E 5.20); Wives submit to your own husbands (C 3.17 E 5.20); Husbands love your wives (Col 3.19 E 5.25); Children obey your parents (C 3.20 E 6.1); Slaves obey your masters (C 3.22 E 6.5); Masters... Master in heaven (C 4.1 E 6.9); [Paul's] chains (C 4.18 E 6.20)

Bibliography

Acts of Paul and Thecla.

Alexander, *Of the Manichaeans.*

Alter, Robert. *The Five Books of Moses, A Translation With Commentary.* New York: W. W. Norton & Company, 2004.

Ambrose, *Exposition of the Christian Faith.*

———. *Three Books on the Duties of the Clergy.*

———. *Three Books on the Holy Spirit.*

———. *Two Books Concerning Repentance.*

Aquinas, Thomas. *Summa Theologica.*

Aristotle, *Metaphysics.*

———. *Politica.*

Arnobius, *Adversus Gentes.*

Athanasius, *Four Discourses Against the Arians.*

Augustine, *A Treatise on Faith and the Creed.*

———. *City of God.*

———. *Confessions.*

———. *Enchiridion.*

———. *In Answer to the Letters of Petilian, the Donatist, Bishop of Certa.*

———. *Letters of Saint Augustine.*

———. *Of the Work of Monks.*

———. *On Christian Doctrine.*

———. *On the Trinity.*

———. *Our Lord's Sermon on the Mount.*

———. *St. Augustine on the Psalms.*

Banks, Dr. Robert. *Paul's Idea of a Community.* Australia: Paternoster Press, 1980.

Bainton, Roland H. *The Reformation of the Sixteenth Century.* Boston, MA: Beacon Press, 1952.

Barnabas, *The Epistle of Barnabas.*

Barnes, Albert. *Barnes' Notes on the New Testament*, Electronic Database, Biblesoft, 1997.

Barnett, Rosalind, and Caryl Rivers. *Same Difference.* New York: Basic Books, 2004.

Barnston, Willis, and Marvin Meyer, eds. *The Gnostic Bible.* Boston, MA: New Seeds, 2003.

Barstow, Anne Llewellyn. *Witchcraze.* San Francisco, CA: Harper, 1994.

Basil. *First Canonical Epistle of Basil*, Archbishop of Caesarea in Cappadocia.

Basil. *On John V.19. The Son Can Do Nothing of Himself.* Prolegomena, Sketch of the Life and Works of St. Basil, II.

Basil. *The Book of Saint Basil on the Spirit*, De Spiritu Sancto.

bin Laden, Carmen. *Inside the Kingdom, My Life in Saudi Arabia.* New York: Warner Books, 2004.

Branch, Taylor. *Parting the Waters.* New York: Simon and Schuster Paperbacks, 1988.

Browning, Don S. *Equality and the Family, A Fundamental, Practical Theology of Children, Mothers, and Fathers in Modern Societies.* Grand Rapids, MI: Wm. B. Eerdmans Publishing Co., 2007.

Cahill, Thomas. *Desire of the Everlasting Hills.* New York: Random House, 2001.

Cairns, Earle E. *Christianity Through the Centuries,* 3rd Edition, revised and expanded. Grand Rapids, MI: Zondervan, 1996.

Canons of the Holy Fathers Assembled at Gangra.

Carter, Nancy A. "Paul and Corinthian Women's Head Coverings." Global Ministries of the United Methodist Church. http://gbgm-umc.org/UMW/corinthians/veils.stm (accessed June 10, 2009).

"The Catholic Encyclopedia," New Advent. www.newadvent.com.

Christenson, Larry. *The Christian Family.* Grand Rapids, MI: Bethany House Publishers, 1970.

Chrysostom, John. *Homilies on First Timothy.*

———. *Homilies on Matthew.*

———. *Homilies on Philippians.*

———. *Homilies on Romans.*

———. *Homilies on Ephesians.*

———. *Homilies on First Corinthians.*

Churton, Tobias. *The Gnostics.* New York: Barnes and Nobles Books, 1987.

Clarke, Adam. *Adam Clarke's Commentary on the Whole Bible.* Biblesoft. Electronic Database, 1996.

Clement of Alexandria. *Stromata.*

———. *The Instructor.*

Clement of Rome. *The First Epistle of Clement to the Corinthians.*

Collins, Gail. *America's Women, 400 years of Dolls, Drudges, Helpmates and Heroines.* New York: Perennial, 2003.

Comer, James P., MD. *Beyond Black and White.* New York: Quadrangle Books, 1972.

Constitutions of the Holy Apostles.

Crabb, Dr. Larry. *Men and Women, Enjoying the Difference.* Grand Rapids, MI: Zondervan, 1991.

Cyprian, *Epistles of Cyprian.*

———. *Of the Discipline and Advantage of Chastity.*

———. *Treatises of Cyprian.*

Dick-Read, Dr. Grantly. *Childbirth Without Fear,* 5th Edition. New York: Perennial Library, 1985.

Dobson, Dr. James C. *Straight Talk to Men and Their Wives.* Waco, TX: Word Books, 1980.

Dyer, Mercedes H., Ph.D., ed. *Prove All Things, A Response to Women in Ministry.* Berrien Springs, MI: Adventists Affirm, 2000.

Eggerichs, Dr. Emerson. *Love and Respect*. Brentwood, TN: Integrity Publishers, 2004.

Ehrenreich, Barbara, and Deidre English. *For Her Own Good*. Anchor, 1989.

Ehrman, Bart D. *Misquoting Jesus*. New York: Harper Collins, 2005.

Eisen, Ute E. *Women Officeholders in Early Christianity*. Collegeville, MN: The Liturgical Press, 2000.

Epiphanius. Epiphanius, Bishop of Salamis, in Cyprus, Letter to John, Bishop of Jerusalem.

Epp, Eldon Jay. *Junia, The First Woman Apostle*. Minneapolis, MN: Fortress Press, 2005.

Eusibius. *Pamphilius, The Church History of Eusibius*.

Freeman, Charles. *Egypt, Greece and Rome*, 2nd Edition. New York: Oxford University Press, 2004.

Friedan, Betty. *It Changed My Life*. Boston, MA: Harvard University Press, 1998.

———. *The Feminine Mystique*. New York: W. W. Norton & Company. Inc., 1963.

Friedman, Richard Elliott. *Commentary on the Torah*. San Francisco, CA: Harper Collins, 2001.

Fromm, Erich. *The Art of Loving*. New York: Bantam Books, 1956.

Getz, Gene A. *Measure of a Woman*. Ventura, CA: Regal Books, 1977.

Goldsmith, Barbara. *Other Powers*. New York: Harper Perennial, 1998.

Goodspeed, Edgar J., trans. *The Bible, An American Translation*. Chicago, IL: The University of Chicago Press, 1931.

Gottman, John, with Nan Silver. *Why Marriages Succeed or Fail…And How You Can Make Yours Last*. New York: A Fireside Book, 1994.

Gregoire, Sheila Wray. *To Honor, Love and Vacuum*. Grand Rapids, MI: Kregel Publications, 2003.

Gregory Nazianzen, *Orations*.

Gregory of Nyssa, *Against Eunomius*.

———. *On the Making of Man, to his Brother Peter, The Servant of God*.

Gregory the Great, Bishop of Rome. *Selected Epistles*.

Grene, Marjorie. "Aristotle and Modern Biology." *Journal of the History of Ideas*, July–Sept. 1972. www.culturaleconomics.atfreeweb.com.

Grimke, Sarah. *Letters on the Equality of the Sexes and the Condition of Woman*.

Grudem, Wayne. *Evangelical Feminism*. Wheaton, IL: Crossway, 2006.

———. *Systematic Theology*. Grand Rapids, MI: Zondervan, 1994.

———. "The Myth of Mutual Submission as an Interpretation of Ephesians 5:21." *Biblical Foundations for Manhood and Womanhood*, John Piper and Wayne Grudem, eds. www.cbmw.org.

Gurko, Miriam. *The Ladies of Seneca Falls, The Birth of the Woman's Rights Movement*. New York: Shocken Books, 1974.

Hamilton, Edith. *The Roman Way*. New York: W. W. Norton & Company, 1964.

Handfrod, Elizabeth Rice. *Me? Obey Him?* Murfreesboro, TN: Sword of the Lord Publishers, 1972.

Handlin, Oscar and Lilian. *Liberty and Equality*. New York: HarperCollins, 1994.

Hastings Adrian, ed. *A World History of Christianity*. Grand Rapids, MI: Wm. B. Eerdmans Publishing Company, 1999.

Hecht, Jennifer Michael. *Doubt, A History, The Great Doubters and Their Legacy of Innovation from Socrates and Jesus to Thomas Jefferson and Emily Dickinson*. San Francisco, CA: Harper, 2003.

Henry, Matthew. *Matthew Henry's Commentary on the Whole Bible: New Modern Edition*. Hendrickson Publishers, Inc. Electronic Database, 1991.

Hilary of Poitiers. *On the Councils, Or the Faith of the Easterns*.

———. *On the Trinity*.

Hippolytus. *Refutation of All Heresies*.

Hirsch, Rabbi Samson Raphael. *The Chumash: The Stone Edition*. Brooklyn, NY: Mesorah Publications, 1996.

Holland, Jack. *Misogyny*. New York: Carroll and Graf Publishers, 2006.

Ignatius, *Epistle to the Magnesians*.

———. *The Epistle of Ignatius to the Philadelphians*.

———. *The Epistle of Ignatius to the Trallians*.

Irenaeus. *Against Heresies*.

———. *The Epistle of Ignatius to the Trallians*.

———. *Fragments from the Lost Writings of Irenaeus*.

Jamieson, Robert, A. R. Fausset, and David Brown. *Jamieson, Fausset, and Brown's Commentary on the Whole Bible*. Biblesoft. Electronic Database, 1997.

Janeway, Elizabeth. *Man's World, Woman's Place*. New York: William Morrow and Company, Inc., 1971.

Jerome, *Against Jovinianus*.

———. *Apology of Jerome*.

———. *The Letters of St. Jerome*.

Jewett, Paul K. *Man as Male and Female*. Grand Rapids, MI: Wm. B. Eerdmans Publishing Company, 1975.

Jewish Study Bible. New York: Oxford University Press, 2004.

Josephus, Flavius. "Against Apion," *Josephus, The Complete Works*. trans.

Justin. *Dialogue of Justin, Philosopher and Martyr, with Trypho, a Jew*.

———. *The First Apology of Justin*.

———. *The Sole Government of God*.

Kaiser, Walter C., Peter H. Davids, E. E. Bruce, and Manfred T. Brauch. *Hard Sayings of the Bible*. Downers Grove, IL: InterVarsity Press, 1996.

Kelly, George A. *The Catholic Marriage Manual*. New York City: Random House, 1958.

Lactantius. *Of the False Wisdom of Philosophers*.

———. *On the Workmanship of God, or the Formation of Man, A Treatise Addressed to His Pupil Demetrianus*.

Lerner, Berel Dov. *The Ten Curses of Eve*. http://jewishbible.blogspot.com/2005/10/ten-curses-of-eve-unpublishable.html.

Lessor, Richard, L. *Love and Marriage and Trading Stamps*. Allen, TX: Argus Communications, 1971.

Luehrs, Bro Kirk, and Stephen C. Graham. *Women's Lib vs. Adam's Rib*. Portland, OR: Telefriend, Inc., 1974.

Luzzatto, Rabbi Moshe Chaim. *The Ways of Reason*, New Revised Edition. Jerusalem, Israel: Feldheim Publishers, 1997.

MacDonald, William. *Believer's Bible Commentary*. Nashville, TN: Thomas Nelson Publishers, Inc., 1980.

Madigan, Kevin, and Carolyn Osiek. *Ordained Women in the Early Church*. Baltimore, MD: The Johns Hopkins University Press, 2005.

Mason, Mike. *The Mystery of Marriage, As Iron Sharpens Iron*. Colorado Springs, CO: Multnomah Press, 1985.

McQuilkin, Robertson. *Understanding and Applying the Bible*. Chicago, IL: Moody Press, 1983.

Mead, Margaret. *Male and Female, A Study of the Sexes in a Changed World*. New York: William Morrow, 1949.

Mernissi, Fatima. *The Veil and the Male Elite*. New York: Basic Books, 1987.

Mill, John Stuart. *The Subjection of Women*. New York: Source Book Press, 1970.

Mouser, Barbara K. "The Womanliness of Deborah: Complementarian Principles from Judges 4–5." The Council on Biblical Manhood and Womanhood. www.cbmw.com.

New Webster Encyclopedic Dictionary of the English Language, The International Edition. New York: Grolier, 1968.

Ojeda, Auriana, ed. *Male/Female Roles*. Chicago, IL: Greenhaven Press, 2005.

Olofsson, Folke T. "God and the Genesis of Gender: The Trustworthy Biblical Design of Man and Woman." *Touchstone Magazine*, Sept. 2001. The Council on Biblical Manhood and Womanhood. www.cbmw.com.

Origen, *Commentary on the Gospel of John*.

———. *Origen de Principiis*.

Osborne, Martha Lee. *Woman in Western Thought*. New York: Random House, 1979.

Pagels, Elaine. *The Gnostic Gospels*. Vintage Books edition. 1989.

Payne, Philip B. *New Testament Study*, Vol. 41. Edmonds, WA: 1995.

Pendergraft, Rachel, "The Shocking Story of Real Slavery in America," The Knights of the Ku Klux Klan. www.kkk.com.

Perseus Digital Library, www.perseus.tufts.edu.

Piper, John, and Wayne Grudem, eds. *Recovering Biblical Manhood and Womanhood*. Wheaton, IL: Crossway, 1994 .

Plaut, W. Hunther. *The Torah, Genesis, A Modern Commentary*. New York: Union of American Hebrew Congregations, 1974.

Polycarp. *The Epistle of Polycarp to the Philippians*.

Pomeroy, Sarah B. *Goddesses, Whores, Wives, and Slaves*. New York: Shocken Books, 1995.

Price, Eugenia. *Woman to Woman*. Grand Rapids, MI: Zondervan, 1959.

Priscilla Papers, Vol. 23, No. 1, Winter 2009.

Rainey, Dennis. *Staying Close*. Dallas, TX: Word Publishing, 1989.

Rhoads, Steven E. *Taking Sex Differences Seriously*. San Francisco, CA: Encounter Books, 2004.

Richards, Sue Poorman, and Lawrence O. Richards. *Women of the Bible*. Nashville, TN: Nelson Reference & Electronic, 2003.

Roberts, Doug, M.D. *To Adam with Love*. Bible Voice, 1974.

Rogers, George A., and R. Frank Saunders. *Swamp Waters and Wiregrass: Historical sketches of Coastal Georgia*. Macon, GA: Mercer University Press, 1984.

Rosenberg, Rosalind. *Beyond Separate Spheres: Intellectual Roots of Modern Feminism*. New Haven, CT: Yale University Press, 1982.

Rothman, Sheila E. *Woman's Proper Place*. New York: Basic Books, 1978.

Rufinus, *The Apology of Rufinus*.

———. *A Commentary on the Apostles' Creed*.

Salley, Columbus, and Ronald Behm. *Your God Is Too White*. Downer's Grove, IL: InterVarsity Press, 1970.

Scanion, Rev. Regis. "Women Deacons: At What Price?" *Catholic Culture*. www.catholicculture.org.

Schaff Philip, D.D and Wace Henry, D.D,. Jerome: *Letters and Select Works, The Nicene and Post-Nicene Fathers*, Second Series, Vol. VI, Logos Research Systems: Oak Harbor 1997.

Schaff, Philip, D.D,. and Henry Wace, D.D. *Historical Introduction to the Council of Nice*, Ante Nice, Second Series, Volume XIV.

Schulz, Mona Lisa M.D., Ph.D., *The New Feminine Brain, Developing Your Intuitive Genius* (New York: Simon and Schuster, 2006).

Seymour, Susan C. *Women, Family, and Child Care in India, A World in Transition*. Cambridge University Press, 1999.

Sozomen, Hermias. *Ecclesiastical History*.

Stearns, Peter N. *Gender in World History*. Routledge, 2000.

Telushkin, Rabbi Joseph. *Biblical Literacy*. New York: Morrow, 1997.

Tertullian, *Against the Valentinians*.

———. *Five Books Against Marcion*.

———. *On Modesty*.

———. *On the Apparel of Women*.

———. *On the Veiling of Virgins*.

———. *The Apology*.

———. *The Chaplet or De Corona*.

———. *The Prescription Against Heretics*.

Theodoret. "Dialogue II—The Unconfounded." *Dialogues*.

Tonsor, Stephen J. *Equality, Decadence, and Modernity*. Wilmington, DE: ISI Books, 2005.

Torjesen, Karen Jo. *When Women Were Priests, Women's Leadership in the Early Church & the Scandal of Their Subordination in the Rise of Christianity*. San Francisco, CA: Harper, 1993.

Unger, Merrill F. *Archeology and the Old Testament*. Grand Rapids, MI: Zondervan, 1954.

Velasquez, Manuel. *Philosophy, a Text with Readings.* Belmont, CA: Thomson Wadsworth, 2008.

Victorinus. *Commentary on the Apocalypse of the Blessed John.*

Viorst, Judith. *Grown-Up Marriage.* The Free Press, 2003.

Ward, Geoffrey C., and Ken Burns. *Not for Ourselves Alone, The Story of Elizabeth Cady Stanton and Susan B. Anthony.* New York: Alfred A. Knopp, 1999.

Whiston, William. *A.M. Nashville,* TN: Thomas Nelson Publishers, 1998.

Wijngaards, John. *Women Deacons in the Early Church.* New York: A Herder and Herder Book, The Crossroad Publishing Company, 2002.

Wycliffe Bible Commentary. Moody Press. Electronic Database,1962.